Programming Distributed Computing Systems

Programming Distributed Computing Systems

A Foundational Approach

Carlos A. Varela

The MIT Press
Cambridge, Massachusetts
London, England

MIT Press books may be purchased at special quantity discounts for business or sales promotional use. For information, please email special_sales@mitpress.mit.edu or write to Special Sales Department, The MIT Press, 55 Hayward Street, Cambridge, MA 02142.

This book was set in Sabon by Westchester Books Group. Printed and bound in the United States of America.

Library of Congress Cataloging-in-Publication Data

Varela, Carlos A.
Programming distributed computing systems : a foundational approach / Carlos A. Varela.
p. cm.
Includes bibliographical references and index.
ISBN 978-0-262-01898-2 (hardcover : alk. paper)
1. Electronic data processing—Distributed processing. 2. Parallel programming (Computer science) 3. Programming languages (Electronic computers) I. Title.
QA76.9.D5V374 2013
005.2′76—dc23
2012038059

10 9 8 7 6 5 4 3 2 1

This book is dedicated with love to my daughters Tatiana and Catalina.

—C.A.V.

Contents

Foreword

From web services to cloud computing, sensor networks to social networking, and multiparty games to data mining, distributed computing systems have acquired a central role in computer science today. There are several good books in the area of programming distributed computing systems. Some cover a particular concurrency theory; others cover a particular programming language for distributed systems. A difficulty has been that the these works provide only a very partial view: they fail to connect theory with practice and sometimes limit coverage to only a single model of concurrency or a single programming language for distributed systems. Moreover, the few textbooks that have broader coverage of programming for distributed computing systems are now dated.

Carlos Varela's *Programming Distributed Computing Systems* is a timely book that fills this gap. It is the first book to explain the best-known foundational models of concurrency. These models have been used to study different aspects of distributed computing systems: autonomy, synchronization, reconfigurability, mobility. That by itself would be a significant achievement. But the book also describes how these theoretical models have been used to build programming languages for distributed computing, and it provides a guide to programming in them. The understanding of these theoretical models is also deepened by providing a careful comparison between them. The comparison not only strengthens the pedagogy in the book, it will be of interest to researchers.

A major strength of Varela's work is its accessibility. Although the book is aimed at graduate students, it will be suitable for advanced undergraduates, as well as for computer scientists who are unfamiliar with the area. The treatment Varela gives to theoretical models of concurrency is not overly technical. Nor does he linger on uninteresting details of programming languages, a common deficiency in books on programming. The book includes a careful comparison of the languages. It provides a valuable case study of a social networking application—a timely topic that will be exciting for students.

The book has a modular structure. The content is not verbose, but it has sufficient details to enable a diligent student to follow. The definitions are precisely stated, and examples of reasoning about systems expressed using the models are provided. These examples illustrate the applications and limitations of the models. The exercises provide a valuable reinforcement mechanism and make this a very useful textbook.

Programming Distributed Computing Systems is in the outstanding tradition of books that serve to define a nascent field. Such books are more than standard textbooks; they not only cover what is already known and understood about an established area, they enrich the area by integrating and organizing knowledge that is otherwise scattered. Indeed, researchers in concurrency are often too specialized in their knowledge and too committed to a single model, which limits their way of looking at problems of representing and building distributed systems. This book provides multiple perspectives, allowing students to get a broad and practical view of distributed programming.

Students at many universities would benefit from a course that covers material in *Programming Distributed Computing Systems*. And there is no better source for practitioners who wish to familiarize themselves with a range of models and languages for distributed programming than this concise work. It will serve them as a useful primer for the research literature.

Gul Agha
University of Illinois at Urbana-Champaign

Preface

This book has two main goals: first, to teach the fundamental theories of concurrent computation, with a special focus on how they help design and reason about distributed and mobile computing systems, and second, to teach programming languages that help develop correct distributed computing systems at a high level of abstraction.

In the theoretical part, we cover modern theories of concurrent computation, including the π calculus, the actor model, the join calculus, and mobile ambients. In the practical part, we present programming languages that follow the aforementioned theoretical models, in particular the Pict programming language, the SALSA programming language, and the JoCaml programming language. While the focus is on those concurrency models and languages, I will also refer to related theoretical models and related programming languages as appropriate to illustrate alternative concurrency models and programming language designs.

This book has been written mainly for researchers and graduate students working in the area of programming technology for distributed computing. The book can also be used as a textbook for advanced undergraduate students in computer science who want to learn to develop distributed computing systems following well-founded concurrent computing models and theories.

This book is unique in helping bridge the gap between the theory and the practice of programming distributed computing systems.

On the Connection between Theory and Practice

The book structure has been designed to make the link between the theories of concurrency and the programming languages as clear as possible. In particular, there is a clear parallel between part I chapters and part II chapters, as outlined in table P.1.

I am not aware as of this writing, of a high-level programming language whose concurrency model follows the mobile ambients theory (chapter 6). However, if and

Table P.1
Concurrent Programming Models and Languages

Model	Language(s)
π calculus (chapter 3)	Pict, Nomadic Pict (chapter 8)
Actors (chapter 4)	SALSA (chapter 9)
Join Calculus (chapter 5)	JoCaml (chapter 10)
Mobile Ambients (chapter 6)	

once such a language becomes available, I would be happy to add relevant material to the book in a subsequent edition.

The highlighted part I and II chapters all follow a structure by which the first section describes syntax and the second section describes semantics. This structure enables a reader to compare different theoretical models to each other, as well as to understand easily how a programming language supports the theoretical model it follows. Indeed, figures 8.1, 9.3, and 10.1 explicitly make the connection between the syntax of the theoretical model and the corresponding syntax of the associated practical programming language.

The third section in each part I chapter (chapters 3–6) describes the main theory developed for each model, usually some form of program equivalence. The third section in each part II chapter (chapters 8–10) goes over programming patterns that each language advocates to facilitate developing distributed and mobile concurrent systems.

Finally, the fourth section of the highlighted chapters in parts I and II goes over examples making the connection between theory and practice as clear as possible. Specifically, subsections x.4.1 all describe how to represent a reference cell in the corresponding theory or programming language. Subsections x.4.2 all describe how to represent mutual exclusion in the corresponding theory or programming language. Subsections x.4.3 all describe how to represent the dining philosophers problem in the corresponding theory or programming language. Finally, subsections x.4.4 all describe the same mobile reference cell example in their respective languages.

I present the theory first because I think that it allows students to focus on the essential components of concurrency, distribution, and mobility without getting bogged down by syntactic details of specific programming languages. In my experience, once the theory is clear in a student's mind, the practical part of implementing a system on an actual programming language becomes much easier. In fact, I have used this material for a few years at a graduate seminar at Rensselaer Polytechnic Institute using this order and structure.

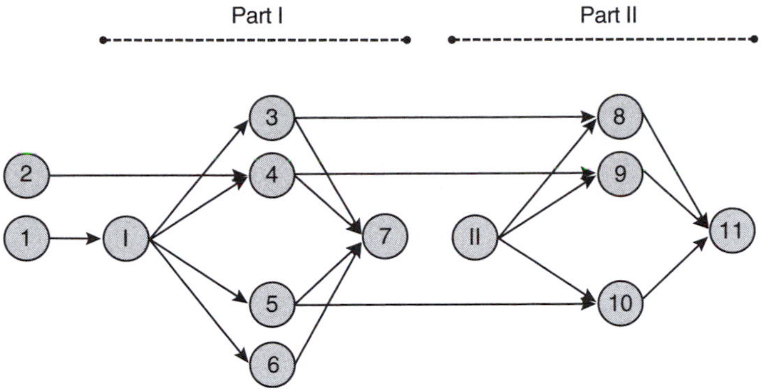

Figure P.1
Chapter dependencies.

Chapter 7 concludes part I with a comprehensive side-by-side analysis of the different theories of concurrent computation. Chapter 11 concludes part II with a comprehensive example, the essential publish-and-subscribe protocol component of social networking applications, implemented in the different programming languages.

Chapter Dependencies and Book Uses

This book has been designed as a textbook for a graduate-level course on the theory and practice of concurrent and distributed computation. The textbook's chapters can therefore be studied sequentially.

Chapter dependencies are outlined in figure P.1. A student or instructor wishing to focus on the theoretical aspects can skip part II. A student or instructor wishing to focus on the pragmatic aspects of distributed computing can skip sections $x.3$ in chapters 3–5, chapters 6 and 7, and sections $y.2$ in chapters 8–10.

An alternative way to study the book is to consider only a subset of the computation models and languages. A student wishing to focus on the π calculus can read chapters 1, 3, 8, and 11 skipping sections 11.4 and 11.5. A student wishing to focus on the actor model can read chapters 1, 4, 9, and 11, skipping sections 11.3 and 11.5. A student wishing to focus on the join calculus can read chapters 1, 5, 10, and 11, skipping sections 11.3 and 11.4. A student wishing to focus on the ambient calculus can read chapters 1 and 6.

Online Supplement and Sample Code

All the source code appearing in the book is available at the book's web site at http://wcl.cs.rpi.edu/pdcs.

Acknowledgments

Gul Agha, my former Ph.D. advisor, has been a constant source of inspiration for me throughout the years, and this book could not possibly have been written without his teaching and guidance. Indeed, many of the ideas behind studying and organizing theories of concurrent programming started shaping in my mind after his Concurrent Object Oriented Programming graduate seminar at the University of Illinois at Urbana-Champaign back in the twentieth century. Gul also provided critical feedback on this book's organization.

Carolyn Talcott has also always been a source of inspiration with her formal mathematical approach to studying concurrent computation. She provided invaluable timely feedback on early drafts of this book.

My current research collaborations with John Field and David Musser on programming models for fault-tolerant distributed computing and formal verification of actor systems respectively have already produced some important results, and I thank them for shaping my thoughts with a direct impact on this book's writing. I expect that future versions of this book or further manuscripts will include some of our ongoing work.

The worldwide computing laboratory (WCL) research group members at Rensselaer Polytechnic Institute over the years have also helped significantly to shape my ideas, in particular with regard to the pragmatics of developing Internet-based distributed computing systems. I would like to especially thank my former Ph.D. students Travis Desell, Kaoutar El Maghraoui, and Wei-Jen Wang. Other WCL research group members that have made significant contributions to the ideas and technologies reported in this book (especially the SALSA programming language and associated software) include Shigeru Imai, Jason LaPorte, and Abe Stephens. My interaction with colleagues in distributed computing projects has also been very valuable. In particular, I would like to acknowledge Malik Magdon-Ismail, Heidi Newberg, and Boleslaw Szymanski.

Many students at Rensselaer Polytechnic Institute have provided feedback on early versions of some of this book's chapters used to teach the graduate seminar

CSCI.6500, Distributed Computing over the Internet and the undergraduate course CSCI.4430, Programming Languages. I would especially like to thank Jeff Baumes for typing out the initial lecture notes on the lambda calculus and Joshua Taylor for excellent comments throughout the book, in particular on part I. Other students who provided feedback on early drafts include Richard Klockowski, Misbah Mubarak, Yousaf Shah, Giovanni Thenstead, and Ping Wang.

Most of this book's chapters were written while on sabbatical at the University of Tokyo and at the University of Melbourne. I would like to acknowledge the candid support and excellent working environment provided by my colleagues Kenjiro Taura and Rajkumar Buyya during my sabbatical year. Members of their research groups that provided feedback on this book include Marcus Assunçao, Alexandre Di Costanzo, and Christian LaVechia. On a more recent visit to Michel Riveill's research group at the University of Nice, Sophia-Antipolis, I received invaluable feedback from Ludovic Henrio on chapters related to the actor model. Their comments have helped me improve the book significantly.

I would like to acknowledge the work of the authors of the theories of concurrent computation and practical programming languages presented in this book, in particular, I want to acknowledge Alonzo Church, Robin Milner, Joachim Parrow, David Walker, Carl Hewitt, Gul Agha, Ian Mason, Scott Smith, Carolyn Talcott, Cédric Fournet, Georges Gonthier, Luca Cardelli, Andrew Gordon, Benjamin Pierce, David Turner, Pawel Wojciechowski, Peter Sewell, Fabrice Le Fessant, Louis Mandel, and Luc Maranget. This is surely a partial list, since significant contributions often build on existing great work. Please excuse any omissions. In any event, without their work, this book would not have been possible.

I would also like to acknowledge the partial funding support provided by Rensselaer Polytechnic Institute, the National Science Foundation, the Air Force Office of Scientific Research, and IBM Research over the more than ten years that it has taken me to write this book.

Last but not least, I want to thank my family for all their support and encouragement. My wife Adriana and my daughters Tatiana and Catalina have been a constant source of love, inspiration and motivation. I want to thank my parents Carlos and Flor Alba, my brothers Javier and Leonardo, and my extended family and friends, for their understanding when I could not be there.

I dedicate this book to Tatiana and Catalina: Let the new generations make the world a better place!

This book has built on top of numerous contributions and has had the benefit of several revisions, including some excellent feedback by anonymous MIT Press reviewers and the MIT Press editorial board. All errors remain the author's. I would appreciate it if you would contact me to let me know of any errors you might find.

Programming Distributed Computing Systems

1 Introduction

1.1 Motivation

Digital computing as a relatively new scientific discipline has enabled revolutionary improvements in its few decades of existence. We have witnessed and enjoyed hardware development technologies that for a long time have improved processor, network, and storage performance exponentially. Moore's law predicted that the number of transistors per chip would double every two years, effectively going from 2,300 transistors in 1971 to more than 2,600,000,000 in 2011. Networking capabilities have also enjoyed significant growth. For example, the backbone network bandwidth has moved from ARPANet's 50,000 bits per second in the United States in 1968 to a U.S.-Japan backbone bandwidth of 500,000,000,000 bits per second in 2011. Storage capabilities have improved from the world's first hard drive in 1956 capable of storing 4,400,000 bytes of data to relatively cheap personal hard drives capable of storing more than 4,000,000,000,000 bytes of data in 2011. Data processing, communication, and storage capabilities have improved by six orders of magnitude in only four decades.[1]

At the same rate of growth, by 2031, we may see a thousandfold further improvement in hardware, resulting in 1,000 plus-core processors in mobile devices, laptops, and desktops, 100-terabit-per-second-plus network backbones, and hard drives storing petabytes of data. The growing number of transistors in emerging multicore architectures can only be translated into practical software applications' performance if software developers understand how to program concurrent systems effectively.

Why Concurrency?

Concurrency can be regarded as potential parallelism. Computing activities can be executed in parallel provided there are no data or control dependencies that require them to be executed sequentially. However, a concurrent computer program can also be executed on a single processor by distributing its activities over time, also known as *interleaving*. When multiple processors are used to execute a concurrent application, we say that it is a *parallel execution* of the concurrent program. If the processors are separated geographically, we say that it is a *distributed execution* of the concurrent program. If the location of the activities can change dynamically, we say it is a *mobile execution* of the concurrent program.

There are several advantages and disadvantages associated with writing concurrent computer programs. Concurrent programs have the potential to execute much faster than their sequential counterparts, provided that there are enough resources to run their independent activities, and provided that the frequency and cost of communication between these activities are not significant with respect to their computation time. In the best case scenario, subactivities are completely independent from each other, and applications scale up to the availability of computing resources. Applications in this category are often called *massively parallel* applications. In the worst case scenario, subactivities have significant data and control dependencies, and sequential execution represents the best execution time. Most applications lie in the middle. For example, a web server may be able to service client requests in parallel, but a database service component may have to serialize writing requests for consistency.

Concurrent software enables better human-computer interaction. For example, a mobile phone can be used for oral communication at the same time that its calendar or contacts features are used to find or update relevant information. Concurrent software also enables better resource utilization. For example, a network interface card can send and receive data from other computers while the processor is busy computing application functions and the graphical coprocessor is busy rendering images for data visualization.

While the advantages of concurrent programs are potentially significant, they also require a different way of thinking about and organizing computer programs. As opposed to sequential programs, concurrent programs are typically *not deterministic*: Different executions of the same program can produce different results. The combinatorial explosion of possible execution orders makes reasoning about correctness and termination harder than it is for sequential code. Programming abstractions designed to help tackle the inherent complexity of concurrent execution can be misused, producing *deadlocks*. Beyond having to consider application *safety*—that is, ensure data consistency—and *liveness*—that is, ensure computation progress—it is not always trivial to obtain *high performance* due to the additional resources required to schedule multiple activities and enable their communication and synchronization.

Why Distribution?

Distributed computing refers to computation that spreads over space and time. As an example, geographically separated database servers may each contain part of the *distributed state* of an application. Banking transactions started by the user of an automated teller machine in any part of the world, or even a simple Google search, may trigger the response of dozens or even hundreds of servers worldwide.

Internet computing, web computing, grid computing, and cloud computing are all forms of distributed computing. One significant advantage of distributed computation is the potential scalability afforded by applications. Data in many domains, including science, engineering, finance, and medicine, are growing exponentially, and computing over the data is imperative to be able to analyze it and derive hypotheses, improve products, and generate wealth and well-being. As a consequence, the need to scale data analyses to large data sets requires ever larger computing infrastructures that can be provided only by multiple geographically distributed data and computing centers.

Distributed systems are more difficult to reason about and to develop than centralized systems. Standards are often required to enable components developed by independent parties to interact. Failures can be partial, whereby only part of the application's distributed state is available at a given point in time. The heterogeneity inherent in geographically distributed computing infrastructures makes resource scheduling and allocation critical to provide a reasonable quality of service to application users. The open nature of the Internet and the World Wide Web make security a key aspect of distributed systems. Data privacy and integrity are fundamental to many applications, for example, in the health and financial industries.

Why Mobility?

We use *mobility* to refer to mobile distributed systems, which exhibit mobile code, mobile data, mobile devices, and/or mobile users.

Mobile code can refer to downloading computer programs or components from the Internet, or it can refer to applications whose components reconfigure themselves at run-time to adapt to changes in their execution environment. The mobility of code enables dynamic application extensibility—for example, web browsers automatically downloading applets or plug-ins—to augment their behavior or to enable viewing of heterogeneous data types. Mobility of code also enables distributed applications to adapt to changing network conditions. For example, a scientific data analysis application can grow to make use of thousands of newly available processors over the Internet by splitting and moving its components dynamically. Likewise, it can shrink by merging its components to run efficiently on a smaller number of resources as distributed computers become unavailable, fail, or are put to sleep to save energy.

Mobile data refers to accessing remote databases, for example as produced by sensors, and requires policies for replication, efficient access, and preservation. The mobility of data, including its potential replication, enables faster access by both human users and computer applications. Data replication also enables fault tolerance. Sensor and actuator networks more and more often produce data at different scales continuously. Applications that produce or consume data continuously are known as *data streaming* applications.

Mobile devices refers to laptops, personal digital assistants, cellular phones, robots, cameras, cars, planes, and other devices that can change physical location and can become connected or disconnected at any time. Typically, mobile devices are highly heterogeneous, and can have significant constraints in terms of processing speed, wireless network access, memory size, and availability (due to being powered by batteries with limited life time.)

Finally, *mobile users* refers to the need of humans to access information and applications from anywhere anytime, even while traveling at different speeds and enjoying different levels of connectivity.

Mobility enables dynamically adaptable applications, real-time streaming data analyses, and information access through heterogeneous devices and from disparate geographical locations. Mobility enables computing with sparse data sets in different application domains, including agriculture, space exploration, weather monitoring and forecasting, and environmental sciences. However, mobility also adds a new dimension of complexity to consider in distributed software development.

1.2 Models of Computation

Theoretical models of computation are critical to be able to reason about properties of software, including the programming languages used to develop the software. Examples of software properties include expressive power, correctness, performance, and reliability. Models of computation also help programming language designers and application developers organize software artifacts to handle complexity and promote reusability and composability.

Church (1941) and Kleene created the λ calculus in the 1930s. The calculus is at the heart of functional programming languages. It is Turing-complete, that is, any computable function can be expressed and evaluated using the calculus. It is useful to study sequential programming language concepts because of its high level of abstraction.

Milner et al. (1992) created the π calculus, which models concurrent computation in terms of communicating processes, which can dynamically change their communication topology. Milner et al. have developed a theory of equivalence of processes that uses a technique called *bisimulation*, whereby two processes are considered equivalent if they can indefinitely mimic each other's interactions with any environment.

Hewitt et al. (1973) created the *actor* model of concurrent computation in the 1970s. Agha (1986) refined it to model open distributed systems. Actors model concurrent units of computation, which communicate by asynchronous and guaranteed message passing. Agha et al. (1997) extended the call-by-value λ calculus with primitives for actor creation and communication, and they provided an operational semantics for the actor model. Sequential computation within an actor is modeled with the λ calculus, and actor configurations model communication and distributed state. Configurations evolve over time using a labeled transition system. A theory of observational equivalence was developed that equates actor programs when no observational context can tell them apart.

Fournet and Gonthier (1996) created the *join calculus* to model concurrent computation as chemical processes, whereby complex expressions can appear as the result of combining simpler expressions according to a dynamic set of bidirectional rewriting rules. The transformation of simpler expressions into more complex expressions and vice versa is inspired by heating molecules and cooling atoms in chemical reactions. An observational congruence is defined as a behavioral equivalence for a restricted yet equally expressive subset (i.e., a core) of the join calculus.

Cardelli and Gordon (2000) created the theory of *mobile ambients* to model mobile code, devices, and users. The ambient calculus defines a hierarchical structure of ambients that contain processes and other ambients. Processes are restricted to only communicate within the same ambient. Primitives in the calculus enable the movement of ambients in and out of other ambients, as well as creation and destruction of ambient boundaries. Ambient calculus expressions can be translated into the pure π calculus, and vice versa. This strategy enables the use of equivalence techniques developed for the π calculus in the ambient calculus.

1.3 Programming Languages

Programming languages have coevolved significantly with new theories of computation and hardware improvements. We can categorize programming languages according to their programming models or paradigms as *imperative*, *object-oriented*, *functional*, *logical*, or *multiparadigm*.

Imperative programming languages include Fortran, created by Backus in 1954 at IBM as one of the first *high-level* (i.e., compiled) programming languages and used for numerical computing (Backus et al., 1957); Algol, created by Naur in 1958, the precursor of many of today's most widely used programming languages (Backus et al., 1960); Cobol, created by Hopper in 1959, an English-like language for business applications (Hopper, 1981); BASIC, created by Kemeny and Kurtz in 1964 (Kurtz, 1981), and Pascal, created by Wirth in 1970 (Wirth, 1971), both developed for teaching computer programming; C, created by Kernighan and Ritchie in 1971 at Bell Labs, and used to program the UNIX operating system (Kernighan and Ritchie, 1978); and Ada, created by Whitaker in 1979 for concurrent applications (Whitaker, 1996).

Object-oriented programming languages include Simula, created by Dahl and Nygaard in 1966 for developing computational physics simulations (Dahl and Nygaard, 1966); Smalltalk, created by Kay in 1980, in which everything is an object including primitive types such as numbers and characters (Kay, 1980); C++, created by Stroustrop in 1980, designed to introduce classes and objects to C programmers (Stroustrup, 1982); Eiffel, created by Meyer in 1985, which includes assertions and invariants (Meyer et al., 1987); Java, created by Gosling at Sun Microsystems in 1994, initially to program appliances and later used to program dynamic web content (Gosling et al., 1996); and C#, created by Hejlsberg at Microsoft in 2000, in response to Java (Hejlsberg et al., 2003).

Functional programming languages include Lisp, created by McCarthy in 1958 (McCarthy, 1978); ML, created by Milner in 1973 (Gordon et al., 1978); Scheme, created by Sussman and Steele in 1975 in an attempt to understand the actor model (Sussman and Steele, 1998); and Haskell, created by Hughes et al. in 1987, which advocates lazy evaluation (Hudak et al., 1992, 2007). The best-known logic programming language is Prolog, created by Colmerauer and Roussel in 1972 initially to process (the French) natural language (Colmerauer and Roussel, 1993). Oz, created by Smolka in 1993, is a more recent multiparadigm programming language that can be used to develop functional, object-oriented, concurrent, and logical programs (Smolka et al., 1993).

Concurrent programming, which encompasses developing parallel, distributed, and mobile systems, has been mostly an afterthought in programming language design. This is in part because early programming languages, such as C and Fortran, predate significant computing developments such as the personal computer, local area networks, and the Internet. Emerging areas such as web computing, grid computing, and cloud computing are fueling renewed efforts to rethink programming languages in order to raise the level of abstraction for programmers and improve the performance and scalability of applications running on highly heterogeneous and dynamic distributed computing infrastructure.

We will focus on programming languages that follow well-founded theories of concurrent computation. While the programming languages we will cover may not be the most popular or widely used in industry today, they serve the educational purpose of helping students think concurrently from the beginning and design systems from first principles. These languages also help us highlight the key differences in programming models from a concurrency perspective. Finally, it is the author's expectation that this book will give insight to developers of new programming languages into how to provide high-level programming abstractions that facilitate the development of correct, flexible, and efficient concurrent systems.

Processes have been a key abstraction used by operating systems to isolate applications from one another when running on the same computer. Processes have also been widely used by parallel application developers, e.g., using the message passing interface (MPI) as an abstraction to separate parallel computation running on multiple computers (Gropp et al., 1994). Unfortunately, processes have not received significant attention from the programming language community: It is assumed that libraries can be written in a programming language to allow multiple processes to establish communication with one another, and all such communication and synchronization is largely left to library developers and application programmers.

We study a programming language that follows the π calculus model and adds the notion of types to interprocess communication channels: Pict (Pierce and Turner, 2000). We also study an extension of Pict to study process mobility: Nomadic Pict, created by Wojciechowski and Sewell in 1998 (Sewell et al., 1998, 2010).

Actor-oriented programming languages include PLASMA (Hewitt, 1975), Act (Lieberman, 1981), ABCL (Yonezawa et al., 1986), Actalk (Briot, 1989), Erlang (Armstrong et al., 1993), E (Miller et al., 2005), and SALSA (Varela and Agha, 2001). SALSA introduces the notion of *universal actors* that can communicate over the Internet enabling the development of *open systems*. AmbientTalk is an actor-oriented programming language that aims to help develop ubiquitous computing applications. Mobile ad-hoc networking issues such as intermittent connectivity over wireless networks and the need for discovery of peers are considered in the language (Dedecker et al., 2006). Scala is a multiparadigm programming language that also advocates the use of actors as a concurrency abstraction (Haller and Odersky, 2007).

A programming language based on the join calculus is JoCaml, which extends OCaml with join patterns (Fournet et al., 2002). OCaml is an object-oriented extention of Caml, an efficient implementation of ML. C# has borrowed some notions from join patterns to implement synchronization at a higher level (Benton et al., 2002).

In this book we will use Pict, Nomadic Pict, SALSA, and JoCaml to illustrate practical aspects of developing concurrent, distributed, and mobile systems. These languages follow respectively the π calculus, the actor model, and the join calculus theories.

1.4 Common Concurrent Programming Examples

For each theory of concurrent computation and for each concurrent programming language, we will illustrate how to encode the same three programs: a *reference cell*, a *mutual exclusion* problem, and the famous *dining philosophers*. This will help the reader directly contrast the theories and programming languages and put them side by side for comparison purposes. These examples can also be used as a starting point for more complex program specifications. In this section, we specify these three examples and we describe their significance in concurrent computation.

1.4.1 Reference Cell

A reference cell models stateful computation, i.e., a cell contains mutable state. A simple cell can be created, updated, and queried by other concurrent computations. A reference cell is perhaps the simplest stateful concurrent program that illustrates issues such as *nondeterminism*: For example, if both an *update* and a *query* are concurrently issued, the order of request processing will determine the result received by the querying process.

Even though a reference cell is a very simple example, it is at the basis of all stateful computation, including databases and more complex information systems.

1.4.2 Mutual Exclusion

Mutual exclusion refers to the need of two or more concurrent computations to coordinate and avoid executing at the same time some critical region of code. For example, if two computations are using a shared resource—for instance, a printer—it is important that they take turns, or else the result will not be as desired. You might thus end up with words from two different documents printed on the same page.

Mutual exclusion is perhaps the simplest illustration of the need for coordination of concurrent activities. A useful abstraction for guaranteeing mutual exclusion is the notion of *semaphores*. It forms the basis for more complex coordination mechanisms such as distributed transactions.

1.4.3 Dining Philosophers

A typical example of the complexities of concurrent computation is the famous *dining philosophers* scenario. Consider n philosophers, $Ph_1, \ldots, Ph_{n-1}$, dining at a round table containing n chopsticks $ch_1, \ldots, ch_{n-1}$ where each chopstick is shared by two consecutive philosophers (see figure 1.1 for an example with $n = 4$). Each philosopher uses the following sequential algorithm:

1. Pick up the *left* chopstick, if available.
2. Pick up the *right* chopstick, if available.
3. Eat.
4. Release both chopsticks.
5. Think.
6. Go to 1.

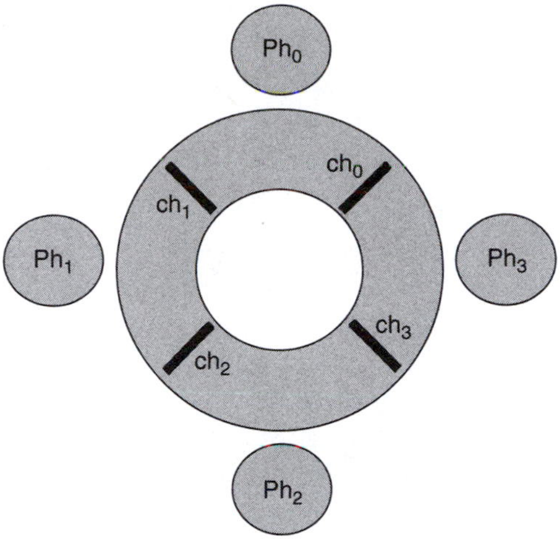

Figure 1.1
A table with four philosophers and four chopsticks.

While each philosopher's algorithm seems to make sense from an individual sequential perspective, the group's concurrent behavior has the potential for *deadlock*: All philosophers can pick up their left chopsticks in step 1 and block forever in step 2, waiting for the philosopher on her/his right to release her/his left chopstick.

This well-known example highlights the potential for deadlock in concurrent systems with shared resources.

Note

1. Four decades of doubling transistors every two years represents approximately six orders of magnitude: $2^{40/2} \simeq 10^6$.

2 λ Calculus

The λ *(lambda) calculus* created by Church and Kleene in the 1930s (Church, 1941) is at the heart of functional programming languages. We will use it as a foundation for sequential computation. The λ calculus is Turing-complete; that is, any computable function can be expressed and evaluated using the calculus. The λ calculus is useful to study programming language concepts because of its high level of abstraction.

In the following sections, we will motivate the λ calculus, introduce its syntax and semantics (section 2.1) and present the notion of scope of variables (section 2.2), the importance of the order of expression evaluation (section 2.3), the notion of combinators (section 2.4), currying (section 2.5), η-conversion (*eta*-conversion) (section 2.6), the sequencing and recursion combinators (sections 2.7 and 2.8), and higher-order programming in the λ calculus, including an encoding of natural numbers and booleans (section 2.9).

2.1 Syntax and Semantics

The mathematical notation for defining a *function* is with a statement such as:

$$f(x) = x^2, \quad f : \mathbf{Z} \to \mathbf{Z},$$

where $\mathbf{Z}$ is the set of all integers. The first $\mathbf{Z}$ represents the *domain* of the function, or the set of values x can take. We denote it as $dom(f) = \mathbf{Z}$. The second $\mathbf{Z}$ represents the *range* of the function, or the set containing all possible values of $f(x)$. We denote it as $ran(f) = \mathbf{Z}$. In programming languages, we call $\mathbf{Z} \to \mathbf{Z}$, the *type* of the function f. The type of a function defines what kinds of values the function can receive and what kinds of values it produces as output.

Suppose $f(x) = x^2$ and $g(x) = x + 1$. Traditional function *composition* is defined as:

$$(f \circ g)(x) = f(g(x)).$$

With our functions f and g,

$$(f \circ g)(x) = f\,(g(x)) = f(x+1) = x^2 + 2x + 1.$$

Similarly,

$$(g \circ f)(x) = g\left(f(x)\right) = g(x^2) = x^2 + 1.$$

Therefore, function composition is not commutative.

In the λ calculus, we can use a different notation to represent the same concepts. To define a function $f(x) = x^2$, we instead may write:[1]

$$\lambda x.x^2.$$

Similarly, for $g(x) = x + 1$, we write:

$$\lambda x.x + 1.$$

To describe a function *application* such as $f(2) = 4$, we write:

$$(\lambda x.x^2 \quad 2) \Rightarrow 2^2 \Rightarrow 4.$$

We can pictorially illustrate function application as shown in figure 2.1.

The *syntax* for λ calculus expressions is

$$\begin{array}{lll} e ::= & v & \text{– variable} \\ \mid & \lambda v.e & \text{– functional abstraction} \\ \mid & (e \quad e) & \text{– function application.} \end{array}$$

The *semantics* of the λ calculus, or the way of evaluating or simplifying expressions, is defined by the *β-reduction* (*beta-reduction*) rule:

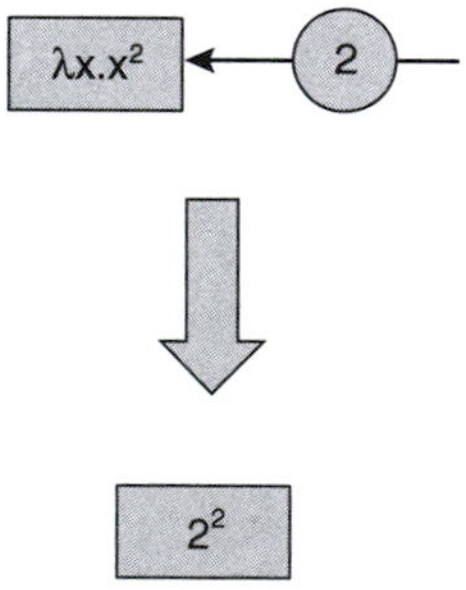

Figure 2.1
A pictorial representation of function application in the λ calculus.

$(\lambda x.E \quad M) \Rightarrow E\{M/x\}.$

The new expression $E\{M/x\}$ can be read as "replace 'free' x's in E with M." Informally, a "free" x is an x that is not nested inside another lambda expression. We will cover free and bound variable occurrences in detail in section 2.2.

For example, in the expression:

$(\lambda x.x^2 \quad 2),$

$E = x^2$ and $M = 2$. To evaluate the expression, we replace x in E with M to obtain:

$(\lambda x.x^2 \quad 2) \Rightarrow 2^2 \Rightarrow 4.$

In the λ calculus, all functions may only have one variable. Functions with more than one variable may be expressed as a function of one variable through *currying*. Suppose we have a function of two variables expressed in the standard mathematical way:

$h(x, y) = x + y, \quad h : (\mathbf{Z} \times \mathbf{Z}) \rightarrow \mathbf{Z}.$

With currying, we can input one variable at a time into separate functions. The first function will take the first argument, x, and return a function that will take the second variable, y, and will in turn provide the desired output. To create the same function with currying, let:

$f : \mathbf{Z} \rightarrow (\mathbf{Z} \rightarrow \mathbf{Z})$

and:

$g_x : \mathbf{Z} \rightarrow \mathbf{Z}.$

That is, f maps every integer x to a function g_x, which maps integers to integers. The function $f(x)$ returns a function g_x that provides the appropriate result when supplied with y. For example,

$f(2) = g_2, \quad \text{where} \quad g_2(y) = 2 + y.$

So:

$f(2)(3) = g_2(3) = 2 + 3 = 5.$

In the λ calculus, this function would be described with currying by:

$\lambda x.\lambda y.x + y.$

To evaluate the function, we nest two function application expressions:

$((\lambda x.\lambda y.x + y \quad 2) \quad 3).$

We may then simplify this expression using β reduction as follows:

$((\lambda x.\lambda y.x + y \quad 2) \quad 3) \;\Rightarrow\; (\lambda y.2 + y \quad 3) \;\Rightarrow\; 2 + 3 \;\Rightarrow\; 5.$

The composition operation $\circ$ can itself be considered a function, also called a *higher-order* function, that takes two other functions as its input and returns a function as its output; that is, if the first function is of type $\mathbf{Z} \to \mathbf{Z}$ and the second function is also of type $\mathbf{Z} \to \mathbf{Z}$, then

$\circ : (\mathbf{Z} \to \mathbf{Z}) \times (\mathbf{Z} \to \mathbf{Z}) \to (\mathbf{Z} \to \mathbf{Z}).$

We can also define function composition in the λ calculus. Suppose we want to compose the *square* function and the *increment* function, defined as

$\lambda x.x^2$ and $\lambda x.x + 1.$

We can define function composition as a function itself with currying as follows:

$\lambda f.\lambda g.\lambda x.(f \quad (g \quad x)).$

Applying the composition function to two variables with currying works the same way as before, except now our variables are functions:

$$
\begin{aligned}
&((\lambda f.\lambda g.\lambda x.(f \quad (g \quad x)) \quad \lambda x.x^2) \quad \lambda x.x + 1) \\
\Rightarrow\; &(\lambda g.\lambda x.(\lambda x.x^2 \quad (g \quad x)) \quad \lambda x.x + 1) \\
\Rightarrow\; &\lambda x.(\lambda x.x^2 \quad (\lambda x.x + 1 \quad x)) \\
\Rightarrow\; &\lambda x.(\lambda x.x^2 \quad x + 1).
\end{aligned}
$$

The resulting function gives the same results as $f(g(x)) = (x + 1)^2$.

In the Scheme programming language (Sussman and Steele, 1998), as well as in most functional programming languages, we can directly use λ calculus expressions. They are defined using a similar syntax. To define a function we use the code

```
(lambda([x y z ...]) expr),
```

where variables `x`, `y`, `z`, etc. are optional. Scheme syntax allows you to have functions of zero variables, one variable, or more than one variable.

The code

```
(lambda(x) (* x x))
```

describes the square function. Note that even common operations, such as $*$, are considered functions and are always used in a prefix format. You may define variables (which can refer to functions) with

```
(define a b).
```

For example,

```
(define f (lambda(x) (* x x)))
```

defines a function $f(x) = x^2$.

To perform a procedure call, use the code

```
(f [x y z ...])
```

where `x`, `y`, `z`, etc. are additional parameters that `f` may require. The code

```
(f 2)
```

evaluates $f(2) = 4$.

2.2 Free and Bound Variables in the λ Calculus

The process of simplifying (or β-reducing) in the λ calculus requires further clarification. The general rule is to find an expression of the form

$(\lambda x.E \quad M)$,

called a *redex* (for *reducible expression*), and replace the "free" x's in E with M's. A *free* variable is one that is not *bound* by a lambda expression representing a functional abstraction. The functional abstraction syntax, $\lambda v.e$, defines the *scope* of the variable v to be e, and effectively *binds* occurrences of v in e. For example, in the expression

$(\lambda x.x^2 \quad x+1)$

the x in x^2 is bound by the λx, because it is part of the expression defining that function, i.e., the function $f(x) = x^2$. The final x, however, is not bound by any function definition, so it is said to be free. Do not be confused by the fact that the variables have the same name. The two occurrences of the variable x are in different scopes, and therefore they are totally independent of each other.

An equivalent C program could look like this:

```
int f(int x) {
  return x*x;
}
```

```
int main() {
  int x;
  ...
  x = x + 1;
  return f(x);
}
```

In this example, we could substitute `y` (or any other variable name) for all `x` occurrences in function `f` without changing the meaning of the program. In the same way, the lambda expression

$(\lambda x.x^2 \quad x + 1)$

is equivalent to the expression

$(\lambda y.y^2 \quad x + 1)$.

We cannot replace the final x, since it is unbound, or free.

To simplify the expression

$(\lambda x.(\lambda x.x^2 \quad x + 1) \quad 2)$,

you could let $E = (\lambda x.x^2 \quad x + 1)$ and $M = 2$. The only free x in E is the final occurrence so the correct reduction is

$(\lambda x.x^2 \quad 2 + 1)$,

where the x in x^2 is not replaced since it is bound.

However, things get more complicated. It is possible when performing β-reduction to inadvertently change a free variable into a bound variable, which changes the meaning of the expression. For example, in the statement

$(\lambda x.\lambda y.(x \quad y) \quad (y \quad w))$,

the y in $(x \quad y)$ is bound to λy whereas the final y is free. Taking $E = \lambda y.(x \quad y)$ and $M = (y \quad w)$, we could mistakenly arrive at the simplified expression

$\lambda y.((y \quad w) \quad y)$.

But now both occurrences of y are bound, because they are both a part of the functional abstraction starting by λy. This is wrong, because one of the y occurrences should remain free, as it was in the original expression. To solve this problem, we can change the λy expression to a λz expression:

$(\lambda x.\lambda z.(x \quad z) \quad (y \quad w))$,

which again does not change the meaning of the expression. This process is called *α-renaming* (*alpha-renaming*). Now when we perform the β-reduction, the original two y variable occurrences are not confused. The result is

$$\lambda z.((y \quad w) \quad z),$$

where the free y remains free.

2.3 Order of Evaluation

There are different ways to evaluate λ calculus expressions. The first method is always to fully evaluate the arguments of a function before evaluating the function itself. This order is called *applicative order*. In the expression

$$(\lambda x.x^2 \quad (\lambda x.x+1 \quad 2)),$$

the argument $(\lambda x.x+1 \quad 2)$ should be evaluated first. The result is

$$\Rightarrow (\lambda x.x^2 \quad 2+1) \Rightarrow (\lambda x.x^2 \quad 3) \Rightarrow 3^2 \Rightarrow 9.$$

Another method is to evaluate the left-most redex first. Recall that a redex is an expression of the form $(\lambda x.E \quad M)$, on which β-reduction can be performed. This order is called *normal order*. The same expression would be reduced from the outside in, with $E = x^2$ and $M = (\lambda x.x+1 \quad 2)$. In this case the result is

$$\Rightarrow (\lambda x.x+1 \quad 2)^2 \Rightarrow (2+1)^2 \Rightarrow 9.$$

As you can see, both orders produced the same result. But is this always the case? It turns out that the answer is a qualified *yes*: only if both orders of expression evaluation terminate. Otherwise, the answer is *no*, since normal-order evaluation may terminate with a result that is never achieved by a nonterminating applicative-order evaluation. Consider the expression

$$(\lambda x.(x \quad x) \quad \lambda x.(x \quad x)).$$

It is easy to see that reducing this expression gives the same expression back, creating an infinite loop. If we consider the expanded expression

$$(\lambda x.y \quad (\lambda x.(x \quad x) \quad \lambda x.(x \quad x))),$$

we find that the two evaluation orders are not equivalent. Using applicative order, the $(\lambda x.(x \quad x) \quad \lambda x.(x \quad x))$ expression must be evaluated first, but this process never terminates. If we use normal order, however, we evaluate the entire expression first, with $E = y$ and $M = (\lambda x.(x \quad x) \quad \lambda x.(x \quad x))$. Since there are no x's in E to replace, the result is simply y. It turns out that it is only in these particular nonterminating cases that the two orders may give different results. The *Church-Rosser theorem* (also called the *confluence property* or the *diamond property*) states that if a λ calculus expression can be evaluated in two different ways and both ways terminate, both ways will yield the same result (Church and Rosser, 1936).

Also, if there is a way for an expression to terminate, using normal order will cause the termination. In other words, normal order is the best if you want to avoid infinite loops. Consider a similar example, written in the C programming language:

```
int loop() {
  return loop();
}

int f(int x, int y) {
  return x;
}

int main() {
  return f(3, loop());
}
```

In this case, using applicative order will cause the program to hang, because the second argument `loop()` will be evaluated. Using normal order will terminate because the unneeded `y` variable will never be evaluated.

Though normal order is better in this respect, applicative order is the one used by most programming languages. Why? Consider the function $f(x) = x + x$. To find $f(4/2)$ using normal order, we hold off on evaluating the argument until after placing the argument in the function, so it yields

$$f(4/2) = 4/2 + 4/2 = 2 + 2 = 4,$$

and the division needs to be done twice. If we use applicative order, we get

$$f(4/2) = f(2) = 2 + 2 = 4,$$

which requires only one division.

Since applicative order avoids repetitive computations, it is the preferred method of evaluation in most programming languages, where short execution time is critical. Some functional programming languages, such as Haskell, use *call-by-need* evaluation, which will avoid performing unneeded computations (such as `loop()` above) yet will memoize the values of needed arguments (such as `4/2` above) so that repetitive computations are avoided. This *lazy evaluation* mechanism is typically implemented with *thunks*, or zero-argument functions that *freeze* the evaluation of an argument until it is actually used, and *futures* or references to these thunks that trigger the *thawing* of the expression when evaluated, and keep its value for further immediate access.

2.4 Combinators

Any λ calculus expression with no free variables is called a *combinator*. Because the meaning of a λ calculus expression is dependent only on the bindings of its free variables, combinators always have the same meaning independently of the context in which they are used.

There are certain combinators that are very useful in the λ calculus:

The *identity* combinator, defined as

$I = \lambda x.x$

simply returns whatever is given to it. For example:

$(I \quad 5) = (\lambda x.x \quad 5) \Rightarrow 5.$

The identity combinator in the Oz programming language[2] can be written

```
fun {I X} X end
```

or equivalently, but closer to the λ calculus syntax:[3]

```
I = fun {$ X} X end
```

Contrast it to, for example, a `Circumference` function:

```
Circumference = fun {$ Radius} 2*PI*Radius end
```

The semantics of the `Circumference` function depends on the definitions of `PI` and `*`. The `Circumference` function is, therefore, *not* a combinator.

The identity combinator is the identity for function composition, i.e., for any function F:

$((\lambda f.\lambda g.\lambda x.(f \quad (g \quad x)) \quad I) \quad F) \quad = \quad ((\lambda f.\lambda g.\lambda x.(f \quad (g \quad x)) \quad F) \quad I) \quad = \quad F.$

The *application* combinator is

$App = \lambda f.\lambda x.(f \quad x),$

and allows you to evaluate a function with an argument. For example,

$$((App \;\; \lambda x.x^2) \;\; 3)$$

$$\Rightarrow ((\lambda f.\lambda x.(f \;\; x) \;\; \lambda x.x^2) \;\; 3)$$

$$\Rightarrow (\lambda x.(\lambda x.x^2 \;\; x) \;\; 3)$$

$$\Rightarrow (\lambda x.x^2 \;\; 3)$$

$$\Rightarrow 9.$$

The application combinator can be converted to the identity combinator by *eta*-reduction (see section 2.6). We will see more combinators in the following sections.

2.5 Currying

The *currying* higher-order function takes a function and returns a curried version of the function. For example, it can take as input the `Plus` function, which has the type

$$(\mathbf{Z} \times \mathbf{Z}) \rightarrow \mathbf{Z},$$

that is, `Plus` takes two integers ($\mathbf{Z} \times \mathbf{Z}$,) and returns an integer ($\mathbf{Z}$).

The definition of `Plus` in Oz is

```
Plus = fun {$ X Y}
          X+Y
       end
```

The currying combinator would then return the curried version of `Plus`, which we call `PlusC`, with type

$$\mathbf{Z} \rightarrow (\mathbf{Z} \rightarrow \mathbf{Z}).$$

That is, `PlusC` takes one integer as input and returns a function from integers to integers ($\mathbf{Z} \rightarrow \mathbf{Z}$). The definition of `PlusC` in Oz is

```
PlusC = fun {$ X}
           fun {$ Y}
             X+Y
           end
        end
```

Notice how `Plus` returns a number whereas `PlusC` returns a function.

The Oz version of the currying combinator, which we call `Curry`, is to work as follows:

```
{Curry Plus} ⇒ PlusC.
```

Using the input and output types above, the type of the `Curry` function must be at least as general as

$$(\mathbf{Z} \times \mathbf{Z} \rightarrow \mathbf{Z}) \rightarrow (\mathbf{Z} \rightarrow (\mathbf{Z} \rightarrow \mathbf{Z})).$$

So the `Curry` function should take as input an uncurried function and return the curried version of the function. In Oz, we can write `Curry` as follows:

```
Curry = fun {$ F}
          fun {$ X}
            fun {$ Y}
              {F X Y}
            end
          end
        end
```

2.6 η-Conversion

Consider the expression

$$(\lambda x.(\lambda x.x^2 \quad x) \quad y).$$

Using β-reduction, we can take $E = (\lambda x.x^2 \quad x)$ and $M = y$. In the reduction we replace only the one x that is free in E to get

$$\xrightarrow{\beta} (\lambda x.x^2 \quad y).$$

We use the symbol $\xrightarrow{\beta}$ to show that we are performing β-reduction on the expression. (As another example, we may write $\lambda x.x^2 \xrightarrow{\alpha} \lambda y.y^2$, since α-renaming is taking place.)

Another type of operation possible on λ calculus expressions is called *η-conversion* (eta-reduction when applied from left to right). We perform η-reduction using the rule

$$\lambda x.(E \quad x) \xrightarrow{\eta} E.$$

η-reduction can only be applied if x does not appear free in E.

Consider the expression $\lambda x.(\lambda x.x^2 \quad x)$. We can perform η-reduction to obtain

$$\lambda x.(\lambda x.x^2 \quad x) \xrightarrow{\eta} \lambda x.x^2.$$

We can also apply η-reduction to subexpressions; i.e., starting with the same expression as before, $(\lambda x.(\lambda x.x^2 \quad x) \quad y)$, we can perform η-reduction to obtain

$$(\lambda x.(\lambda x.x^2 \quad x) \quad y) \xrightarrow{\eta} (\lambda x.x^2 \quad y),$$

which gives the same result as β-reduction.

η-reduction can be considered a program optimization. For example, consider the following Oz definitions:

```
Increment = fun {$ X} X+1 end

Inc = fun {$ X} {Increment X} end
```

Using η-reduction, we could statically reduce `{Inc Y}` to `{Increment Y}` avoiding one extra function call (or β reduction step) at run-time. This compiler optimization is also called *inlining*.

In λ calculus terms, where *i* corresponds to `Increment`, we are performing the following reduction:

$$(\lambda x.(i \quad x) \quad y) \xrightarrow{\eta} (i \quad y).$$

Notice that in this example, we could also have applied β-reduction, to get to the same expression:

$$(\lambda x.(i \quad x) \quad y) \xrightarrow{\beta} (i \quad y).$$

Now consider:

```
IncTwice = fun {$ X} {Inc {Inc X}} end
```

Compiler inlining can convert a call `{IncTwice Y}` to `{Inc {Inc Y}}` and then to `{Increment {Increment Y}}`, avoiding three extra function calls at run-time.

In λ calculus terms, we would write:

$$(\lambda x.(\lambda x.(i \quad x) \quad (\lambda x.(i \quad x) \quad x)) \quad y) \xrightarrow{\eta}\xrightarrow{\eta}\xrightarrow{\beta} (i \quad (i \quad y)).$$

In this case, we must perform at least one β-reduction step, since the expression $(\lambda x.(i \quad (i \quad x)) \quad y)$ has no η-redex. This example illustrates that the function inlining compiler optimization is more generally a static application of β-reduction.

However, there are also expressions without a β-redex that can be η-reduced. An example follows:

$\lambda x.(i \quad x) \xrightarrow{\eta} i.$

A compiler optimization strictly corresponding to η-reduction is able to convert a more complex function into a simpler one, without the function necessarily being applied. In Oz terms, the compiler could generate code for:

```
Inc = Increment,
```

whether the function `Inc` is directly applied to an argument in the body of the program.

η-conversion can also affect termination of expressions in applicative order expression evaluation. For example, the Y recursion combinator has a terminating applicative order form that can be derived from the normal order combinator form (see section 2.8) by using η-expansion, i.e., η-conversion from right to left.

2.7 Sequencing Combinator

The *normal order sequencing* combinator is:

$Seq = \lambda x.\lambda y.(\lambda z.y \quad x),$

where z is chosen so that it does not appear free in y.

This combinator guarantees that x is evaluated before y, which is important in programs with side-effects. Assuming we had a "display" function sending output to the console, an example is

$((Seq \quad (\text{display "hello"})) \quad (\text{display "world"})).$

The combinator would not work in applicative order (call by value) evaluation because evaluating the `display` functions before getting them passed to the `Seq` function would defeat the purpose of the combinator: to sequence execution. In particular, if the arguments are evaluated *right to left*, execution would not be as expected.

The *applicative-order sequencing* combinator can be written as follows:

$ASeq = \lambda x.\lambda y.(y \quad x),$

where y is a lambda abstraction that *wraps* the original last expression to evaluate.

The same example above would be written as follows:

$((ASeq \quad (\text{display "hello"})) \quad \lambda x.(\text{display "world"})),$

with x fresh, that is, not appearing free in the second expression.

This strategy of *wrapping* a λ calculus expression to make it a value and delay its evaluation is very useful. It enables the expression to simulate *call by name* parameter passing in languages using *call by value*. The process of wrapping is also called *freezing* an expression, and the resulting frozen expression is called a *thunk*. Evaluating a thunk to get back the original expression is also called *thawing*.

2.8 Recursion Combinator

The *recursion* combinator allows defining recursive computations in the λ calculus. For example, suppose we want to implement a recursive version of the factorial function:

$$f(n) = n! = \begin{cases} 1 & \text{if } n = 0 \\ n(n-1)! & \text{if } n > 0. \end{cases}$$

We could start by attempting to write the recursive function f in the λ calculus (assuming it has been extended with conditionals, and numbers) as follows:[4]

$$\begin{aligned} f = \lambda n.(\text{if} \;\; & (= \;\; n \;\; 0) \\ & 1 \\ & (* \;\; n \;\; (f \;\; (- \;\; n \;\; 1)))). \end{aligned}$$

The problem is that this function definition uses a free variable f, which is the very factorial function that we are trying to define. To avoid this circular definition, we can extend the definition with another functional abstraction (lambda expression) to take the factorial function itself as follows:

$$\begin{aligned} f' = \lambda f.\lambda n.(\text{if} \;\; & (= \;\; n \;\; 0) \\ & 1 \\ & (* \;\; n \;\; (f \;\; (- \;\; n \;\; 1)))). \end{aligned}$$

Before we can input an integer to the function, we must input a function to satisfy f so that the returned function computes the desired factorial value. Let us call this function X. Notice that the function X must behave just like f, i.e., $X = f$. The function f' will return the proper recursive function f with the type $\mathbf{Z} \to \mathbf{Z}$, but only when supplied with the correct function X. We can write the type of f' as

$$f' : (\mathbf{Z} \to \mathbf{Z}) \to (\mathbf{Z} \to \mathbf{Z}).$$

What we need is a function X that, when we apply f' to it, it returns the correct recursive factorial function f, that is,

$$(f' \;\; X) = \lambda n.(\text{if} \;\; (= n \;\; 0) \;\; 1 \;\; (* \;\; n \;\; (X \;\; (- \;\; n \;\; 1)))) = f = X,$$

and so we need to solve the fixed point X of the function f', i.e., the solution to the equation $(f' \;\; X) = X$.

We could try applying f' to itself, i.e.,

$$(f' \;\; f').$$

This does not work, because f' expects a function of type $\mathbf{Z} \to \mathbf{Z}$, but it is taking another f', which has the more complex type $(\mathbf{Z} \to \mathbf{Z}) \to (\mathbf{Z} \to \mathbf{Z})$. A function that has the correct input type is the identity combinator, $\lambda x.x$. Applying f' to the identity combinator, we get:

$$\begin{aligned}(f' \;\; I) \Rightarrow \;\; & \lambda n.(\text{if} \;\; (= \;\; n \;\; 0) \\ & \qquad\quad 1 \\ & \qquad\quad (* \;\; n \;\; (I \;\; (- \;\; n \;\; 1)))) \\ \Rightarrow \;\; & \lambda n.(\text{if} \;\; (= \;\; n \;\; 0) \\ & \qquad\quad 1 \\ & \qquad\quad (* \;\; n \;\; (- \;\; n \;\; 1))),\end{aligned}$$

which is equivalent to

$$g(n) = \begin{cases} 1 & \text{if } n = 0 \\ n * (n - 1) & \text{if } n > 0. \end{cases}$$

We need to find the correct expression X such that when f' is applied to X, we get X, the recursive factorial function. It turns out that the X that works is:

$$\begin{aligned}X = \;\; & (\lambda x.(\lambda f.\lambda n.(\text{if} \;\; (= \;\; n \;\; 0) \;\; 1 \;\; (* \;\; (n \;\; (f \;\; (- \;\; n \;\; 1))))) \;\; (x \;\; x)) \\ & \;\lambda x.(\lambda f.\lambda n.(\text{if} \;\; (= \;\; n \;\; 0) \;\; 1 \;\; (* \;\; (n \;\; (f \;\; (- \;\; n \;\; 1))))) \;\; (x \;\; x))).\end{aligned}$$

Note that this λ calculus expression has a structure similar to the nonterminating expression

$$(\lambda x.(x \;\; x) \;\; \lambda x.(x \;\; x)),$$

and explains why the recursive function can keep going.

X can be defined as $(Y \;\; f')$ where Y is the recursion combinator,

$$(f' \;\; X) = (f' \;\; (Y \;\; f')) \Rightarrow (Y \;\; f') = X = f.$$

The recursion combinator that works for normal order evaluation is defined as:

$$\begin{aligned}Y = \lambda f.(& \lambda x.(f \;\; (x \;\; x)) \\ & \lambda x.(f \;\; (x \;\; x))).\end{aligned}$$

The applicative order evaluation version of the recursion combinator is:

$$\begin{aligned}Y = \lambda f.(& \lambda x.(f \;\; \lambda y.((x \;\; x) \;\; y)) \\ & \lambda x.(f \;\; \lambda y.((x \;\; x) \;\; y))).\end{aligned}$$

How do we get from the normal order evaluation recursion combinator to the applicative order evaluation recursion combinator? We use η-expansion (see section 2.6). This is an example where η-conversion can have an impact on the termination of an expression in applicative order evaluation.

To sum up, we can write the factorial function in the λ calculus, as follows:

$$
\begin{aligned}
(Y\ \lambda f.\lambda n.(\text{if}\ \ & (=\ n\ 0)\\
& 1\\
& (*\ n\ (f\ (-\ n\ 1))))).
\end{aligned}
$$

2.9 Higher-Order Programming

Most imperative programming languages, for example, Java and C++, do not allow us to treat functions or procedures as first-class entities, for example, we cannot create and return a new function that did not exist before. A function that can deal only with primitive types (i.e., not other functions) is called a *first-order* function. For example, `Increment`, whose type is $\mathbf{Z} \rightarrow \mathbf{Z}$, can only take integer values and return integer values. Programming only with first-order functions is called *first-order* programming.

If a function can take another function as an argument, or if it returns a function, it is called a *higher-order* function.

For example, the `Curry` combinator, whose type is:

`Curry` : $(\mathbf{Z} \times \mathbf{Z} \rightarrow \mathbf{Z}) \rightarrow (\mathbf{Z} \rightarrow (\mathbf{Z} \rightarrow \mathbf{Z}))$,

is a higher-order (third order) function. It takes a function of type $\mathbf{Z} \times \mathbf{Z} \rightarrow \mathbf{Z}$ and returns a function of type $\mathbf{Z} \rightarrow (\mathbf{Z} \rightarrow \mathbf{Z})$. That is, `Curry` takes a first-order function and returns a second-order function. The ability to view *functions* as data is called *higher-order programming*.[5]

2.9.1 Currying as a Higher-Order Function

Higher-order programming is a very powerful technique, as shown in the following Oz example. Consider an exponential function, `Exp`, as follows:

```
Exp = fun {$ B N}
        if N==0 then
          1
        else
          B * {Exp B N-1}
        end
      end.
```

And recall the Curry combinator in Oz:

```
Curry = fun {$ F}
          fun {$ X}
            fun {$ Y}
              {F X Y}
            end
          end
        end.
```

We can create a function to compute the powers of 2, `TwoE`, by just using

```
TwoE = {{Curry Exp} 2}.
```

To illustrate the execution of this expression, consider the following Oz computation steps (equivalent to two β-reduction steps in the λ calculus):

```
TwoE = {{Curry Exp} 2}
     = {{fun {$ F}
             fun {$ X}
                fun {$ Y}
                   {F X Y}
                end
             end
          end Exp} 2}
     = {fun {$ X}
            fun {$ Y}
               {Exp X Y}
            end
         end 2}
     = fun {$ Y}
          {Exp 2 Y}
        end
```

If we want to create a `Square` function, using `Exp`, we can create a *reverse curry* combinator, `RCurry`, as:

```
RCurry = fun {$ F}
           fun {$ X}
             fun {$ Y}
               {F Y X}
             end
           end
         end,
```

where the arguments to the function are simply reversed.

We can then define `Square` as

```
Square = {{RCurry Exp} 2}.
```

2.9.2 Numbers in the λ Calculus

The λ calculus is a *Turing-complete* language, that is, any computable function can be expressed in the pure λ calculus. In many of the previous examples, however, we have used numbers and conditionals.

Let us see one possible representation of numbers in the pure λ calculus:

$$\begin{aligned} |0| &= \lambda x.x \\ |1| &= \lambda x.\lambda x.x \\ \ldots \\ |n+1| &= \lambda x.|n|. \end{aligned}$$

That is, zero is represented as the identity combinator. Each succesive number $(n+1)$ is represented as a functional (or procedural) abstraction that takes any value and returns the representation of its predecessor (n.) You can think of zero as a first-order function, one as a second-order function, and so on.

In Oz, this would be written:

```
Zero = I

Succ = fun {$ N}
          fun {$ X}
             N
          end
       end
```

Using this representation, the number 2, for example, would be the λ calculus expression: $\lambda x.\lambda x.\lambda x.x$, or equivalently in Oz:

```
{Succ {Succ Zero}}.
```

2.9.3 Booleans in the λ Calculus

Now, let us see one possible representation of booleans in the pure λ calculus:

$$\begin{aligned} |\texttt{true}| &= \lambda x.\lambda y.x \\ |\texttt{false}| &= \lambda x.\lambda y.y \\ |\texttt{if}| &= \lambda b.\lambda t.\lambda e.((b\ \ t)\ \ e). \end{aligned}$$

That is, `true` is represented as a (curried) function that takes two arguments and returns the first, while `false` is represented as a function that takes two arguments and returns the second. `if` is a function that takes:

- a function b representing a boolean value (either `true` or `false`),
- an argument t representing the *then* branch, and
- an argument e representing the *else* branch,

and returns either t if b represents `true`, or e if b represents `false`.

Let us see an example evaluation sequence for (((`if true`) 4) 5):

$$(((\lambda b.\lambda t.\lambda e.((b\ \ t)\ \ e)\ \ \lambda x.\lambda y.x)\ \ 4)\ \ 5)$$

$$\xrightarrow{\beta} ((\lambda t.\lambda e.((\lambda x.\lambda y.x\ \ t)\ \ e)\ \ 4)\ \ 5)$$

$$\xrightarrow{\beta} (\lambda e.((\lambda x.\lambda y.x\ \ 4)\ \ e)\ \ 5)$$

$$\xrightarrow{\beta} ((\lambda x.\lambda y.x\ \ 4)\ \ 5)$$

$$\xrightarrow{\beta} (\lambda y.4\ \ 5)$$

$$\xrightarrow{\beta} 4.$$

Note that this definition of booleans works properly in normal evaluation order, but has problems in applicative evaluation order. The reason is that applicative order evaluates *both* the *then* and the *else* branches, which is a problem if used in recursive computations (where the evaluation may not terminate) or if used to guard improper operations (such as division by zero). The applicative order evaluation versions of `if`, `true`, and `false` can *wrap* the *then* and *else* expressions inside functional abstractions, so that they are values and do not get prematurely evaluated, similarly to how the applicative order evaluation sequencing operator wrapped the expression to be evaluated last in the sequence (see section 2.7).

In Oz, the following (uncurried) function definitions can be used to test this representation:

```
LambdaTrue  = fun {$ X Y}
                X
              end

LambdaFalse = fun {$ X Y}
                Y
              end
```

```
LambdaIf      = fun {$ B T E}
                   {B T E}
                end
```

2.10 Discussion and Further Reading

The λ calculus is a formal theoretical model of sequential computation invented by Alonzo Church and his student Kleene in the 1930s (Church, 1941). The Church-Rosser theorem, proved in 1936, demonstrates that expressions in the λ calculus have normal forms, i.e., $(e \Rightarrow e_1) \wedge (e \Rightarrow e_2) \implies \exists e' \mid (e_1 \Rightarrow^* e') \wedge (e_2 \Rightarrow^* e')$ (Church and Rosser, 1936). While normal-order evaluation is better behaved since reduction terminates where other evaluation orders may not, applicative-order evaluation is the most commonly used strategy in practical programming languages due to its efficiency. Lazy evaluation, in languages such as Haskell (Hudak et al., 1992), is a strategy to delay expression evaluation until (and only if) needed, and then memoize the result to avoid redundant computation.

Currying is a technique that allows to define a function of n arguments as a higher-order function of only one argument that returns another function that takes the remaining $n - 1$ arguments and returns the value of the original n-arity function. Because of currying, the λ calculus can use a single abstraction for function definition and a single abstraction for function evaluation, and yet be more generally applicable. Some programming languages, such as ML (Gordon et al., 1978) and Haskell (Hudak et al., 1992), have first-class currying, i.e., all their functions have single arity. Combinators are λ calculus expressions with no free variables, which makes their meaning context-independent. The recursive combinator, Y, discovered by Haskell Curry, allows to define recursive functions in the λ calculus, proving it Turing-complete (Curry, 1941).

Higher-order programming, which is natural in the λ calculus, enables us to view functions as data. Lisp is a functional programming language that uses the same syntax for programs and for data (lists). This enables *metacircular* interpretation: a full Lisp interpreter, written in Lisp, can be an input to itself (McCarthy, 1960).

The simplicity and expressive power of the λ calculus make it one of the most commonly used formal models to study sequential programming languages, and it has influenced the design of many modern programming languages. The actor model of concurrent computation, which we study in chapter 4, uses the λ calculus as the formalism for sequential computation within communicating actors. The reader interested in a more extensive treatment of the λ calculus is referred to Barendregt (1981).

2.11 Exercises

1. α-convert the outer-most x to y in the following λ calculus expressions, if possible:
(a) $\lambda x.(\lambda x.x\,x)$
(b) $\lambda x.(\lambda x.x\,y)$

2. β-reduce the following λ calculus expressions, if possible:
(a) $(\lambda x.\lambda y.(x\,y)\,(y\,w))$
(b) $(\lambda x.(x\,x)\,\lambda x.(x\,x))$

3. Simulate the execution of `Square` in Oz, using the definition of `RCurry` given in section 2.9.1.
4. Using the number representation in section 2.9.2, define functions `Plus`, `PlusC` (its curried version) in Oz, and test them using Mozart (Oz's run-time system).
5. Write a function composition combinator in the λ calculus.
6. Define a curried version of `Compose` in Oz, `ComposeC`, without using the `Curry` combinator. *Hint*: It should look very similar to the λ calculus expression from exercise 5.
7. η-reduce the following λ calculus expressions, if possible:
(a) $\lambda x.(\lambda y.x\,x)$
(b) $\lambda x.(\lambda y.y\,x)$

8. Use η-reduction to get from the applicative order Y combinator to the normal order Y combinator.
9. What would be the effect of applying the reverse currying combinator, `RCurry`, to the function composition combinator?

```
Compose = fun {$ F G}
            fun {$ X}
              {F {G X}}
            end
          end
```

Give an example of using the `{RCurry Compose}` function.
10. Give an alternative representation of numbers in the λ calculus. Test your representation using Oz. *Hint*: Find out about *Church numerals*.
11. Define a + operation for your representation of numbers from the preceding exercise. Test your addition operation in Oz.
12. Give an alternative representation of booleans in the λ calculus. Test your representation using Oz. *Hint*: One possibility is to use $\lambda x.x$ for `true` and $\lambda x.\lambda x.x$ for `false`. You need to figure out how to define `if`.

13. Create an alternative representation of booleans in the λ calculus so that conditional execution works as expected in applicative evaluation order. Test your representation using Oz. *Hint*: Use the strategy of wrapping the *then* and *else* branches to turn them into values and prevent their premature evaluation.
14. For a given function f, prove that $(Y \quad f) \Rightarrow (f \quad (Y \quad f))$.

Notes

1. Being precise, the λ calculus does not directly support number constants (such as "1") or primitive operations (such as "+" or x^2) but these can be encoded as we shall see in section 2.9. We use this notation here for pedagogical purposes only. If you would rather follow the syntax precisely, think of x^2 as $(s\ x)$ and $x + 1$ as $(i\ x)$ where s and i denote *square* and *increment* functions.

2. We use examples in different programming languages (e.g., Scheme, C, Oz) to illustrate that the concepts in the λ calculus are ubiquitous and apply to many different sequential programming languages.

3. The $ notation in Oz converts a language statement into an expression (with a return value), which we use here to create an anonymous function.

4. We will use prefix notation for mathematical expressions to be more consistent with function application syntax in the λ calculus as introduced in section 2.1.

5. The ability in some imperative programming languages to pass pointers to functions, as in a generic sort routine that can receive different element ordering functions, is only half of the equation. Truly higher-order programming requires the ability to create arbitrarily *new* functions as done in the currying example in section 2.5. This requires the language to support *closures*, i.e., functions whose free variables become bound to environment variable values at the time of function creation.

I Theoretical Models of Concurrency, Distribution, and Mobility

I.1 Models of Concurrent Computing

In this part of the book, we will introduce the main modern theories of concurrent, distributed, and mobile computation. The first two chapters discuss the π calculus and the actor model of concurrent computation, whereas the following two chapters discuss more recent theories—the join calculus and mobile ambients—that attempt to model more explicitly distribution and mobility issues, respectively. Each of these chapters presents the syntactic constructs of a formal language embodying the model, the operational semantics of the language, usually as a labeled transition system, and reasoning capabilities afforded by the model, typically some form of observational equivalence. A set of common examples—a reference cell, mutual exclusion, and the famous dining philosophers problem—are presented in each model's language to enable the reader to compare side by side each model's encoding of the same examples. Finally, in chapter 7, we categorize the fundamental properties of each of these models for a direct comparison of their characteristics: e.g., What are their ontological commitments? What is their expressive power? How well do they support reasoning about concurrent, distributed, and mobile computer systems?

The π calculus (Milner et al., 1992), discussed in chapter 3, is the main representative of a family of process algebra-based models, which has its roots in earlier models of concurrency such as the calculus of communicating systems (CCS) (Milner, 1980, 1989) and communicating sequential processes (CSP) (Hoare, 1985). The key feature that the π calculus attempts to model, which makes it depart from earlier process algebras, is *mobility* of processes, according to Milner's Turing Award lecture (Milner, 1993). Such mobility is represented in the π calculus as the dynamic reconfiguration of the topology of communicating processes. Modeling dynamic topologies of communication and interaction was inspired by the actor model and makes the π calculus closer to practical distributed and mobile systems. Process algebras have been used as theoretical frameworks to reason about concurrency, and there are important techniques that have been devised in the context of process algebras, such as bisimulation, in order to study equivalence of concurrent programs.

The actor model of concurrent computation (Hewitt, 1977; Agha, 1986; Agha et al., 1997), discussed in chapter 4, in contrast to process algebras, formalizes concurrency by modeling interaction between independent, uniquely named, history-sensitive computational entities, termed *actors*. The actor model explicitly disallows shared memory (such as channels in process algebras): The only way for an actor to communicate with another actor is by sending it messages, which requires knowing the actor's (unique) name. Messages are received and processed asynchronously (as opposed to the synchronous nature of communication in process algebras), which makes actors more naturally model distributed and mobile systems. The model affords unbounded concurrency by allowing actors to create new actors in response to messages. Actor creation is synchronous, returning the actor's name, which can be used for future communication with the actor, or can be passed along in messages to other actors, thereby making the topology of communication dynamic. Fairness is a key property of actor systems that enables compositional reasoning.

The join calculus (Fournet and Gonthier, 1996) and the ambient calculus (Cardelli and Gordon, 2000), described in chapters 5 and 6 respectively, belong to the same family of process algebras as the π calculus, and attempt to address more explicitly distribution and mobility aspects.

The join calculus models computation as a multiset of *chemical reaction sites*, where processes, modeled as *molecules* (i.e., parallel composition of *atoms*) interact according to local *rules*, which can change over time. Reaction rules define patterns that must be matched by the molecules in the site for reactions to take place. In response to an atomic reaction, molecules disappear and new molecules may appear in the reaction site. Also in response to an atomic reaction, new reaction rules may be created, which makes the model *reflective*. The reaction rule patterns define names with static scope, i.e., affecting only local molecules. Distribution and mobility of processes are modeled as heating and cooling of reaction rules to enable interaction between molecules.

The ambient calculus creates the notion of *boundaries* that contain and restrict interaction between processes: only processes in the same boundary, or *ambient*, can communicate with each other. Ambients can also contain other ambients, creating a nested hierarchical structure of interaction. Ambients are *mobile*, which allows the topology of interaction to change dynamically. Ambients move *subjectively*, i.e., in response to a contained process requesting such movement. When ambients move, all contained inner ambients and processes also move with the parent ambient. Therefore, process mobility is modeled as the mobility of the surrounding ambient enclosing the moving process. While interprocess communication is asynchronous, ambient movement (and destruction) primitives are synchronous and modeled as *capabilities* that can be communicated.

To conclude this part, chapter 7 compares these four models of concurrent, distributed, and mobile computation side by side and illustrates their strengths and weaknesses.

A natural question to ask is why to study more than one fundamental model of concurrency? Clearly, the π calculus attempts to be as simple as possible, and to enable an elegant formal mathematical (algebraic) treatment of concurrent programs. The π calculus attempts to model all concurrent computation as the λ calculus models all sequential computation. The actor model, on the other hand, is much closer to practical distributed computer systems due to its primitive asynchronous mode of communication, its assumption of no shared memory, and its requirement for fairness and uniqueness of actor identities (or names). The actor model is closer to real-world distributed systems, but also and arguably because of that, it is harder to reason about. The actor language that we study in chapter 4 is an extension of the λ calculus, and therefore it more naturally subsumes sequential computation.

Should spatial distribution and process mobility be explicitly modeled? Or should they be left to concurrent programming languages and distributed and mobile systems run-time infrastructure? Both the join calculus and mobile ambients attempt to explicitly model spatial locality and restrict interprocess communication to *purely local* interaction. Formalizing locations and movement significantly increases the complexity of concurrency models. On the other hand, it enables reasoning about important distributed system properties, such as partial failures, atomic group failures, administrative boundaries such as firewalls, and efficiency of communication.

Computing models serve at least two important purposes: First, they help reason theoretically (mathematically) about the nature and the limits of computing; second, they help formalize computation and specify precisely different paradigms or ways to think about, organize, and develop computer systems. Concurrent computing models that address explicitly distribution, mobility, failures, and/or adaptivity of computer systems tend to deviate from the first purpose due to the added inherent complexity, but also tend to serve more effectively for the second purpose, in particular, pragmatically influencing programming language and system designers.

I.2 Other Approaches to Modeling Concurrency

One of the first models of concurrency was Petri nets (Petri, 1962). A Petri net is a graph with two types of nodes: nodes containing tokens and nodes representing potential transitions of tokens between nodes. Transitions can fire if all the nodes that point to a transition node contain at least one token. After the transition fires,

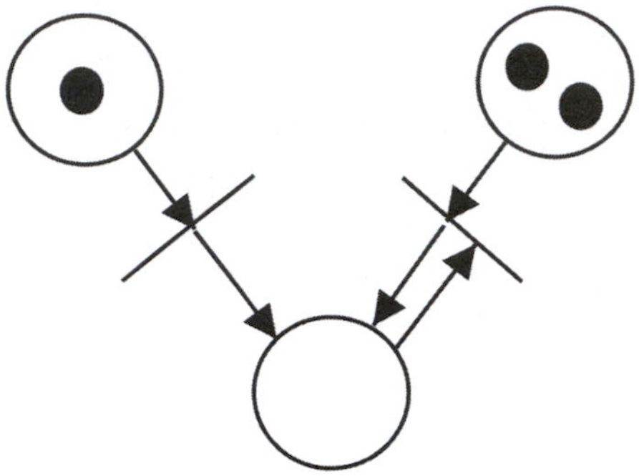

Figure I.1
A simple Petri net. Tokens are filled circles. Token-containing nodes are unfilled circles. Nodes representing potential transitions are drawn as lines. Edges between nodes are represented as arrows.

tokens get removed from the nodes pointing to the transition node and get created in any nodes that transition nodes point to.

Consider, for example, the Petri net illustrated in figure I.1. In this example, only one of the two transitions is enabled, the leftmost transition. The rightmost transition is not enabled since the bottom node does not contain any tokens. After the leftmost transition fires, the transition is no longer enabled since the left node will not contain any tokens; however, the rightmost transition will become enabled, since a token will have appeared in the bottom node after the leftmost transition fired. After the rightmost transition fires twice, the net will reach a quiescent state with no transitions any longer enabled and a single token in the bottom node.

Petri nets have been studied significantly in the literature and have been successfully used, e.g., to model hardware; however, at least in the simplest form described here, they are not able to model the dynamicity of concurrent software: in particular, the creation of new nodes and dynamic changes in the nodes' communication topology. While adding more information in tokens (e.g., "color" in colored Petri nets) increases their expressive power significantly, Petri nets still do not support the compositional reasoning afforded by more modern models of concurrency.

3 π Calculus

The π calculus is a formal model for specification, analysis, and verification of systems composed of communicating concurrent processes (Milner et al., 1992).

In the following sections, we will introduce the π calculus syntax, its semantics, a technique called *bisimulation* to prove equivalence of processes, and some examples illustrating the usage of the π calculus. Finally, we will refer the interested reader to literature describing variants and further developments of the calculus.

3.1 Syntax

Concurrent computation is modeled in the π calculus as processes communicating over shared channels. Process variables are denoted by uppercase letters such as P, Q, R; channel names are denoted by lowercase letters such as a, b, c; interaction on channels (reading, writing) is denoted by the *prefix* α. The π calculus syntax is shown in figure 3.1.

A simple interaction between two processes over a channel a can be modeled as follows in the π calculus

$$a(x).P \mid \bar{a}b.Q.$$

In this expression, there are two concurrently executing processes (separated by $|$.) The first process denoted by $a(x).P$ is blocked, waiting for another process to write a value over channel a, which will be replacing variable x in process P upon communication. The second process denoted by $\bar{a}b.Q$ is similarly blocked, waiting for another process to read the value b (a channel name) over channel a, before proceeding as Q. This example illustrates a synchronous communication. A pictorial representation of this interaction is depicted in figure 3.2.

After interaction between these two processes, the π calculus expression evolves as

$$P\{b/x\} \mid Q.$$

α	::=	$\bar{c}x$	Write x on channel c
		$c(x)$	Read x on channel c
		τ	No interaction
P, Q	::=	0	Empty process
		$\alpha.P$	Prefixed process
		$P \mid Q$	Concurrent composition of P and Q
		$P + Q$	Nondeterministic choice of P or Q
		$(\nu c)P$	New channel c, scope restricted to P
		$\texttt{if}\ x = y\ \texttt{then}\ P$	Conditional execution (match)
		$\texttt{if}\ x \neq y\ \texttt{then}\ P$	Conditional execution (mismatch)
		$A(y_1, \ldots, y_n)$	Process invocation
Δ	::=	$A(x_1, \ldots, x_n) \triangleq P$	Process declaration

Figure 3.1
π calculus syntax.

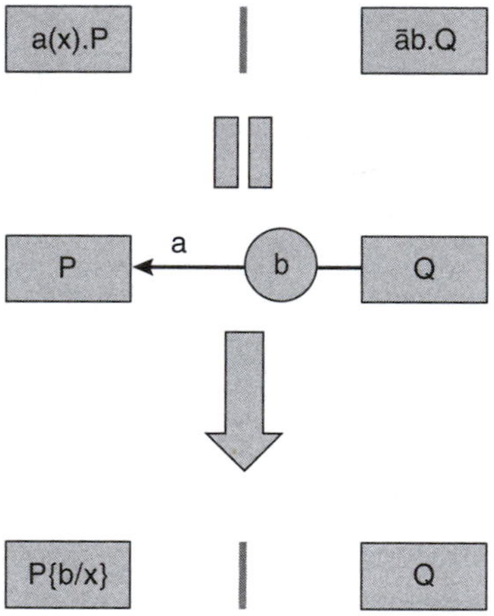

Figure 3.2
A pictorial representation of process interaction in the π calculus.

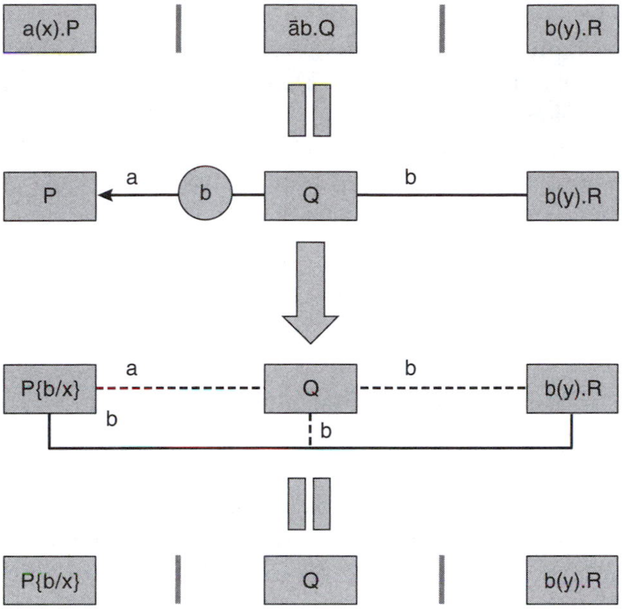

Figure 3.3
Movement of process R from Q to P. Dashed lines represent the possibility of channel a still connecting P and Q, and channel b still connecting Q and R, and after communication P.

That is, P becomes unblocked and can continue execution with any *free occurrences* of x replaced by b. Similarly, Q continues execution.

Notice that channel names are used uniformly as *subjects* and as *objects* of communication. In the previous example, the communication of (object) channel b over (subject) channel a from process Q to process P can be interpreted as the "*movement*" of any processes that the channel b points to from process Q to process P. We can represent this pictorially as in figure 3.3. In this example, channel b connects processes Q and R. After communication, channel b connects processes P and R. This can be interpreted as process R having moved from Q to P. For example, P may denote a web client, Q a web server, and R an applet that has moved from server to client.

Any remaining free instances of a in P and Q would represent channel a still connecting these two processes (denoted by a dotted line in the diagram). The same is true for any remaining free instances of b in Q, which would represent a potential channel of communication not only between Q and R, but also between Q and P (which also shares channel b).

3.1.1 Free and Bound Variables

It is important to understand the notion of scope of variables, since the same channel name, e.g., x, may refer to different channels if it appears in different scopes. The notion of scope of variables is very similar to the λ calculus (see section 2.2). Whereas λ was the only variable binder in the λ calculus, in the π calculus, the input prefix $a(x).P$ and the new channel operator $(\nu x)P$ both *bind* x in P. Conversely, the output prefix $\bar{a}x.P$ *does not bind* x in P.

For example, in the expression

$$c(x).\bar{d}x.P,$$

the variable x refers to the same channel, whose name is read over channel c and subsequently written over channel d. On the other hand, in the expression

$$\bar{c}x.d(x).P,$$

the two occurrences of variable x are in two different scopes: the first x refers to a channel whose name is to be written over channel c, and the second x is creating a *new* scope to represent a channel whose name is read over channel d and potentially subsequently used in P.

We let $\mathbf{fn}(P)$ and $\mathbf{bn}(P)$ respectively denote the sets of free names and bound names in the π calculus expression P. For example, $\mathbf{fn}(a(x).0) = \{a\}$, while $\mathbf{bn}(a(x).0) = \{x\}$. We also let $\mathbf{fn}(\alpha)$ and $\mathbf{bn}(\alpha)$ respectively denote the sets of free names and bound names in prefixes, as follows: $\mathbf{fn}(a(x)) = \{a\}$, $\mathbf{bn}(a(x)) = \{x\}$, $\mathbf{fn}(\bar{a}x) = \{a, x\}$, and $\mathbf{bn}(\bar{a}x) = \mathbf{fn}(\tau) = \mathbf{bn}(\tau) = \emptyset$.

3.1.2 Structural Congruence

Two process expressions P and Q are said to be *structurally congruent,* denoted as $P \equiv Q$, if they represent the same process, although they may be syntactically different. Figure 3.4 specifies the conditions under which two expressions are structurally congruent.

Variants of α-conversion[1] refer to expressions that can be translated into each other by substituting their bound variables with other variable names, respecting the scope of (not capturing) existing free variables. For example, $a(x).\bar{b}x.0$ can be α-converted to $a(y).\bar{b}y.0$ without changing its meaning: Read a channel name on channel a and write it back on channel b. In this example, we replaced the bound occurrences of x to y in the original expression without changing its meaning. Thus, we can say that $a(x).\bar{b}x.0 \equiv a(y).\bar{b}y.0$. We could not, however, replace variable occurrences of x to b, because in such an erroneous case, we would get the π calculus

P and Q are structurally congruent, $P \equiv Q$, in any of the following cases:

1. P and Q are variants of α-conversion.
2. P and Q are related by the Abelian monoid laws for $|$ and $+$:

$$\begin{array}{llll} P \mid Q & \equiv Q \mid P & P + Q & \equiv Q + P \\ (P \mid Q) \mid R & \equiv P \mid (Q \mid R) & (P + Q) + R & \equiv P + (Q + R) \\ P \mid 0 & \equiv P & P + P & \equiv P \end{array}$$

3. P and Q are related by the unfolding law:

$$A(\vec{y}) \equiv P\{\vec{y}/\vec{x}\} \qquad \text{if } A(\vec{x}) \quad \triangleq \quad P$$

4. P and Q are related by the scope extension laws:

$$\begin{array}{lll} (\nu x)0 & \equiv 0 & \\ (\nu x)(P \mid Q) & \equiv P \mid (\nu x)Q & \text{if } x \notin \mathbf{fn}(P). \\ (\nu x)(P + Q) & \equiv P + (\nu x)Q & \text{if } x \notin \mathbf{fn}(P). \\ (\nu x)\texttt{if } u = v \texttt{ then } P & \equiv \texttt{if } u = v \texttt{ then } (\nu x)P & \text{if } x \notin \{u, v\}. \\ (\nu x)\texttt{if } u \neq v \texttt{ then } P & \equiv \texttt{if } u \neq v \texttt{ then } (\nu x)P & \text{if } x \notin \{u, v\}. \\ (\nu x)(\nu y)P & \equiv (\nu y)(\nu x)P & \end{array}$$

Figure 3.4
π calculus structural congruence rules.

expression $a(b).\bar{b}b.0$, in which we would have *captured* the originally free occurrence of b in $a(x).\bar{b}x.0$, and therefore we would have changed the meaning of the expression.

The second scope extension law is important (when applied from right to left) because it allows to extend the scope of a variable x from a single process Q to the concurrent composition $P \mid Q$, provided it does not capture free occurrences of x in P. For example, consider the expression

$$a(x).P \mid (\nu b)\bar{a}b.Q. \tag{3.1}$$

Assuming that $b \notin \mathbf{fn}(P) \cup \{a\}$, we can apply scope extension to make it structurally congruent to:

$$(\nu b)(a(x).P \mid \bar{a}b.Q).$$

The latter expression can evolve by communication of the concurrent embedded processes over channel a into

$$(\nu b)(P\{b/x\} \mid Q).$$

If $b \in \mathbf{fn}(P)$ in expression 3.1, we can α-convert b in $(\nu b)\bar{a}b.Q$ to b', where $b' \notin \mathbf{fn}(P)$ and subsequently apply the scope extension law and a communication over channel a, resulting in the following expression:

$$(\nu b')(P\{b'/x\} \mid Q\{b'/b\}).$$

For example, consider expression 3.1 where P is $\bar{b}x.0$ and Q is 0:

$$a(x).\bar{b}x.0 \mid (\nu b)\bar{a}b.0.$$

We cannot directly apply the scope extension law, since b appears *free* in P. However, we can α-convert the expression by replacing bound occurrences of b to d in the subexpression $(\nu b)\bar{a}b.0$, resulting in the structurally congruent expression

$$a(x).\bar{b}x.0 \mid (\nu d)\bar{a}d.0$$

$$\equiv (\nu d)(a(x).\bar{b}x.0 \mid \bar{a}d.0)$$
$$\xrightarrow{\tau} (\nu d)(\bar{b}d.0 \mid 0)$$
$$\equiv (\nu d)(\bar{b}d.0).$$

Notice that we use $\xrightarrow{\tau}$ to represent an evolution of the π calculus expression without any input from the environment. The final expression can be interpreted as a process that creates a new channel name, d, and sends d over channel b.

To illustrate process declarations and invocations, consider the following *executor* example:

$$\texttt{Exec}(x) \quad \triangleq \quad x(y).\bar{y}. \tag{3.2}$$

$$\texttt{A}(x) \quad \triangleq \quad (\nu z)(\bar{x}z \mid z.P). \tag{3.3}$$

Notice that we use $\bar{x}z$ to denote the process $\bar{x}z.0$. We will also use $a(x)$ to denote the process $a(x).0$. Also notice that we use a and $\bar{a}$ to denote reading and writing on channel a, where the actual value being written and read is unimportant (i.e., it does not appear free in the scope of the reading process). What matters is that there is a communication over the channel, signaling synchronization or coordination between processes. That is, $a.P \mid \bar{a}.Q \xrightarrow{\tau} P \mid Q$. Assuming that $z \notin \mathbf{fn}(P)$, the process $\texttt{A}(x)$ will behave as P when composed with $\texttt{Exec}(x)$.

Another useful process declaration enables recursive and nonterminating programs to be modeled:

$$!P \quad \triangleq \quad P \mid\, !P.$$

For example, a process, P, that can indefinitely receive values on channel a can be modeled in the π calculus as:

$$P = \,!a(x).$$

α	$::=$	$\bar{c}\langle x_1, \ldots, x_n \rangle$	Write $x_1, \ldots, x_n$ on channel c
		$c(x_1, \ldots, x_n)$	Read $x_1, \ldots, x_n$ on channel c

Figure 3.5
Polyadic π calculus syntax extension.

If P interacts with another process, $Q = \bar{a}y$, which writes a value over channel a, $P \mid Q$ can be unfolded as follows:

$$P \mid Q = !a(x) \mid \bar{a}y \equiv (a(x) \mid !a(x)) \mid \bar{a}y \equiv (a(x) \mid \bar{a}y) \mid !a(x) \xrightarrow{\tau} 0 \mid !a(x) \equiv !a(x) = P.$$

3.1.3 Polyadic π Calculus

The π calculus syntax is *monadic*, i.e., it only allows for one value to be communicated over a channel at a given interaction between two processes. A useful extension to the syntax to enable multiple values to be communicated when writing to or reading from a channel is shown in figure 3.5.

The intent is that two processes communicate as follows:

$$\bar{c}\langle x_1, \ldots, x_n \rangle.P \mid c(y_1, \ldots, y_n).Q \xrightarrow{\tau}{}^{*} P \mid Q\{x_1, \ldots, x_n / y_1, \ldots, y_n\}.$$

Notice that we cannot simply translate the polyadic calculus into the monadic calculus by expanding the writing process expression $\bar{c}\langle x_1, \ldots, x_n \rangle.P$ into $\bar{c}x_1.\bar{c}x_2.\cdots.\bar{c}x_n.P$. Instead, we must create a private communication link that is subsequently used to communicate all values over

$$(\nu d)\bar{c}d.\bar{d}x_1.\bar{d}x_2.\cdots.\bar{d}x_n.P. \tag{3.4}$$

The channel variable name d must be *fresh*, i.e., $d \notin \mathbf{fn}(P) \cup \{c, x_1, \ldots, x_n\}$, to ensure that we do not capture free variable occurrences,[2] thereby erroneously changing the meaning of process $\bar{c}\langle x_1, \ldots, x_n \rangle.P$.[3]

We can then decode the polyadic π calculus reading process expression $c(y_1, \ldots, y_n).Q$ into

$$c(d).d(x_1).d(x_2).\cdots.d(x_n).Q, \tag{3.5}$$

where d is fresh.

The reader may want to take a look at the reference cell example in section 3.4.1 for a more elaborate process expression modeling stateful concurrent programs in the π calculus.

3.2 Operational Semantics

The semantics of a concurrency model explains precisely the behavior of its elements. An operational semantics of the π calculus can be expressed in terms of a *labeled transition system*, where process expressions can evolve, modeling computation over time, according to a set of well-defined structural inference rules. When the system evolves from a state P, into a state Q, according to the label α, we write:

$$P \xrightarrow{\alpha} Q.$$

In the π calculus, the label α denotes interaction with the environment surrounding the process execution. For example,

$$\bar{a}x.P \xrightarrow{\bar{a}x} P$$

denotes that the π calculus expression $\bar{a}x.P$ can evolve as P if the environment allows for the value x to be sent over channel a.

More generally, we can use a prefix α to range over possible actions that a π calculus process may evolve with, and write:

$$\alpha.P \xrightarrow{\alpha} P.$$

Notice that the input prefix can make a process evolve in infinitely many possible ways according to its environment. For example,

$$a(b).\bar{b}c.0 \xrightarrow{a(u)} \bar{u}c.0 \xrightarrow{\bar{u}c} 0$$

or

$$a(b).\bar{b}c.0 \xrightarrow{a(v)} \bar{v}c.0 \xrightarrow{\bar{v}c} 0.$$

The complete set of rules defining the π calculus operational semantics is described in figure 3.6.

The transition above, $a(b).\bar{b}c.0 \xrightarrow{a(u)} \bar{u}c.0$, is a direct consequence of applying the PREFIX and STRUCT rules as follows:

$$\dfrac{a(b).\bar{b}c.0 \equiv a(u).\bar{u}c.0 \qquad \dfrac{}{a(u).\bar{u}c.0 \xrightarrow{a(u)} \bar{u}c.0}\ \texttt{PREFIX} \qquad \bar{u}c.0 \equiv \bar{u}c.0}{a(b).\bar{b}c.0 \xrightarrow{a(u)} \bar{u}c.0}\ \texttt{STRUCT}.$$

From the operational semantics rules, it is also possible to deduce that the process $(\nu x)\bar{x}a.P$ is semantically equivalent to the empty process 0. That is because

PREFIX $$\frac{}{\alpha.P \xrightarrow{\alpha} P}$$

STRUCT $$\frac{P' \equiv P \qquad P \xrightarrow{\alpha} Q \qquad Q \equiv Q'}{P' \xrightarrow{\alpha} Q'}$$

SUM $$\frac{P \xrightarrow{\alpha} P'}{P + Q \xrightarrow{\alpha} P'}$$

MATCH $$\frac{P \xrightarrow{\alpha} P'}{\texttt{if } x = x \texttt{ then } P \xrightarrow{\alpha} P'}$$

MISMATCH $$\frac{P \xrightarrow{\alpha} P' \qquad x \neq y}{\texttt{if } x \neq y \texttt{ then } P \xrightarrow{\alpha} P'}$$

PAR $$\frac{P \xrightarrow{\alpha} P' \qquad \mathbf{bn}(\alpha) \cap \mathbf{fn}(Q) = \emptyset}{P \mid Q \xrightarrow{\alpha} P' \mid Q}$$

COM $$\frac{P \xrightarrow{a(x)} P' \qquad Q \xrightarrow{\bar{a}u} Q'}{P \mid Q \xrightarrow{\tau} P'\{u/x\} \mid Q'}$$

RES $$\frac{P \xrightarrow{\alpha} P' \qquad x \notin \alpha}{(\nu x)P \xrightarrow{\alpha} (\nu x)P'}$$

Figure 3.6
π calculus operational semantics.

no inference rules apply to either expression. This intuitive notion of equivalence is formalized in section 3.3.

The semantic rules are composed of two parts: the *preconditions* under which each transition can occur, which are written above the horizontal line, and the *consequent* of the rule that specifies how a process expression can evolve into another one, which is written below the horizontal line.

The PREFIX rule has no preconditions and specifies that any $\alpha.P$ expression can evolve as P using a transition with label α.

The STRUCT rule formalizes the intuition that structural congruence is a syntactic form of equivalence of processes. The rule specifies that if $P \xrightarrow{\alpha} Q$ then any expression P', structurally congruent to P, can also evolve into any expression Q', structurally congruent to Q.

For example, one may derive the following:

$$\dfrac{\bar{a}x.P \mid 0 \equiv \bar{a}x.P \qquad \dfrac{}{\bar{a}x.P \xrightarrow{\bar{a}x} P}\ \text{PREFIX} \qquad P \equiv P \mid 0}{\bar{a}x.P \mid 0 \xrightarrow{\bar{a}x} P \mid 0}\ \text{STRUCT}.$$

More interestingly, the STRUCT rule helps us avoid needing dual rules for many π calculus primitives. For example, it is not necessary to have a dual SUM rule:

$$\text{SUM2} \qquad \dfrac{Q \xrightarrow{\alpha} Q'}{P + Q \xrightarrow{\alpha} Q'},$$

since it can be infered from STRUCT and SUM:

$$\dfrac{P + Q \equiv Q + P \qquad \dfrac{Q \xrightarrow{\alpha} Q'}{Q + P \xrightarrow{\alpha} Q'}\ \text{SUM} \qquad Q' \equiv Q'}{P + Q \xrightarrow{\alpha} Q'}\ \text{STRUCT}.$$

Assuming that $P \xrightarrow{\alpha} P'$ and $Q \xrightarrow{\alpha'} Q'$, then the expression $P + Q$ can evolve in two possible ways: $P + Q \xrightarrow{\alpha} P'$ according to the SUM rule, or $P + Q \xrightarrow{\alpha'} Q'$ according to the inferred SUM2 rule. This is exactly the intent of the $+$ operator in the π calculus: non-deterministic choice between P and Q.

The MATCH and MISMATCH rules also precisely specify how process expressions of the form if $x = y$ then P and if $x \neq y$ then P may evolve. Notice in particular, that we can deduce that if $x = y$ then P is semantically equivalent to the empty process, 0, when $x \neq y$, since no transition rules apply. The same is true for the process if $x \neq x$ then P.

The PAR rule specifies independent progress for a process P interacting with the environment when it is part of a concurrent process composition expression $P \mid Q$, and the COM rule specifies how both processes P and Q can make progress synchronously as a result of a communication between them over a shared channel a.

The precondition $\mathbf{bn}(\alpha) \cap \mathbf{fn}(Q) = \emptyset$ of the PAR rule is necessary to prevent erroneously capturing free variable occurrences in the process Q as a result of applying both the rules PAR and COM as follows:

$$\dfrac{\dfrac{\dfrac{}{a(x).P \xrightarrow{a(x)} P}\ \text{PREFIX}}{(a(x).P) \mid Q \xrightarrow{a(x)} P \mid Q}\ \text{PAR} \qquad \dfrac{}{\bar{a}u.R \xrightarrow{\bar{a}u} R}\ \text{PREFIX}}{((a(x).P) \mid Q) \mid \bar{a}u.R \xrightarrow{\tau} (P \mid Q)\{u/x\} \mid R}\ \text{COM}.$$

Therefore, ensuring that x (bound in $a(x)$) does not appear free in Q is critical to the correctness of the substitution $(P \mid Q)\{u/x\}$.

The RES rule specifies the behavior of processes that create a new channel x, namely $(\nu x)P$. The RES rule allows *internal* progress within P, as long as the communication with the environment does not have anything to do with the restricted channel x. If the label α is τ, then there is no interaction with the environment, and RES applies trivially:

$$\dfrac{\dfrac{\dfrac{}{a(b).P \xrightarrow{a(b)} P}\ \texttt{PREFIX} \qquad \dfrac{}{\bar{a}c.Q \xrightarrow{\bar{a}c} Q}\ \texttt{PREFIX}}{a(b).P \mid \bar{a}c.Q \xrightarrow{\tau} P\{c/b\} \mid Q}\ \texttt{COM}}{(\nu x)(a(b).P \mid \bar{a}c.Q) \xrightarrow{\tau} (\nu x)(P\{c/b\} \mid Q)}\ \texttt{RES}. \tag{3.6}$$

Notice in the former example that any of a, b, and c could have been x; and the RES rule would still apply.

The two less clear cases are when α is $a(b)$ or $\bar{a}b$, namely, how should processes $(\nu x)a(b).P$ and $(\nu x)\bar{a}b.P$ evolve?

According to the RES rule, the only way that these processes can evolve is if $x \neq a$ and $x \neq b$. When $a = x$, we have the expressions $(\nu x)x(b).P$ and $(\nu x)\bar{x}b.P$, which should be semantically equivalent to 0, since we are trying to communicate over a channel name that is private. Therefore, by construction no rule should apply. When $b = x$, we have the expressions $(\nu x)a(x).P$ and $(\nu x)\bar{a}x.P$. We do not want to allow

$$(\nu x)a(x).P \xrightarrow{a(x)} (\nu x)P,$$

since the input $a(x)$ from the environment allows for any arbitrary name to be input over channel a. However, if x itself is sent over channel a, any free occurrences of x in P would become erroneously captured by the (νx) using this transition.

Finally, we have the expression $(\nu x)\bar{a}x.P$. In this case, we want the semantics to capture the intuitive notion that the expression

$$a(b).P \mid (\nu x)\bar{a}x.Q$$

can evolve as

$$(\nu x)(P\{x/b\} \mid Q),$$

assuming that $x \notin \mathbf{fn}(P) \cup \{a\}$. The PREFIX, COM, RES and STRUCT rules could be used to make this derivation as follows:

$$\dfrac{x \notin \mathbf{fn}(P) \cup \{a\}}{a(b).P \mid (\nu x)\bar{a}x.Q \equiv (\nu x)(a(b).P \mid \bar{a}x.Q)} \tag{3.7}$$

$$\text{OPEN} \qquad \frac{P \xrightarrow{\bar{a}x} P' \qquad a \neq x}{(\nu x)P \xrightarrow{\bar{a}\nu x} P'}$$

$$\text{RCOM} \qquad \frac{P \xrightarrow{a(x)} P' \qquad Q \xrightarrow{\bar{a}\nu u} Q' \qquad u \notin \mathbf{fn}(P)}{P \mid Q \xrightarrow{\tau} (\nu u)(P'\{u/x\} \mid Q')}$$

Figure 3.7
π calculus operational semantics rules for explicit restricted channel communication.

$$\frac{(3.7)\quad \dfrac{(3.6)}{(\nu x)(a(b).P \mid \bar{a}x.Q) \xrightarrow{\tau} (\nu x)(P\{x/b\} \mid Q)}}{a(b).P \mid (\nu x)\bar{a}x.Q \xrightarrow{\tau} (\nu x)(P\{x/b\} \mid Q)} \ \text{STRUCT.} \tag{3.8}$$

However, for completeness, we want to make it explicit that process $(\nu x)\bar{a}x.P$ can make progress by creating a new channel x and writing it over channel a to the environment. The optional additional rules in figure 3.7 make this restricted channel communication explicit.

In the OPEN rule, the new label $\bar{a}\nu x$ denotes this operation, where $\mathbf{fn}(\bar{a}\nu x) = \{a\}$ and $\mathbf{bn}(\bar{a}\nu x) = \{x\}$.

In order to make the derivation 3.8 using OPEN, we need another operational semantics rule, similar to COM, except enabling communication of restricted channels. We call that rule RCOM and it assumes that the name of the restricted channel u does not appear free in P, otherwise these free occurrences of u would be erroneously captured in the final expression $(\nu u)(P'\{u/x\}|Q')$. With these new rules, the alternative derivation of 3.8 follows, assuming that $x \notin \mathbf{fn}(P)$:

$$\frac{\dfrac{}{a(b).P \xrightarrow{a(b)} P}\ \text{PREFIX} \qquad \dfrac{\dfrac{}{\bar{a}x.Q \xrightarrow{\bar{a}x} Q}\ \text{PREFIX}\ , a \neq x}{(\nu x)\ \bar{a}x.Q \xrightarrow{\bar{a}\nu x} Q}\ \text{OPEN}}{a(b).P \mid (\nu x)\bar{a}x.Q \xrightarrow{\tau} (\nu x)(P\{x/b\} \mid Q)}\ \text{RCOM.}$$

Notice that the additional rules OPEN and RCOM are optional, since we could make the same derivation 3.8 for communicating restricted channels only with the rules in figure 3.6. The only difference if not using the additional optional rules is that process $(\nu x)\bar{a}x.P$ could make no progress in isolation, but this is also a reasonable semantics, since it can really make progress only when combined with another process $a(b).Q$.

3.3 Equivalence of Processes

We have said that $(\nu x)\bar{x}a.P$ is *semantically equivalent* to 0, since neither expression can make any progress based on the operational semantics presented in section 3.2. That is to say, no transition rules apply to either expression. While this is a proper intuition, and it is correct, the more general question is: *When are two arbitrary processes P and Q semantically equivalent?*

Informally, bisimulation is a procedure through which two process expressions are compared to determine whether they are semantically equivalent. More formally, bisimulation is a symmetric binary relation $\mathcal{R}$ on process expressions, such that:

$$P \mathcal{R} Q \quad \wedge \quad P \xrightarrow{\alpha} P' \qquad \Rightarrow \qquad \exists Q' : \quad Q \xrightarrow{\alpha} Q' \quad \wedge \quad P' \mathcal{R} Q'.$$

That is, two processes, P and Q are *bisimilar* if they can indefinitely mimic (or *simulate*) the transitions of each other.

3.3.1 Strong Bisimilarity

In the π calculus, we need to refine the notion of bisimilarity to consider α labels representing input from the environment, since each process must be able to mimic the other *under any possible inputs* from the environment. Therefore, we define *strong bisimulation* as a symmetric binary relation $\mathcal{R}$ on process expressions, such that

$$P \mathcal{R} Q \quad \wedge \quad P \xrightarrow{\alpha} P',$$

where $\mathbf{bn}(\alpha)$ is *fresh* (i.e., $\mathbf{bn}(\alpha) \cap (\mathbf{fn}(P) \cup \mathbf{fn}(Q)) = \emptyset$.) implies that:

1. If $\alpha = a(x)$ then[4]

$$\exists Q' : \quad Q \xrightarrow{a(x)} Q' \quad \wedge \quad \forall u : P'\{u/x\} \mathcal{R} Q'\{u/x\}.$$

2. If α is not an input then

$$\exists Q' : \quad Q \xrightarrow{\alpha} Q' \quad \wedge \quad P' \mathcal{R} Q'.$$

P and Q are *strongly bisimilar*, written $P \dot{\sim} Q$, if they are related by a strong bisimulation.

Let us illustrate this definition by using some examples:

Example 3.1

$P = a \mid \bar{b}$

$Q = a.\bar{b}.$

Notice that process expression P has two possible transition paths:

$$P \xrightarrow{a} \bar{b} \xrightarrow{\bar{b}} 0$$

$$P \xrightarrow{\bar{b}} a \xrightarrow{a} 0,$$

while process expression Q has only one:

$$Q \xrightarrow{a} \bar{b} \xrightarrow{\bar{b}} 0.$$

Therefore, we say that Q cannot simulate P, in particular, it cannot simulate the transition $P \xrightarrow{\bar{b}} a$, and therefore, P and Q are not strongly bisimilar, denoted $P \not\dot{\sim} Q$.

Example 3.2

$$P = a \mid \bar{b}$$

$$Q = a.\bar{b} + \bar{b}.a.$$

Notice that each process expression has only two possible transition paths:

$$P \xrightarrow{a} \bar{b} \xrightarrow{\bar{b}} 0$$

$$P \xrightarrow{\bar{b}} a \xrightarrow{a} 0$$

and

$$Q \xrightarrow{a} \bar{b} \xrightarrow{\bar{b}} 0$$

$$Q \xrightarrow{\bar{b}} a \xrightarrow{a} 0.$$

Therefore, we say $P \dot{\sim} Q$.

Example 3.3

$$P = a(u)$$

$$Q = a(x).(\nu v)\bar{v}u$$

The transition $P \xrightarrow{a(u)} 0$ cannot be simulated by Q because x cannot be α-converted to u in Q, since u appears free in Q. Therefore, P and Q are not bisimilar, even though intuitively P and Q behave the same. Because strong bisimilarity only requires to consider transitions where $\mathbf{bn}(\alpha)$ is *fresh*, it holds that P and Q are strongly bisimilar, i.e., $P \dot{\sim} Q$.

In general, if P and Q are strongly bisimilar, i.e., $P \dot{\sim} Q$, we cannot conclude that P and Q are bisimilar.

Example 3.4

$P = a(x).\bar{b}x$

$Q = a(y).\bar{b}y.$

The process P can evolve as follows:

$P \xrightarrow{a(x)} \bar{b}x.$

The process Q can also evolve after α-conversion $(a(y).\bar{b}y \equiv a(x).\bar{b}x)$ by using the STRUCT rule as follows:

$Q \xrightarrow{a(x)} \bar{b}x.$

We also have $\forall u : \bar{b}x\{u/x\}\ \mathcal{R}\ \bar{b}x\{u/x\}$ since $\bar{b}u \dot{\sim} \bar{b}u$. So Q can simulate P.

Similarly, P can simulate Q, i.e., $P \xrightarrow{a(y)} \bar{b}y$, using α-conversion, the STRUCT rule, and $\bar{b}u \dot{\sim} \bar{b}u$. Therefore, $P \dot{\sim} Q$.

In general, $P \equiv Q$ implies $P \dot{\sim} Q$.

Example 3.5

$P_1 = a(x).P + a(x).0$

$P_2 = a(x).P + a(x).\texttt{if } x = u \texttt{ then } P.$

If we assume that $P \dot{\nsim} 0$ then $P_1 \dot{\nsim} P_2$ since the transition $P_1 \xrightarrow{a(x)} 0$ cannot be simulated by P_2, $P_2 \xrightarrow{a(x)} \texttt{if } x = u \texttt{ then } P$, for the substitution $\{u/x\}$.

Example 3.6

$P_1 = a(x).P + a(x).0$

$P_2 = a(x).P + a(x).0 + a(x).\texttt{if } x = u \texttt{ then } P.$

P_1 and P_2 are bisimilar since they can indefinitely mimic each other. In particular, $P_2 \xrightarrow{a(u)} \texttt{if } u = u \texttt{ then } P$ can be simulated by $P_1 \xrightarrow{a(u)} P$ and $P_2 \xrightarrow{a(y)} \texttt{if } y = u \texttt{ then } P$ can be simulated by $P_1 \xrightarrow{a(y)} 0$. However, if we assume that $P \dot{\nsim} 0$ then $P_1 \dot{\nsim} P_2$ since the transition $P_2 \xrightarrow{a(x)} \texttt{if } x = u \texttt{ then } P$ can not be simulated by P_1, for all substitutions $\{u/x\}$.

In general, if P and Q are bisimilar, we cannot conclude that P and Q are strongly bisimilar, i.e., $P \dot{\sim} Q$.

Example 3.7

$$P = a \mid \bar{a}$$

$$Q_1 = a.\bar{a} + \bar{a}.a + \tau$$

$$Q_2 = a.\bar{a} + \bar{a}.a.$$

$P \dot{\sim} Q_1$ but $P \dot{\not\sim} Q_2$, since the empty transition cannot be simulated by Q_2. However, recall from example 3.2 that $(a \mid \bar{b}) \dot{\sim} (a.\bar{b} + \bar{b}.a)$.

In general, $\dot{\sim}$ is not closed under substitutions, i.e., from $P \dot{\sim} Q$ we cannot conclude $P\sigma \dot{\sim} Q\sigma$.

Example 3.8

$$P = c(a).(a \mid \bar{b})$$

$$Q = c(a).(a.\bar{b} + \bar{b}.a).$$

$P \dot{\not\sim} Q$ since for substitution $\{b/a\}$, $(a \mid \bar{b}) \dot{\not\sim} (a.\bar{b} + \bar{b}.a)$, i.e., $(b \mid \bar{b}) \dot{\not\sim} (b.\bar{b} + \bar{b}.b)$.

In general, $\dot{\sim}$ is not preserved by input prefix, i.e., from $P \dot{\sim} Q$ we cannot conclude $a(x).P \dot{\sim} a(x).Q$.

Proposition 3.1 If $P \dot{\sim} Q$ and σ is injective, then $P\sigma \dot{\sim} Q\sigma$.

Proposition 3.2 $\dot{\sim}$ is an equivalence (reflexive, symmetric, and transitive).

Proposition 3.3 $\dot{\sim}$ is preserved by all operators except the input prefix.

3.3.2 Congruence

Two processes P and Q are (strongly) *congruent*, written $P \sim Q$, if $P\sigma \dot{\sim} Q\sigma$ for all substitutions σ.

Example 3.9

$$P = a \mid \bar{b}$$

$$Q = a.\bar{b} + \bar{b}.a + \texttt{if } a = b \texttt{ then } \tau.$$

$P \sim Q$ since every substitution σ (including $\{b/a\}$ and $\{a/b\}$) preserves $P\sigma \dot{\sim} Q\sigma$.

STR	If $P \equiv Q$	then	$P = Q$	
CG1	If $P = Q$	then	$\bar{a}u.P = \bar{a}u.Q$	
			$\tau.P = \tau.Q$	
			$P + R = Q + R$	
			$P \mid R = Q \mid R$	
			$(\nu x)P = (\nu x)Q$	
CG2	If $P\{y/x\} = Q\{y/x\}$ for all $y \in \mathbf{fn}(P, Q, x)$ then $a(x).P = a(x).Q$			

S	$P + P = P$			
M1	$\texttt{if } x = x \texttt{ then } P$	$=$	P	
M2	$\texttt{if } x = y \texttt{ then } P$	$=$	0	if $x \neq y$
MM1	$\texttt{if } x \neq x \texttt{ then } P$	$=$	0	
MM2	$\texttt{if } x \neq y \texttt{ then } P$	$=$	P	if $x \neq y$
R1	$(\nu x)\alpha.P = \alpha.(\nu x)P$			if $x \notin \alpha$
R2	$(\nu x)\alpha.P = 0$			if $\alpha = \bar{x}y$ or $\alpha = x(y)$
R3	$(\nu x)(P + Q) = (\nu x)P + (\nu x)Q$			

Figure 3.8
Equational theory—axioms for strong bisimilarity.

3.3.3 Algebraic Theory

The (strong) bisimulation and (strong) congruence relations effectively can be understood as notions of semantic equality between process expressions. Figures 3.8 and 3.9 present sets of axioms for an equational theory based on strong bisimilarity and congruence, respectively. These axiomatizations only hold for the finite subcalculus, that is, the π calculus without process invocation and declarations, which are used for recursion and replication. Proofs of soundness and completeness of these axiomatizations can be found in Parrow (2001).

3.4 Common Examples

3.4.1 Reference Cell in the π Calculus

A reference cell, described in section 1.4.1, can be defined in the π calculus as follows:

$$\begin{aligned}
\texttt{Ref}(g, s, i) &\triangleq (\nu l)(\bar{l}i \mid \texttt{GetServer}(l, g) \mid \texttt{SetServer}(l, s)) \\
\texttt{GetServer}(l, g) &\triangleq\ !g(c).l(v).(\bar{c}v \mid \bar{l}v) \\
\texttt{SetServer}(l, s) &\triangleq\ !s(c, v').l(v).(\bar{c} \mid \bar{l}v').
\end{aligned}$$

The cell's invariant is to keep the current value of the cell in a private channel, namely l. Initially, the value i is written to that channel l (in subexpression $\bar{l}i$).

STR	If $P \equiv Q$ then $P = Q$
CG	"=" is preserved by all operators
S	$P + P \quad = \quad P$
MM1	$\texttt{if}\ x \neq x\ \texttt{then}\ P \quad = \quad 0$
GM1	$\texttt{if}\ M\ \texttt{then}\ P \quad = \quad \texttt{if}\ N\ \texttt{then}\ P$ if $M \Leftrightarrow N$
GM2	$\texttt{if}\ x = y\ \texttt{then}\ P + \texttt{if}\ x \neq y\ \texttt{then}\ P \quad = \quad P$
GM3	$\texttt{if}\ M\ \texttt{then}\ (P + Q) \quad = \quad \texttt{if}\ M\ \texttt{then}\ P + \texttt{if}\ M\ \texttt{then}\ Q$
GM4	$\texttt{if}\ M\ \texttt{then}\ \alpha.P \quad = \quad \texttt{if}\ M\ \texttt{then}\ (\alpha.\texttt{if}\ M\ \texttt{then}\ P)$ if $\mathbf{bn}(\alpha) \notin M$
GM5	$\texttt{if}\ x = y\ \texttt{then}\ \alpha.P \quad = \quad \texttt{if}\ x = y\ \texttt{then}\ (\alpha\{x/y\}).P$
GM6	$(\nu x)\texttt{if}\ x = y\ \texttt{then}\ P \quad = \quad 0$ if $x \neq y$
R1	$(\nu x)\alpha.P = \alpha.(\nu x)P$ if $x \notin \alpha$
R2	$(\nu x)\alpha.P = 0$ if $\alpha = \bar{x}y$ or $\alpha = x(y)$
R3	$(\nu x)(P + Q) = (\nu x)P + (\nu x)Q$

Figure 3.9
Equational theory—axioms for strong congruence.

Concurrently, two processes are started: a *get server* and a *set server*, both of which have access to the private channel l. The get server and set server export two channels, respectively g and s, which they use to interact with client processes. They also use replication (the ! definition) to model nonterminating behavior.

When the get server reads a customer channel name c over channel g from a client in subexpression $g(c)$, the get server reads the current cell's value off l in subexpression $l(v)$ and concurrently sends it over channel c and l in subexpression $(\bar{c}v \mid \bar{l}v)$. Writing it over channel c satisfies the client's *get* query, while writing it over channel l preserves the reference cell's invariant.

Similarly, when the set server reads two channel names over s from a client in subexpression $s(c, v')$,[5] the set server reads the current cell's value off l in subexpression $l(v)$ and concurrently sends a completion signal to the client over channel c in subexpression $\bar{c}$ and updates the reference cell's value by writing the new value to the private channel l in sub-expression $\bar{l}v'$.

The following is an example process expression representing a client of the reference cell:

$$(\nu c)\bar{s}\langle c, v\rangle.c.(\nu d)\bar{g}d.d(e).P.$$

In this example, process P will eventually receive the value of the reference cell over channel variable e. If no other processes are interacting with the cell, it will receive the value v.

The following is an alternative expression for the client of the reference cell:

$(\nu c)\bar{s}\langle c, v\rangle.c \mid (\nu d)\bar{g}d.d(e).P.$

In this example, process P will eventually receive the value of the reference cell over channel variable e. However, this time, it may receive either i or v depending upon the order of processing of the *set* and *get* operations.

3.4.2 Mutual Exclusion in the π Calculus

The mutual exclusion problem, described in section 1.4.2, can be solved by using a *semaphore*, as follows:

$$\begin{aligned}
\texttt{Sem}(r) &\triangleq \bar{r}\\
\texttt{Get}(r) &\triangleq r\\
\texttt{Rel}(r) &\triangleq \bar{r}
\end{aligned}$$

Processes P and Q can mutually exclude each other, assuming that r is *fresh*, that is, $r \notin \mathbf{fn}(P) \cup \mathbf{fn}(Q)$, as follows:

$(\nu r)(\texttt{Sem}(r) \mid !\texttt{Get}(r).P.\texttt{Rel}(r) \mid !\texttt{Get}(r).Q.\texttt{Rel}(r)).$

Notice that the π calculus does not specify any *fairness* constraints, that is, even though P and Q can both make progress, there is no guarantee that both eventually will. For example, suppose $P = \bar{a}b.\bar{a}b$ and $Q = \bar{a}c.\bar{a}c$. The semaphore ensures that the processes send over channel a sequences of two bs and sequences of two cs, that is, if composed only with a process $R = a(x_0).a(x_1).a(x_2).a(x_3)$, there can never be a reception in R where $x_0 \neq x_1$ or $x_2 \neq x_3$. However, there is no guarantee that $x_0 \ldots x_3$ are not all equal to b or c. The same is true even if $R = !a(x)$. In theory, an *unfair* execution where P is always chosen over Q or vice versa is admissible.

3.4.3 Dining Philosophers in the π Calculus

The dining philosophers problem, described in section 1.4.3, can be encoded in the π calculus as follows:

$$\begin{aligned}
\texttt{Phil}(l, r) &\triangleq !l.r.(\bar{l} \mid \bar{r})\\
\texttt{Chopstick}(c) &\triangleq \bar{c}
\end{aligned}$$

A table with two philosophers and two chopsticks can be modeled as follows:

$\texttt{Phil}(c_0, c_1) \mid \texttt{Phil}(c_1, c_0) \mid \texttt{Chopstick}(c_0) \mid \texttt{Chopstick}(c_1).$

Notice that each chopstick is modeled as a channel (c) that is written to when it is available ($\bar{c}$) and that is read from when it is picked up (c). Each philosopher is thus in a continuous loop (denoted by the !) picking up the left chopstick (l), then the right chopstick (r), and then releasing both chopsticks concurrently ($\bar{l} \mid \bar{r}$).

A table with n philosophers can be modeled as follows:[6]

$$\prod_{0 \leq i < n} (\texttt{Phil}(c_i, c_{(i+1) \bmod n}) \mid \texttt{Chopstick}(c_i)).$$

3.5 Discussion and Further Reading

The π calculus is one of the most recent and best-studied models of concurrent computation. It was created by Robin Milner, Joachim Parrow, and David Walker in the late 1980s (Milner et al., 1992). Its roots can be traced to process algebras such as Robin Milner's calculus of communicating systems (CCS) (Milner, 1980, 1989) and C. A. R. Hoare's communicating sequential processes (CSP) (Hoare, 1985). The key difference between previous concurrency models such as CCS, CSP, and Petri nets (Reisig, 1983) and the π calculus is the latter's ability to pass channel names around, enabling dynamic process intercommunication topologies. This so-called *mobility* of processes was inspired by the Actor model of concurrent computation (Milner, 1993), which we will study in chapter 4. Other models with explicit distribution and mobility of processes are the join calculus, which we will study in chapter 5, and the mobile ambient calculus, which we will study in chapter 6.

Chapter 3 followed the syntax, semantics, and several examples of the π calculus from the thorough presentation by Joachim Parrow (Parrow, 2001). Parrow's presentation differs from the original presentation (Milner et al., 1992) in introducing the conditional mismatch operator and some notational differences, for example, new channel is denoted (νc) instead of (c) and conditional execution is denoted $\texttt{if}\ x = y\ \texttt{then}\ P$ instead of $[x = y]P$. Readers interested in learning about variants and extensions of the π calculus are referred to Parrow (2001) and Milner (1999).

3.6 Exercises

1. Define the following sets in terms of a, x, $\mathbf{fn}(P)$ and $\mathbf{bn}(P)$.

(a) $\mathbf{fn}(a(x).P) =$

(b) $\mathbf{fn}((\nu x)P) =$

(c) $\mathbf{fn}(\bar{a}x.P) =$

(d) $\mathbf{bn}(a(x).P) =$

(e) $\mathbf{bn}((\nu x)P) =$

(f) $\mathbf{bn}(\bar{a}x.P) =$

2. Determine whether the following π calculus expressions are structurally congruent. Justify why or why not.
(a) $b(x).\bar{x}d.0 \equiv b(y).\bar{y}d.0$?
(b) $(\nu x)\bar{x}y.0 \equiv 0$?
(c) $\bar{x}y.\bar{a}b \equiv \bar{x}y + \bar{a}b$?
(d) $\bar{x}y \mid \bar{a}b \equiv \bar{x}y.\bar{a}b + \bar{a}b.\bar{x}y$?

3. Can you apply the scope extension law to the following π calculus expressions? If so, write the resulting expression. If not, explain why not.
(a) $a(d).\bar{c}d.0 \mid (\nu b)\bar{a}b.0$
(b) $a(b).\bar{c}b.0 \mid (\nu b)\bar{a}b.0$
(c) $(\nu a)\bar{a}b.P \mid \bar{a}c.Q \mid a(x).R$

4. Reduce the following π calculus expression according to the definitions 3.2 and 3.3:

$\mathtt{A}(x) \mid \mathtt{Exec}(x)$

5. Prove proposition 3.1 from section 3.3.
6. Prove proposition 3.2 from section 3.3.
7. Prove proposition 3.3 from section 3.3.
8. Using the axioms in figure 3.9, prove the following equality:

$$(\nu x)\bar{a}x.\mathtt{if}\ x = y\ \mathtt{then}\ P \quad = \quad (\nu x)\bar{a}x.0$$

9. Expand the following polyadic π calculus expression into the monadic π calculus by using the expansions 3.4 and 3.5 described in section 3.1.3 and reduce the expanded expression to confirm intended behavior:

$\bar{c}\langle x_1, \ldots, x_n\rangle.P \mid c(y_1, \ldots, y_n).Q.$

10. Consider the following polyadic π calculus expression:

$\bar{a}\langle u, v\rangle.P \mid a(x, y).Q \mid a(x, y).R.$

(a) Expand the expression by translating $\bar{c}\langle x_1, \ldots, x_n\rangle.P$ into $\bar{c}x_1.\bar{c}x_2.\cdots.\bar{c}x_n.P$ and $c(y_1, \ldots, y_n).Q$ into $c(y_1).c(y_2).\cdots.c(y_n).Q$. What goes wrong with this naïve translation scheme?
(b) Expand into the monadic π calculus according to the expansion rules 3.4 and 3.5 described in section 3.1.3 and reduce the expression.

11. Consider the π calculus reference cell defined in section 3.4.1.
(a) Reduce the following expression:

$\mathtt{Ref}(r, w, i) \mid (\nu c)\bar{w}\langle c, v\rangle.c.(\nu d)\bar{r}d.d(e).P.$

(b) How can you change the preceding process expression to ensure that no other interacting processes may interfere with process P receiving the value v over channel d in variable e from the reference cell?

12. Consider the dining philosophers example illustrated in section 3.4.3.
(a) Expand the process expression corresponding to a table with two philosophers demonstrating how deadlock may occur.
(b) Modify the example definitions to eliminate the possibility of deadlock.

Notes

1. Notice that we are overloading α: here, α is not referring to a π calculus expression prefix, but instead to α renaming as in the λ calculus (see section 2.2).

2. See section 3.1.1 for an explanation of free and bound variable occurrences.

3. See sections 2.2 and 3.1.2 for examples of the significance of erroneously capturing a free variable during α-conversion.

4. *Late* bisimilarity results in a different equivalence relationship following the modified condition: $\forall u : \exists Q' : Q \xrightarrow{a(x)} Q' \wedge P'\{u/x\} \mathcal{R} Q'\{u/x\}$, where Q can simulate P by taking different transition steps depending on the input on channel a. We refer the interested reader to Parrow (2001).

5. This example uses polyadic communication as explained in section 3.1.3.

6. We use the product notation for parallel process composition, i.e., $\prod_{0 \leq i < n} P_i \triangleq P_0 \mid P_1 \mid \ldots \mid P_{n-1}$.

4 Actors

Open systems must support the addition of new components, the replacement of existing components, and dynamic changes in component interconnections. The actor model formalizes concurrent computation in open distributed systems (Hewitt, 1977; Agha, 1986).

The actor model assumes asynchronous communication to be the most primitive interaction mechanism. In the model, the communication medium is not explicit. Actors are first-class history-sensitive entities with an explicit identity used for communication. In response to an asynchronous message, an actor a may perform one or more of the following actions:

1. send a message to an *acquaintance*, an actor whose identity is known to the actor a,
2. create a new actor a', with a given *behavior* b, or
3. become *ready* to receive a new message with new behavior b.

Openness in the actor model is thus supported as follows: new components can be added by creating new actors dynamically, replacement of existing components is modeled by modifying an actor's behavior, and dynamic changes in component interconnections are modeled by passing actor identities in messages and subsequently modifying actor behaviors, thereby altering the actor reference graph and potential future communications.

The actor model theory assumes *fair* communication and computation:

- message delivery is guaranteed, and
- an actor infinitely often ready to process a message eventually processes the message.

Fairness is very useful for reasoning about equivalences of actor programs but can be hard and expensive to guarantee in practical systems when distribution, failures, and potentially complex scheduling policies must be considered.

In the following sections, we will introduce a simple actor language extending the λ calculus, its operational semantics, a technique called *observational equivalence* to prove equivalence of actor programs, and some examples illustrating the usage of the actor language. Finally, we will refer the reader to literature describing variants and further developments of the actor model.

4.1 Actor Language Syntax

The actor language uses the call-by-value λ calculus for sequential computation, and extends it with actor model primitives for coordination. An actor's behavior is modeled as a λ calculus functional abstraction that is applied to incoming messages.

As shown in Figure 4.1, first, we extend the λ calculus with atoms (including booleans to facilitate conditional expressions), numbers, and primitive operators (including pair constructors and destructors to facilitate building arbitrary data structures).[1] We then incorporate *actor primitives*: send(a, v) sends value v to actor

$\mathcal{A}$	=	{ true, false, nil, ...}	***Atoms***
$\mathcal{N}$	=	{ 0, 1, 2, ...}	***Natural numbers***
$\mathcal{X}$	=	{ x, y, z, ...}	***Variable names***
$\mathcal{F}$	=	{ +, *, =, ispr?, 1st, 2nd, ...}	***Primitive operators***
$\mathcal{V}$	::=		***Values***
		$\mathcal{A} \mid \mathcal{N} \mid \mathcal{X}$	
	|	$\lambda\mathcal{X}.\mathcal{E}$	*Functional abstraction*
	|	pr($\mathcal{V}, \mathcal{V}$)	*Pair constructor*
$\mathcal{E}$	::=		***Expressions***
		$\mathcal{V}$	
	|	pr($\mathcal{E}, \mathcal{E}$)	*Pair constructor*
	|	$\mathcal{E}(\mathcal{E})$	*Function application*
	|	$\mathcal{F}(\mathcal{E}, \ldots, \mathcal{E})$	*Primitive function application*
	|	br($\mathcal{E}, \mathcal{E}, \mathcal{E}$)	*Conditional execution*
	|	letrec $\mathcal{X} = \mathcal{E}$ in $\mathcal{E}$	*Recursive definition*
	|	send($\mathcal{E}, \mathcal{E}$)	*Message send*
	|	new($\mathcal{E}$)	*Actor creation*
	|	ready($\mathcal{E}$)	*Behavior change*

Figure 4.1
Actor language syntax.

$\texttt{let}\ x = e_1\ \texttt{in}\ e_2$	$\triangleq$	$\lambda x.e_2(e_1)$	
$\texttt{seq}(e_1, e_2)$	$\triangleq$	$\texttt{let}\ z = e_1\ \texttt{in}\ e_2$	z *fresh*
$\texttt{seq}(e_1, \ldots, e_n)$	$\triangleq$	$\texttt{seq}(e_1, \texttt{seq}(e_2, \ldots, \texttt{seq}(e_{n-1}, e_n))\ldots)$	$n \geq 3$
$\texttt{if}(e_1, e_2, e_3)$	$\triangleq$	$\texttt{br}(e_1, \lambda z.e_2, \lambda z.e_3)(\texttt{nil})$	z *fresh*
$\texttt{rec}(f)$	$\triangleq$	$\lambda x.f(\lambda y.x(x)(y))(\lambda x.f(\lambda y.x(x)(y)))$	

Figure 4.2
Actor language syntactic sugar.

a, $\texttt{new}(b)$ creates a new actor with behavior b and returns the identity of the newly created actor, and $\texttt{ready}(b)$ becomes ready to receive a new message with behavior b.

In this chapter, we use the notation $f(x)$ for function application, as opposed to the notation $(f\ x)$ used in chapter 2. We also use standard syntactic sugar to make it easier to read and write actor programs. These defined forms are depicted in figure 4.2.[2]

For example, the actor program

$$b5 = \texttt{rec}(\lambda y.\lambda x.\texttt{seq}(\texttt{send}(x, 5), \texttt{ready}(y)))$$

receives an actor name x, sends the number 5 to that actor, and then it becomes ready to process new messages with the same behavior y ($b5$.)

To create an actor with the $b5$ behavior, and interact with the actor, we can write the following:

$$\texttt{send}(\texttt{new}(b5), a).$$

When executing this code, an actor with the behavior $b5$ is created and eventually actor a receives a message with value 5 from that newly created actor. A pictorial representation of this interaction is shown in figure 4.3.

Another example is

$$sink = \texttt{rec}(\lambda b.\lambda m.\texttt{ready}(b)),$$

a behavior for an actor that disregards all incoming messages.

An actor does not always necessarily know its own name, as in the $b5$ and $sink$ examples. However, a recursive definition can be used to let an actor know its own name. For example, a *ticker* can be encoded as:

$$ticker = \texttt{rec}(\lambda b.\lambda t.\lambda n.\lambda m.\texttt{seq}(\texttt{send}(t, \texttt{nil}), \texttt{ready}(b(t)(n+1)))).$$

The ticker has as its state an actor name (t) and a natural number (n), and in response to (tick) messages (m), it sends the actor a new message and becomes ready to process the next message with an incremented internal time.

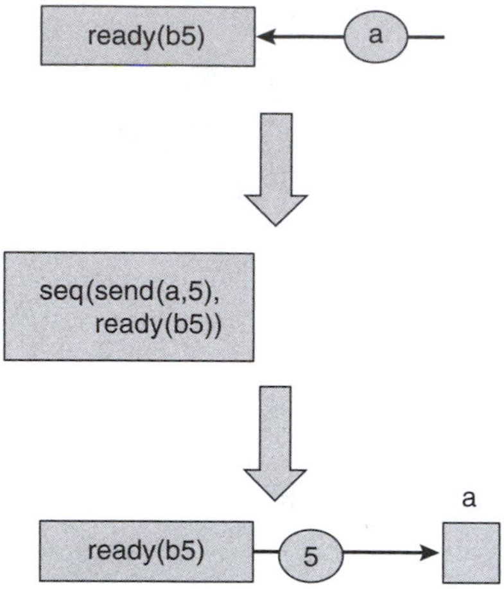

Figure 4.3
A pictorial representation of asynchronous message passing in the actor model.

To create a ticker actor with its own name and get it started, we can write the following:

letrec $t =$ new($ticker(t)(0)$) in send(t, nil).

This actor expression creates a new ticker, initialized with its own name and time 0, and starts the ticker by sending it a tick message, represented as nil.

4.1.1 Join Continuations

Consider the functional programming code to compute the product of numbers in the leaves of a binary tree:

$$
\begin{aligned}
treeprod = \texttt{rec}(\ &\lambda f.\lambda tree.\\
&\quad \texttt{if}(\texttt{isnat?}(tree),\\
&\qquad tree,\\
&\qquad f(left(tree)) \times f(right(tree))))
\end{aligned}
$$

We could write actor code to compute the left and right branches concurrently. In *italics*, we denote auxiliary definitions that can be defined in terms of the pairing primitives. Messages to the tree product actor are pairs containing the tree and the customer actor to send the result to. These are accessible by *tree*(m) and *cust*(m) respectively. Likewise, binary trees can be represented as either number values (leaves) or pairs with the left and right subtrees (nonleaves). In summary, $tree = left = \texttt{1}^{\texttt{st}}$, and $cust = right = \texttt{2}^{\texttt{nd}}$.

```
tprod = rec( λb.λm.
          seq( if( isnat?(tree(m)),
                   send(cust(m), tree(m)),
                   let  newcust = new(joincont(cust(m))),
                        lp = new(tprod),
                        rp = new(tprod)
                    in  seq( send(lp, pr(left(tree(m)), newcust)),
                             send(rp, pr(right(tree(m)), newcust)))),
               ready(b)))

joincont =λcustomer.λfirstnum.
        ready(λnum.seq( send(customer, firstnum × num),
                        ready(sink)))
```

In this example, a tree product actor receives a request as a pair containing a binary tree and a customer to receive the result of computing the product of the numbers in the tree. If the tree is a leaf, then the number is returned to the customer. Otherwise, two new tree product actors are created, as well as a new customer, in charge of getting the partial results from the left and right subtrees and composing the final result for the original customer.

The new customer is also called a *join continuation*, since its behavior is to wait for two concurrent computations executing asynchronously and perform an action when they both complete. The join continuation actor has an initial state containing a *customer* to be notified of completion. On reception of the *first number* containing the result of the first computation completed, it becomes ready to receive the *second number* and notify the *customer* with the product of the two subcomputations. Finally, it becomes a *sink*, since its goals have been met.

Notice that you could create a relatively more efficient version that does not create two new actors for the left and right subtrees, but rather uses the same tree product actor for one of the two subtrees without sacrificing concurrency. The new behavior contains an additional state variable representing its own name (*self*.) The code follows:

```
tprod2 = rec( λb.λself.λm.
          seq( if( isnat?(tree(m)),
                   send(cust(m), tree(m)),
                   letrec  newcust = new( joincont(cust(m))),
                           rp = new(tprod2(rp))
                    in seq( send(self, pr(left(tree(m)), newcust)),
                            send(rp, pr(right(tree(m)), newcust)))),
               ready(b(self))))
```

4.2 Operational Semantics

The operational semantics of our actor language is defined as a set of labeled transition rules from *actor configurations* to actor configurations specifying valid computations. Concurrent systems' evolution over time can be followed by applying the rules specified in the operational semantics in a manner consistent with fairness.

4.2.1 Actor Configurations

Actor configurations model concurrent system components, frozen in time, as viewed by an idealized observer. An actor configuration is composed of:

- a set of individually named actors, and
- messages "en route."

An *actor configuration*, κ, denoted as

$$\alpha \parallel \mu,$$

contains an actor map, α, which is a function mapping actor names to actor expressions, and a multiset of messages, μ. A message to actor named a with content v is denoted as $\langle a \Leftarrow v \rangle$.

There are two syntactic restrictions that valid actor configurations must conform to:

1. If $a \in dom(\alpha)$, then $fv(\alpha(a)) \subseteq dom(\alpha)$.
2. If $\langle a \Leftarrow v \rangle \in \mu$, then $\{a\} \cup fv(v) \subseteq dom(\alpha)$.

The first restriction ensures that free variables in an actor expression—representing its state—refer to valid actor names in the actor configuration. The second restriction does the same for free variables in messages. The only two variable binders in actor expressions are $\lambda x.\ldots$ and `letrec` $x = \ldots$ (i.e., they bind occurrences of variable x in the expression). All other variable occurrences are said to be *free*.

4.2.2 Reduction Contexts and Lambda Reduction Rules

Lemma 4.1 An actor expression, e, is either a value v, or otherwise it can be uniquely decomposed into a *reduction context*, R, filled with a *redex*, r, denoted as $e = \mathsf{R} \blacktriangleright \mathsf{r} \blacktriangleleft$.

The redex r represents the next subexpression to evaluate in a standard left-first, call-by-value evaluation strategy. The reduction context R is represented as the surrounding expression with a *hole* replacing the redex. Figure 4.4 shows the syntax

$\mathcal{E}_r$ ::=		***Redexes***
	$\mathcal{V}(\mathcal{V})$	*Lambda application*
|	$\mathcal{F}(\mathcal{V},\ldots,\mathcal{V})$	*Primitive function application*
|	$\texttt{br}(\mathcal{V},\mathcal{E},\mathcal{E})$	*Conditional execution*
|	$\texttt{letrec}\ \mathcal{X}=\mathcal{V}\ \texttt{in}\ \mathcal{E}$	*Recursive definition*
|	$\texttt{send}(\mathcal{V},\mathcal{V})$	*Message send*
|	$\texttt{new}(\mathcal{V})$	*Actor creation*
|	$\texttt{ready}(\mathcal{V})$	*Behavior change*
$\mathcal{R}$ ::=		***Reduction Contexts***
	$\square$	*Hole*
|	$\texttt{pr}(\mathcal{V},\mathcal{R})$	*Pair constructor*
|	$\texttt{pr}(\mathcal{R},\mathcal{E})$	*Pair constructor*
|	$\mathcal{V}(\mathcal{R})$	*Lambda application*
|	$\mathcal{R}(\mathcal{E})$	*Lambda application*
|	$\mathcal{F}(\mathcal{V},\ldots,\mathcal{V},\mathcal{R},\mathcal{E}\ldots,\mathcal{E})$	*Primitive function application*
|	$\texttt{br}(\mathcal{R},\mathcal{E},\mathcal{E})$	*Conditional execution*
|	$\texttt{letrec}\ \mathcal{X}=\mathcal{R}\ \texttt{in}\ \mathcal{E}$	*Recursive definition*
|	$\texttt{send}(\mathcal{V},\mathcal{R})$	*Message send*
|	$\texttt{send}(\mathcal{R},\mathcal{E})$	*Message send*
|	$\texttt{new}(\mathcal{R})$	*Actor creation*
|	$\texttt{ready}(\mathcal{R})$	*Behavior change*

Figure 4.4
Redexes and reduction contexts.

of redexes and reduction contexts for the actor language. We let r and R range over $\mathcal{E}_r$ and $\mathcal{R}$ respectively. For example, the actor expression $\texttt{send}(\texttt{new}(b5),a)$ can be decomposed into reduction context $\texttt{send}(\square,a)$ filled with redex $\texttt{new}(b5)$. We denote this decomposition as:

$$\texttt{send}(\texttt{new}(b5),a) \quad = \quad \texttt{send}(\square,a) \blacktriangleright \texttt{new}(b5) \blacktriangleleft$$

Redexes are of two kinds: *purely functional redexes* and *actor redexes*. Figure 4.5 depicts standard λ reduction rules for purely functional redexes. These include standard β reduction from the λ calculus, as well as branching, pair destructors, recursive definitions, and primitive operations.

4.2.3 Actor Configuration Transition Rules

The transition rules depicted in figure 4.6 are of the form $\kappa_1 \xrightarrow{l} \kappa_2$, where κ_1 is the initial configuration, κ_2 is the final configuration, and l is the transition label.[3]

$$
\begin{array}{rcll}
\lambda x.e(v) & \rightarrow_\lambda & e\{v/x\} & \\
f(v_1,\ldots,v_n) & \rightarrow_\lambda & v & f \in \mathcal{F}, v = [\![f]\!](v_1,\ldots,v_n) \\
\texttt{br}(\texttt{true}, e, \_) & \rightarrow_\lambda & e & \\
\texttt{br}(\texttt{false}, \_, e) & \rightarrow_\lambda & e & \\
\texttt{1}^{\texttt{st}}(\texttt{pr}(v, \_)) & \rightarrow_\lambda & v & \\
\texttt{2}^{\texttt{nd}}(\texttt{pr}(\_, v)) & \rightarrow_\lambda & v & \\
\texttt{letrec}\ x = v\ \texttt{in}\ e & \rightarrow_\lambda & e\{v\{(\texttt{letrec}\ x = v\ \texttt{in}\ v)/x\}/x\} &
\end{array}
$$

Figure 4.5
Extended λ calculus reduction rules.

$$
\frac{e \rightarrow_\lambda e'}{\alpha, [\mathsf{R} \blacktriangleright e \blacktriangleleft]_a \parallel \mu \xrightarrow{[\mathbf{fun}:a]} \alpha, [\mathsf{R} \blacktriangleright e' \blacktriangleleft]_a \parallel \mu}
$$

$$
\alpha, [\mathsf{R} \blacktriangleright \texttt{new}(b) \blacktriangleleft]_a \parallel \mu \xrightarrow{[\mathbf{new}:a,a']} \alpha, [\mathsf{R} \blacktriangleright a' \blacktriangleleft]_a, [\texttt{ready}(b)]_{a'} \parallel \mu \qquad a' \textit{ fresh}
$$

$$
\alpha, [\mathsf{R} \blacktriangleright \texttt{send}(a', v) \blacktriangleleft]_a \parallel \mu \xrightarrow{[\mathbf{snd}:a]} \alpha, [\mathsf{R} \blacktriangleright \texttt{nil} \blacktriangleleft]_a \parallel \mu \uplus \{\langle a' \Leftarrow v\rangle\}
$$

$$
\alpha, [\mathsf{R} \blacktriangleright \texttt{ready}(b) \blacktriangleleft]_a \parallel \{\langle a \Leftarrow v\rangle\} \uplus \mu \xrightarrow{[\mathbf{rcv}:a,v]} \alpha, [b(v)]_a \parallel \mu
$$

Figure 4.6
Actor language operational semantics.

There are four rules, all of which apply to an actor a, which we call *in focus*: the first one, labeled **fun**, specifies sequential progress within the actor. The other three rules specify creation of and communication with other actors, and apply respectively to actor redexes: new(b), send(a', v), and ready(b).

The **fun** rule subsumes functional computation using the extended λ calculus reduction rules presented in section 4.2.2.

The rule labeled **new** specifies actor creation, which applies when the focus actor a's redex is new(b): actor a creates a new actor a'. The behavior of a' is set to the value ready(b), the actor a's redex is replaced by the new actor's name a'. a' must be fresh, that is, $a' \notin dom(\alpha) \cup \{a\}$.

The rule labeled **snd** specifies asynchronous message sending, which applies when the focus actor a's redex is send(a', v): actor a sends a message containing value v to its acquaintance a'. Actor a continues execution, and the network μ is extended with a new message $\langle a' \Leftarrow v\rangle$.

The rule labeled **rcv** specifies message reception, which applies when the focus actor a's redex is ready(b), and there is a message in μ directed to a, e.g., $\langle a \Leftarrow v\rangle$.

The actor a's new state becomes $b(v)$, that is, its behavior b is applied to the incoming message value v. Notice that the reduction context R is discarded.[4]

4.2.4 Fairness

Computation Sequences and Paths

If κ is a configuration, then the *computation tree* $\tau(\kappa)$ is the set of all finite sequences of labeled transitions $[\kappa_i \xrightarrow{l_i} \kappa_{i+1} \mid i < n]$ for some $n \in \mathcal{N}$, with $\kappa = \kappa_0$. Such sequences are called *computation sequences*. These sequences are partially ordered by the initial segment relation. A *computation path* from κ is a maximal linearly ordered set of computation sequences in the computation tree, $\tau(\kappa)$. We denote a computation path by its maximal sequence. $\tau^{\infty}(\kappa)$ denotes the set of all (possibly infinite) paths from κ.

Fair Computation Paths

Not all computation paths are admissible. Unfair computation paths, where enabled transitions never happen, are ruled out. A transition labeled l is *enabled* in a configuration κ, if and only if there is a configuration κ' such that $\kappa \xrightarrow{l} \kappa'$.

A path $\pi = [\kappa_i \xrightarrow{l_i} \kappa_{i+1} \mid i < \infty]$ in the computation tree $\tau^{\infty}(\kappa)$ is *fair* if each enabled transition eventually happens or becomes permanently disabled. A transition with label of the form $[\mathbf{rcv} : a, v]$ becomes permanently disabled if the actor a starts processing another message and never again becomes ready to accept a new message. For a configuration κ we define $\mathcal{F}(\kappa)$ to be the subset of paths in $\tau^{\infty}(\kappa)$ that are fair. Notice that finite computation paths are fair by maximality, since all enabled transitions must have happened.

Since transition labels have sufficient information to determine computation paths, we can refer to a computation path $[\kappa_i \xrightarrow{l_i} \kappa_{i+1} \mid i < \infty]$ as $\pi = \kappa_i; l_i, l_{i+1}, \ldots,$ where $\kappa_j \xrightarrow{l_j} \kappa_{j+1}$, for $j \geq i$.

4.3 Equivalence of Actor Programs

Programs (expressions) are considered to be *equivalent* if they behave the same when placed in any observing context.

In deterministic functional languages, such as the call-by-value λ calculus, an observing context is a complete program with a hole, such that all the free variables in the expressions being observed are captured when the expressions are placed in the hole. "Behave the same" typically means that both converge or both diverge.

In actor expressions, we define *observing configurations* as "observing contexts," and three different notions of "behave the same" to account for nondeterministic computation.

4.3.1 Events, Observing Configurations, and Observations

An *observing configuration* is a configuration that contains an actor state with a hole. Instead of termination as the criterion for similar behavior, we introduce an observer primitive, `event`, and observe whether in a given computation `event` is executed.

We extend the operational semantics by adding the following rule:

$$\alpha, [\mathsf{R} \blacktriangleright \texttt{event()} \blacktriangleleft]_a \parallel \mu \quad \overset{[\mathrm{ev}:a]}{\longrightarrow} \quad \alpha, [\mathsf{R} \blacktriangleright \texttt{nil} \blacktriangleleft]_a \parallel \mu.$$

The *observing configurations* are configurations over the extended language of the form $\alpha, [\mathsf{C}]_a \parallel \mu$, where C is a *hole-containing* expression or *context*. See figure 4.7 for the syntax of contexts. We assume that the context C has exactly one hole. We use $\mathcal{O}$ to denote the set of observing configurations, and let O range over $\mathcal{O}$. For a given expression e, the observing configurations for e are those $\mathsf{O} \in \mathcal{O}$ such that filling the hole in O with e results in a valid configuration. That is, any free variables in e must refer to actor names in the configuration: $fv(e) \subseteq dom(\alpha) \cup \{a\}$.

Since the actor language is nondeterministic, we distinguish between three different possible scenarios:

- `event` occurs in *all* possible computation paths, or
- `event` occurs in *some* computation paths, but not others, or
- `event` occurs in *no* computation paths.

$\mathcal{C}$ ::=		***Contexts***
|	$\square$	*Hole*
|	$\mathcal{A} \mid \mathcal{N} \mid \mathcal{X}$	*Value*
|	$\texttt{pr}(\mathcal{C},\mathcal{C})$	*Pair constructor*
|	$\lambda\mathcal{X}.\mathcal{C}$	*Functional abstraction*
|	$\mathcal{C}(\mathcal{C})$	*Function application*
|	$\mathcal{F}(\mathcal{C},\ldots,\mathcal{C})$	*Primitive function application*
|	$\texttt{br}(\mathcal{C},\mathcal{C},\mathcal{C})$	*Conditional execution*
|	$\texttt{letrec}\ \mathcal{X} = \mathcal{C}\ \texttt{in}\ \mathcal{C}$	*Recursive definition*
|	$\texttt{send}(\mathcal{C},\mathcal{C})$	*Message send*
|	$\texttt{new}(\mathcal{C})$	*Actor creation*
|	$\texttt{ready}(\mathcal{C})$	*Behavior change*
|	`event()`	*Observation event*

Figure 4.7
Contexts (expressions with holes) syntax.

We define the *observation of a computation path*, $obs(\pi)$, as *successful* if `event` is observed in that computation path. We then define the *observation of a configuration*, $Obs(\kappa)$, as a function of the observations of all its fair computation paths.

Let κ be a configuration of the extended language, and let $\pi = [\kappa_i \xrightarrow{l_i} \kappa_{i+1} \mid i < \infty]$ be a fair path, i.e., $\pi \in \mathcal{F}(\kappa)$. Then, we define:

$$obs(\pi) = \begin{cases} \text{s} & \text{if } (\exists i < \infty)(l_i = [\textbf{ev} : \_]) \\ \text{f} & \text{otherwise} \end{cases}$$

$$Obs(\kappa) = \begin{cases} \text{s} & \text{if } (\forall \pi \in \mathcal{F}(\kappa))(obs(\pi) = \text{s}) \\ \text{f} & \text{if } (\forall \pi \in \mathcal{F}(\kappa))(obs(\pi) = \text{f}) \\ \text{sf} & \text{otherwise} \end{cases}$$

Consider, for example, the following actor expressions and observing context:

$$e_1 = \texttt{send}(a, 1)$$

$$e_2 = \texttt{send}(a, 2)$$

$$e_3 = \texttt{seq}(\texttt{send}(a, 1), \texttt{send}(a, 2))$$

$$e_4 = \texttt{seq}(\texttt{send}(a, 2), \texttt{send}(a, 1))$$

$$\mathsf{O} = \emptyset, [\texttt{ready}(\lambda n.\texttt{if}(n = 1, \texttt{event}(), \texttt{ready}(sink)))]_a, [\square]_{a'} \parallel \emptyset$$

In the case of $\kappa_1 = \mathsf{O} \blacktriangleright e_1 \blacktriangleleft$, we observe the computation path

$$\pi_1 = \kappa_1; [\textbf{snd} : a'], [\textbf{rcv} : a, 1], [\textbf{fun} : a], \ldots, [\textbf{fun} : a], [\textbf{ev} : a],$$

so we say that $obs(\pi_1) = \text{s}$. There are no more computation paths in the computation tree of κ_1, i.e., $\mathcal{F}(\kappa_1) = \{\pi_1\}$, because it is a deterministic computation. So we can conclude that $Obs(\kappa_1) = \text{s}$.

In the case of $\kappa_2 = \mathsf{O} \blacktriangleright e_2 \blacktriangleleft$, we observe the computation path

$$\pi_2 = \kappa_2; [\textbf{snd} : a'], [\textbf{rcv} : a, 2], [\textbf{fun} : a], \ldots, [\textbf{fun} : a],$$

in which `event` never happens, so we say that $obs(\pi_2) = \text{f}$. There are no more computation paths in the computation tree of κ_2, i.e., $\mathcal{F}(\kappa_2) = \{\pi_2\}$, because it is a deterministic computation. So we can conclude that $Obs(\kappa_2) = \text{f}$.

In the cases of $\kappa_3 = \mathsf{O} \blacktriangleright e_3 \blacktriangleleft$ and $\kappa_4 = \mathsf{O} \blacktriangleright e_4 \blacktriangleleft$, there are computation paths that are successful and computation paths that fail to observe the event. For example, take a computation sequence that focuses on actor a' until there are no more enabled transitions on that actor. The ending configuration for both κ_3 and κ_4 would be

$$\emptyset, [\texttt{ready}(\lambda n.\texttt{if}(n = 1, \texttt{event}(), \texttt{ready}(sink)))]_a, [\texttt{nil}]_{a'} \parallel \{\langle a \Leftarrow 1\rangle, \langle a \Leftarrow 2\rangle\}.$$

$\equiv_1$	s	sf	f
s	✓	×	×
sf	×	✓	×
f	×	×	✓

$\equiv_2$	s	sf	f
s	✓	×	×
sf	×	✓	✓
f	×	✓	✓

$\equiv_3$	s	sf	f
s	✓	✓	×
sf	✓	✓	×
f	×	×	✓

Figure 4.8
Testing ($\equiv_1$), must ($\equiv_2$), and may ($\equiv_3$) equivalences. Rows denote $Obs(\mathsf{O}[e_1])$, while columns denote $Obs(\mathsf{O}[e_2])$ for all observing contexts $\mathsf{O} \in \mathcal{O}$. A check mark (✓) denotes $e_1 \equiv e_2$.

In this configuration there are two enabled transitions. The path that continues with the transition labeled $[\mathbf{rcv} : a, 1]$, similarly to π_1, will be successful; while the path that continues with the transition labeled $[\mathbf{rcv} : a, 2]$, similarly to π_2, will fail. So, we say $Obs(\kappa_3) = Obs(\kappa_4) = \mathbf{sf}$.

Notice that the requirement of fairness on admissible paths is critical, since otherwise we could create an observing configuration with a *ticker* actor, in which actors a and a' would never make progress, and therefore we would fail to observe the event in *all* computation paths.

4.3.2 Testing, Must, and May Equivalences

The *natural* equivalence is when equal observations are made in all observing configuration contexts. However, (weaker) equivalences arise if **sf** observations are considered as good as **s** observations, or if **sf** observations are considered as bad as **f** observations. See figure 4.8 for a diagrammatic representation of these equivalences.

Definition 4.1 **Testing Equivalence (or Convex, or Plotkin, or Egli-Milner)**
$e_1 \equiv_1 e_2$ if and only if $Obs(\mathsf{O}[e_1]) = Obs(\mathsf{O}[e_2])$ for all observing contexts $\mathsf{O} \in \mathcal{O}$.

Definition 4.2 **Must Equivalence (or Upper, or Smyth)**
$e_1 \equiv_2 e_2$ if and only if $Obs(\mathsf{O}[e_1]) = \mathbf{s} \iff Obs(\mathsf{O}[e_2]) = \mathbf{s}$ for all observing contexts $\mathsf{O} \in \mathcal{O}$.

Definition 4.3 **May Equivalence (or Lower, or Hoare)**
$e_1 \equiv_3 e_2$ if and only if $Obs(\mathsf{O}[e_1]) = \mathbf{f} \iff Obs(\mathsf{O}[e_2]) = \mathbf{f}$ for all observing contexts $\mathsf{O} \in \mathcal{O}$.

4.3.3 Equivalence Properties and Congruence

Congruence

By construction, testing, must, and may equivalence relations are congruences:

$$e_1 \equiv_j e_2 \quad \Longrightarrow \quad \mathsf{C} \blacktriangleright e_1 \blacktriangleleft \equiv_j \mathsf{C} \blacktriangleright e_2 \blacktriangleleft \qquad \text{for } j \in \{1,2,3\}.$$

Partial Collapse

While it is clear that $e_1 \equiv_1 e_2$ implies $e_1 \equiv_2 e_2 \ \wedge \ e_1 \equiv_3 e_2$, the other directions are not obvious.

Agha, Mason, Smith, and Talcott (Agha et al., 1997) proved that $e_1 \equiv_2 e_2$ implies $e_1 \equiv_1 e_2$ under the assumption of fairness. This effectively collapses testing and must equivalences into one. That is, $e_1 \equiv_1 e_2 \iff e_1 \equiv_2 e_2$. Agha et al. (1997) also shows that $e_1 \equiv_3 e_2$ does not imply $e_1 \equiv_1 e_2$.

4.4 Common Examples

4.4.1 Reference Cell in the Actor Language

A reference cell, described in section 1.4.1, can be encoded in the actor language as follows:

$$
\begin{aligned}
cell = \texttt{rec(}\ & \lambda b.\lambda c.\lambda m.\\
&\quad \texttt{if(}\ get?(m),\\
&\qquad \texttt{seq(}\ \texttt{send}(cust(m), c),\\
&\qquad\qquad \texttt{ready}(b(c))),\\
&\qquad \texttt{if(}\ set?(m),\\
&\qquad\quad \texttt{ready}(b(contents(m))),\\
&\qquad\quad \texttt{ready}(b(c)))))
\end{aligned}
$$

A client of the cell can be encoded as follows:

$$
\begin{aligned}
\texttt{let}\ a = \texttt{new}(cell(0))\ \texttt{in}\ \texttt{seq(}\ & \texttt{send}(a, mkset(7)),\\
& \texttt{send}(a, mkset(2)),\\
& \texttt{send}(a, mkget(c)))
\end{aligned}
$$

A new reference cell actor a is created and three messages are sent to the cell where *mkset* and *mkget* create appropriate pairs representing *set* and *get* messages. Actor c will receive a message containing either 0, 2, or 7, depending on the order of message arrival at a.

The auxiliary functions *mkset*, *mkget*, *get?*, *set?*, *cust*, and *contents* can be defined in terms of booleans and the actor language pairing primitives (`pr`, `ispr?`, $\texttt{1}^{\texttt{st}}$, $\texttt{2}^{\texttt{nd}}$) as follows:

$$
\begin{aligned}
mkget &= \lambda c.\texttt{pr}(\texttt{true}, c)\\
mkset &= \lambda n.\texttt{pr}(\texttt{false}, n)\\
get? &= \lambda m.\texttt{if}(\texttt{ispr?}(m), \texttt{1}^{\texttt{st}}(m), \texttt{false})\\
set? &= \lambda m.\texttt{if}(\texttt{ispr?}(m), \texttt{not}(\texttt{1}^{\texttt{st}}(m)), \texttt{false})\\
cust &= \lambda m.\texttt{if}(\texttt{ispr?}(m), \texttt{2}^{\texttt{nd}}(m), \texttt{nil})\\
contents &= \lambda m.\texttt{if}(\texttt{ispr?}(m), \texttt{2}^{\texttt{nd}}(m), \texttt{nil})
\end{aligned}
$$

4.4.2 Mutual Exclusion in the Actor Language

The mutual exclusion problem, described in section 1.4.2, can be solved by using a *semaphore*, as follows:

```
sem = rec( λb.λh.λm.
            if( get?(m),
                if( h = nil,
                    seq( send(cust(m), true),
                         ready(b(cust(m)))),
                    seq( send(cust(m), false),
                         ready(b(h)))),
                if( release?(m),
                    ready(b(nil)),
                    ready(b(h)))))
```

The semaphore contains state that represents who currently holds access to the shared resource, or `nil` if the resource is available. The semaphore replies `true` to the customer requesting access if allowed, and `false` otherwise.

A customer that keeps trying to get access to the shared resource may be encoded as follows:

```
customer = rec( λb.λself.λs.λm.
                 seq( if( m,
                          seq( <critical code>,
                               send(s, mkrelease())),
                          send(s, mkget(self))),
                      ready(b(self)(s))))
```

Two actors a and a' that mutually exclude each other during the critical code sections can be written as:

```
letrec s = new(sem(nil)),
       a = new(customer(a)(s)),
       a' = new(customer(a')(s)) in seq(send(a, false),
                                        send(a', false))
```

Auxiliary functions *get?*, *release?*, *cust*, *mkget*, and *mkrelease* can be written in terms of the actor language pairing primitives.

4.4.3 Dining Philosophers in the Actor Language

The dining philosophers problem, described in section 1.4.3, can be encoded in the actor language as follows:

```
phil = rec( λb.λl.λr.λself.λsticks.λm.
            if( picked?(m),
                if( eq?(sticks, 0),
                    ready(b(l)(r)(self)(1)),
                    seq( send(l, mkrelease(self)),
                         send(r, mkrelease(self)),
                         ready(b(l)(r)(self)(2)))),
                if( released?(m),
                    if( eq?(sticks, 2),
                        ready(b(l)(r)(self)(1)),
                        seq( send(l, mkpickup(self)),
                             send(r, mkpickup(self)),
                             ready(b(l)(r)(self)(0)))),
                    ready(b(l)(r)(self)(sticks)))))
```

```
chopstick = rec( λb.λh.λw.λm.
                 if( pickup?(m),
                     if( eq?(h, nil),
                         seq( send(getphil(m), mkpicked()),
                              ready(b(getphil(m))(nil))),
                         ready(b(h)(getphil(m)))),
                     if( release?(m),
                         seq( send(getphil(m), mkreleased()),
                              if( eq?(w, nil),
                                  ready(b(nil)(nil)),
                                  seq( send(w, mkpicked()),
                                       ready(b(w)(nil))))),
                         ready(b(h)(w)))))
```

A philosopher is an actor containing as internal state: its own behavior *b*; left and right chopsticks, *l* and *r*; a reference to its own name, *self*; and the number of chopsticks it currently holds, *sticks*. On receipt of a *picked?* message *m*, it checks whether it has any chopsticks. If not, it changes its internal state to now hold one chopstick. If it already has a chopstick, it is receiving the second one, thus it can eat and release its chopsticks by sending each of them a message *mkrelease*(*self*). On receipt of a *released?* message *m*, it decreases its number of chopsticks, and if it only had one, it can think and attempt to pick up the left and right chopsticks again by sending them messages *mkpickup*(*self*); the philosopher becomes ready to accept new messages with changes to its internal state to hold no chopsticks. On receipt of a different type of message, the philosopher ignores it (ready(*b*(*l*)(*r*)(*self*)(*sticks*))).

A chopstick is an actor containing as internal state: its own behavior b, a holding philosopher h, and a waiting philosopher w. On receipt of a message m, it checks whether it is a *pick up* message, a *release* message, or neither of these. If it is a pick up message, it checks whether a philosopher already holds the chopstick($\texttt{eq?}(h, \texttt{nil})$). If not, it sends a message to the philosopher attempting to pick it up (acknowledging it is the new chopstick holder) and changes its internal state accordingly. If a philosopher already holds the chopstick, it saves the waiting philosopher in its internal state. If it is a release message, it sends an acknowledgement to the philosopher releasing the chopstick, and checks whether any philosopher is waiting for the chopstick ($\texttt{eq?}(w, \texttt{nil})$). If so, it sends a message to the waiting philosopher (acknowledging it is the new chopstick holder) and changes its internal state accordingly. If not, it becomes available (and ready to be picked up). On receipt of a different type of message (not a pick up or a release message), the chopstick ignores it ($\texttt{ready}(b(h)(w))$).

A table with two philosophers and two chopsticks can be modeled as follows:

$$
\begin{aligned}
\texttt{letrec}\ c_0 &= \texttt{new}(\mathit{chopstick}(\texttt{nil})(\texttt{nil})),\\
c_1 &= \texttt{new}(\mathit{chopstick}(\texttt{nil})(\texttt{nil})),\\
p_0 &= \texttt{new}(\mathit{phil}(c_0)(c_1)(p_0)(0)),\\
p_1 &= \texttt{new}(\mathit{phil}(c_1)(c_0)(p_1)(0))\ \texttt{in}\quad e
\end{aligned}
$$

where e is defined as:

$$
\begin{aligned}
e = \texttt{seq}(&\texttt{send}(c_0, \mathit{mkpickup}(p_0)),\\
&\texttt{send}(c_1, \mathit{mkpickup}(p_0)),\\
&\texttt{send}(c_0, \mathit{mkpickup}(p_1)),\\
&\texttt{send}(c_1, \mathit{mkpickup}(p_1)))
\end{aligned}
$$

To complete this example, we need to provide the auxiliary definitions:

$$
\begin{aligned}
&\mathit{mkpicked}() &&= \texttt{true}\\
&\mathit{mkreleased}() &&= \texttt{false}\\
&\mathit{mkpickup} &&= \lambda p.\texttt{pr}(\texttt{true}, p)\\
&\mathit{mkrelease} &&= \lambda p.\texttt{pr}(\texttt{false}, p)\\
&\mathit{pickup?} &&= \lambda m.\texttt{if}(\texttt{ispr?}(m), 1^{\texttt{st}}(m), \texttt{false})\\
&\mathit{release?} &&= \lambda m.\texttt{if}(\texttt{ispr?}(m), \texttt{not}(1^{\texttt{st}}(m)), \texttt{false})\\
&\mathit{picked?} &&= \lambda m.\texttt{eq?}(m, \texttt{true})\\
&\mathit{released?} &&= \lambda m.\texttt{eq?}(m, \texttt{false})\\
&\mathit{getphil} &&= \lambda m.\texttt{if}(\texttt{ispr?}(m), 2^{\texttt{nd}}(m), \texttt{nil})
\end{aligned}
$$

4.5 Discussion and Further Reading

The π calculus presented in chapter 3 as well as other process algebras (such as CCS and CSP) take synchronous communication as the most primitive form of communication. In contrast, the actor model assumes asynchronous communication as the most primitive one. In the π calculus, channels explicitly model the interprocess communication medium. Multiple processes can share a channel, potentially causing unexpected interference, whereby two processes can be listening on the same channel. In contrast, actors have unique identities used for communication that can still be passed around to dynamically change the communication topology, but that do not cause potential interference, since all messages directed to an actor eventually reach it.

This chapter followed closely the thorough presentation of the actor model by Agha, Mason, Smith, and Talcott (Agha et al., 1997). We used a very similar actor language syntax, semantics, and borrowed several examples from the referred article. Following are key differences for the interested reader.

Agha et al.'s language uses `become` as an actor primitive rather than our `ready` primitive. The key difference is that `become` creates a new anonymous actor to carry out the rest of the computation (represented by the reduction context surrounding the `become` primitive) and makes the actor in focus immediately ready to receive new messages. In contrast, our `ready` semantics discards the rest of the computation (it assumes that code after `ready` is *dead*, which is not an issue if `ready` always appears in tail form position). The advantage of our semantics is that it resembles more closely practical actor language implementations, where new actor creation is expensive and should be avoided if unnecessary. It also resembles more closely actor languages that extend object-oriented programming languages, where messages are modeled as potential method invocations (see chapter 9).

Agha et al.'s language uses `letactor` as syntactic sugar over actor primitives `newadr` and `initbeh` for actor creation. In our presentation, we chose to use a `new` primitive actor expression that creates an actor and returns its (fresh) address. We combine it with a `letrec` construct to enable an actor to be initialized with its own address. Once again, the advantage of `new` over `letactor/newadr/initbeh` is that it is easier to understand the model, and it more closely resembles practical language implementations where (extended and modified) objects are used to model actors.

Agha et al.'s presentation discusses *composability* of actor configurations. To this extent, it presents configurations as explicitly including an interface with their surrounding environment, modeled by a set of *receptionists*, and a set of *external actors*. However, the composition of two configurations is only allowed if their internal actor names do not collapse, that is, there is no operation equivalent to α-renaming in the λ or π calculi. In part, this is due to the nonlocal effect of such an operation (an actor name may have been *exported* to other configurations,) however, it should be possible for *nonreceptionist* actors to perform α-renaming. For the purpose of simplicity and ease of understanding, we chose not to include composability in this chapter's presentation, and rather defer its presentation to section 7.3.2.

Agha et al. distinguish values from *communicable values* with the specific purpose to disallow an actor to modify another actor's behavior, as shown in the following sequence:

$$\emptyset, [\mathsf{R} \blacktriangleright \texttt{send}(a', \lambda x.\texttt{ready}(b')) \blacktriangleleft]_a, [\texttt{ready}(\lambda b.b(nil))]_{a'} \parallel \emptyset$$

$$\xrightarrow{[\text{snd}:a]} \emptyset, [\mathsf{R} \blacktriangleright \texttt{nil} \blacktriangleleft]_a, [\texttt{ready}(\lambda b.b(nil))]_{a'} \parallel \{\langle a' \Leftarrow \lambda x.\texttt{ready}(b')\rangle\}$$

$$\xrightarrow{[\text{rcv}:a', \lambda x.\texttt{ready}(b')]} \alpha, [\lambda b.b(nil)(\lambda x.\texttt{ready}(b'))]_{a'} \parallel \emptyset$$

$$\xrightarrow{[\text{fun}:a']} \alpha, [\lambda x.\texttt{ready}(b')(nil))]_{a'} \parallel \emptyset$$

$$\xrightarrow{[\text{fun}:a']} \alpha, [\texttt{ready}(b')]_{a'} \parallel \emptyset,$$

where actor a has successfully modified actor a''s behavior to b'. However, for this interaction to succeed, actor a' would have to "cooperate" by initially applying the incoming message to a value as shown above. If we were to send the abstraction $\lambda x.\texttt{ready}(b')$ to an actor such as the reference cell described in section 4.4.1, the message would simply be ignored. In the spirit of the dynamic type checking philosophy of the presented actor language, we have unified values and communicable values in this chapter's presentation.

Finally, Agha et al. present basic expression equivalence laws for actor primitives, as well as techniques for proving actor expression equivalence. Readers interested in these equational laws and proof techniques are referred to Agha et al. (1997).

From a programming language perspective, actors can be thought of as *active objects*, reactive entities that process messages sequentially from a *mailbox* buffering asynchronous messages (which can be modeled as potential method invocations). From an artificial intelligence perspective, actors can be thought of as the core of *software agents*. Actors model the most elemental computation and communication capabilities of software agents. Additional agent capabilities such as higher-level coordination, planning, and knowledge, must be explicitly formalized in higher-level models.

Several works have extended the actor model presented in this chapter to formalize higher-level aspects of distributed computing. Following are some examples for the interested reader. Field and Varela created the τ-calculus to model globally consistent distributed state in the face of failures (Field and Varela, 2005). Frølund and Agha studied higher-level language primitives for synchronization: *synchronizers* to coordinate multiple actors and denote atomic operations, and *local synchronization constraints* for partial ordering of message processing within a single-actor (Frølund and Agha, 1993; Frølund, 1996). Varela and Agha created abstractions for grouping actors into *casts* managed by *directors* to accomplish hierarchical coordination (Varela and Agha, 1999). Toll and Varela introduced primitives for mobility and security to model authentication and access control in open environments (Toll and Varela, 2003). Morali and Varela incorporated trust management primitives to model trust propagation in electronic commerce systems (Morali, 2006). Jamali and Agha defined a *cyberorganism* abstraction to model shared and constrained resources (Jamali, 2004). Ren and Agha explored real-time synchronization primitives to model soft real-time computing (Ren and Agha, 1995). Callsen and Agha explored the integration of the actor model with Linda tuple-space coordination (Carriero and Gelernter, 1990), in the *actorspace* model (Callsen and Agha, 1994). Venkatasubramanian, Talcott, and Agha defined a reflective *two-level* actor model (TLAM) for coordination, adaptation, and resource management in middleware (Venkatasubramanian and Talcott, 1995; Venkatasubramanian et al., 2001).

The actor model has influenced the development of several programming languages. Sussman and Steele developed Scheme in 1975 in an attempt to understand the actor model first conceived by Carl Hewitt (Sussman and Steele, 1998). Early actor languages developed at MIT include PLASMA (Hewitt, 1975) and Act1 (Lieberman, 1981). More recent actor languages include Acore (Manning, 1989), Rosette (Tomlinson et al., 1989), ABCL (Yonezawa et al., 1986), Erlang (Armstrong et al., 1993), E (Miller et al., 2005), and SALSA (Varela and Agha, 2001).

4.6 Exercises

1. Write a functional expression that computes *fib(n)*. Then, write a behavior for an actor that computes *fib(n)* concurrently using a join continuation.
2. Modify the reference cell example in section 4.4.1 to notify a customer when the cell value is updated (such as is done in the π calculus example in section 3.4.1).
3. Consider the mutual exclusion example in section 4.4.2. Write the auxiliary functions *get?*, *release?*, *cust*, *mkget*, and *mkrelease* using the actor language defined in figure 4.1.
4. Consider the dining philosophers example in section 4.4.3. An alternative definition of auxiliary functions *mkpickup* and *mkrelease* follows:

$$
\begin{aligned}
mkpickup &= \lambda p.p \\
mkrelease &= \lambda p.\texttt{nil}
\end{aligned}
$$

Define the remaining auxiliary functions using this alternative definition:

$$
\begin{aligned}
pickup? &= \ldots \\
release? &= \ldots \\
getphil &= \ldots
\end{aligned}
$$

5. Modify the dining philosophers example in section 4.4.3 so that philosophers use a *semaphore* to access the chopsticks. You should reuse the *semaphore* example in section 4.4.2. Discuss the advantages and disadvantages of each implementation.
6. Considering the *b5* behavior example in section 4.1 and the following actor configuration:

$$\kappa = \alpha, [\texttt{send}(\texttt{new}(b5), a)]_{a'} \parallel \emptyset,$$

use the operational semantics rules to evolve the configuration to a final state, where no further transitions are enabled.

7. Modify the *ticker* example in section 4.1 to accept two kinds of messages: `nil` to tick and continue to increment the time, or an actor name as a customer to be sent the current ticker's time. Is a value *always* sent to the customer? *Hint:* Recall the requirement of fairness on valid actor computation paths.[5]
8. What problems may arise if an actor configuration does not follow the syntactic restrictions described in section 4.2.1? Does the model prevent ill-formed messages (e.g., a message directed to a number) from appearing in actor configurations? What about ill-formed behaviors (e.g., nonlambda abstractions)?
9. Modify the actor semantics so that on message reception, the reduction context of the $\mathtt{ready}(b)$ redex is not discarded. Instead, a new anonymous actor should be created to carry out the remaining computation.[6] This new anonymous actor can create other actors and send messages, but it cannot receive new messages, since its name is unknown. *Hint*: You need to modify the **rcv** rule.
10. Given the actor expression $\mathtt{seq}(\mathtt{send}(a, 2), \mathtt{send}(a, 1))$, eliminate syntactic sugar (`seq`) and decompose the expression into a reduction context and a redex.
11. Prove lemma 4.1, i.e., prove that all actor expressions are uniquely decomposable into a reduction context and a redex.
12. Consider the following two expressions:

$$e_1 = \mathtt{ready}(\lambda n.\mathtt{seq}(\mathtt{send}(a, \mathtt{nil}), \mathtt{ready}(sink)))$$

$$e_2 = \mathtt{ready}(\lambda n.\mathtt{if}(n = 1, \mathtt{send}(a, \mathtt{nil}), \mathtt{ready}(sink)))$$

(a) Create an observing context that cannot distinguish between e_1 and e_2.
(b) Create an observing context that can distinguish between e_1 and e_2.

13. Prove that $e_1 \equiv_3 e_2$ does not imply $e_1 \equiv_1 e_2$.

Notes

1. Chapter 2 discussed how we can encode booleans, conditionals, numbers, and pairs in the pure λ calculus.

2. Sections 2.7 and 2.8 discussed in detail the sequencing (`seq`) and recursion (`rec`, which is the same as Y) combinators that we use here.

3. We use $\alpha, [e]_a$ to denote the extended map α', which is the same as α except that it maps a to e, i.e., $\alpha'[a] = e \wedge \forall a' \neq a, \alpha'[a'] = \alpha[a']$. We use $\uplus$ to denote multiset union.

4. See exercise 9 for an alternative definition.

5. Find out about *unbounded nondeterminism*, a property that distinguishes actor computation from other models of concurrent computation such as the π calculus and from more general models of computation such as Turing machines.

6. This is the semantics of the `become` primitive in Agha et al. (1997).

5 Join Calculus

The join calculus is a formal model of concurrency that enables explicit reasoning about *distribution* and *mobility* issues (Fournet and Gonthier, 1996).

Processes are restricted to interact only in *reaction sites* that model localities and correspond to reaction rules with static scoping of names. In order for processes to interact, they must *move* to the appropriate reaction site, and therefore interaction is purely *local* after process mobility. The locality of interaction and mobility of processes is modeled by *reflective* rules that enable chemical abstract machine reaction rules (*join definitions*) to move back and forth between the multiset of rules and the multiset of *molecules* modeling processes, thereby moving processes in and out of scope of the join definitions.

In the following sections, we will introduce the join calculus syntax, its semantics, an observational equivalence notion for join calculus expressions, and some examples illustrating the usage of the join calculus. Finally, we will refer the interested reader to literature describing variants and further developments of the calculus.

5.1 Syntax

Concurrent computation is modeled in the join calculus as a reflective chemical abstract machine, where heating and cooling of molecules and atoms occurs according to *reaction rules* that can evolve over time. We will use $\mathcal{R}$ to denote the multiset of reaction rules and $\mathcal{M}$ to denote the multiset of molecules. Molecules represent processes running in parallel, which can combine and evolve into other processes according to the reaction rules. We use $\mathcal{R} \vdash \mathcal{M}$ to denote the higher-order *solution* where reactions take place.

As in the π calculus, only names are first-class values. Atoms are denoted as $x\langle y\rangle$. Atoms connected by "$|$" are molecules, as in $x\langle y\rangle \mid z\langle w\rangle$. For example, the following expressions are examples of an atom and a molecule, respectively:

$ready\langle laser\rangle$

$ready\langle laser\rangle \mid job\langle f1\rangle$.

Reactions are denoted D or $J \triangleright P$, where J denotes a *join pattern* that existing molecules in the solution must match for the reaction to take place, and P denotes the molecules that result from the reaction. For example:

$$D \quad = \quad ready\langle printer\rangle \mid job\langle file\rangle \triangleright printer\langle file\rangle .$$

Notice that $\mid$ has precedence over $\triangleright$, i.e., the preceding definition means $(ready\langle printer\rangle \mid job\langle file\rangle) \triangleright printer\langle file\rangle$.

Combining a multiset of reaction rules with a multiset of molecules produces the higher-order solution, $\mathcal{R} \vdash \mathcal{M}$. For example:

$$\begin{array}{lll} & D & = ready\langle printer\rangle \mid job\langle file\rangle \triangleright printer\langle file\rangle \\ & D & \vdash ready\langle laser\rangle \mid job\langle f1\rangle \\ \longrightarrow & D & \vdash laser\langle f1\rangle. \end{array}$$

Notice that the formal parameters of J have been instantiated to the actual arguments that caused the join pattern to match, that is, the substitution $\{(laser, f1)/(printer, file)\}$ was applied to P. A pictorial representation of this interaction is shown in figure 5.1.

Since the join calculus is a *reflective* model, reaction rules can be added to the solution by molecules, using the *defining* molecule primitive, `def` D `in` P. For example, the following derivation adds the reaction rule to the solution, before the reaction takes place:

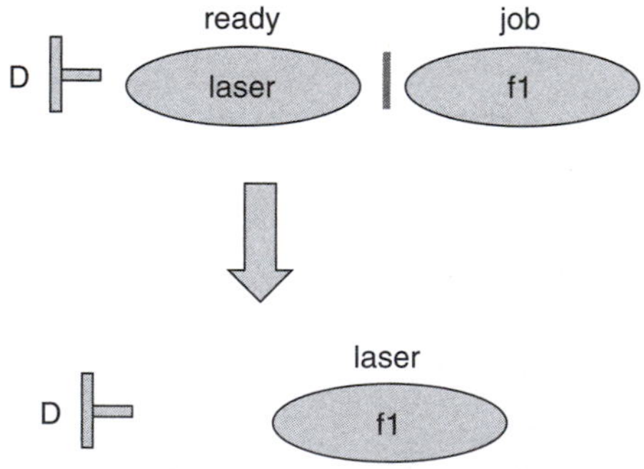

Figure 5.1
A pictorial representation of a chemical reaction in the join calculus.

P	::=		**Processes**
		$x\,\langle \tilde{v} \rangle$	*Atom*
		$\texttt{def}\ D\ \texttt{in}\ P$	*Definition*
		$P \mid P$	*Molecule*
D	::=		**Definitions**
		$J \triangleright P$	*Reaction rule*
		$D \wedge D$	*Multiset constructor*
J	::=		**Join patterns**
		$x\,\langle \tilde{v} \rangle$	*Atom pattern*
		$J \mid J$	*Molecule pattern*

Figure 5.2
Join calculus syntax.

$$\begin{array}{lcl} & \emptyset & \vdash \texttt{def}\ D\ \texttt{in}\ \mathit{ready}\langle \mathit{laser} \rangle \mid \mathit{job}\langle \mathit{f1} \rangle \\ \rightleftharpoons & D & \vdash \mathit{ready}\langle \mathit{laser} \rangle \mid \mathit{job}\langle \mathit{f1} \rangle. \end{array}$$

Structural equivalence, denoted by $\rightleftharpoons$ relates these two solutions.

The formal syntax of the join calculus is depicted in figure 5.2. Processes are either *atoms* which can be regarded as asynchronous polyadic messages $x\,\langle \tilde{v} \rangle$, definitions of new reaction rules, or parallel compositions of other processes. Definitions are multisets of reaction rules, of the form $J \triangleright P$, connected by the $\wedge$ operator, that match patterns J joining messages to guarded processes P.

Join patterns are compositions of atom patterns of the form $x\,\langle \tilde{v} \rangle$, where x is called a *defined port name* and $\tilde{v}$ are called *received names*. There is a syntactic restriction on join patterns, which disallows a received variable from appearing twice in the same pattern J. This prevents using join patterns for comparison of names.

5.1.1 Free and Bound Variables

The sets of received, bound, and free variables are inductively defined as depicted in figure 5.3. We use the notation $\{u \in \tilde{v}\}$ to mean the set $\{v_0, \ldots, v_n\}$, if $\tilde{v} = v_0, \ldots, v_n$. The only binding construct is the definition primitive $\texttt{def}\ J \triangleright P\ \texttt{in}\ P'$, however it binds differently defined variables and received variables. Received variables in J are only bound in the consequent of the reaction rule P, while defined variables in J are bound in the whole defining process, that is in both P and P'.

For example, consider again the join calculus expression:

$$\texttt{def}\ \mathit{ready}\langle \mathit{printer} \rangle \mid \mathit{job}\langle \mathit{file} \rangle \triangleright \mathit{printer}\langle \mathit{file} \rangle\ \texttt{in}\ \mathit{ready}\langle \mathit{laser} \rangle \mid \mathit{job}\langle \mathit{f1} \rangle.$$

Received Variables (Join patterns J)

$$\begin{array}{lll} \mathbf{rv}(x\,\langle\tilde{v}\rangle) & \triangleq & \{u \in \tilde{v}\} \\ \mathbf{rv}(J \mid J') & \triangleq & \mathbf{rv}(J) \cup \mathbf{rv}(J') \quad \text{assuming } \mathbf{rv}(J) \cap \mathbf{rv}(J') = \emptyset \end{array}$$

Defined Variables (Join patterns J, and definitions D)

$$\begin{array}{lll} \mathbf{dv}(x\,\langle\tilde{v}\rangle) & \triangleq & \{x\} \\ \mathbf{dv}(J \mid J') & \triangleq & \mathbf{dv}(J) \cup \mathbf{dv}(J') \end{array}$$

$$\begin{array}{lll} \mathbf{dv}(J \rhd P) & \triangleq & \mathbf{dv}(J) \\ \mathbf{dv}(D \wedge D') & \triangleq & \mathbf{dv}(D) \cup \mathbf{dv}(D') \end{array}$$

Free Variables (Definitions D, and processes P)

$$\begin{array}{lll} fv(J \rhd P) & \triangleq & \mathbf{dv}(J) \cup (fv(P) - \mathbf{rv}(J)) \\ fv(D \wedge D') & \triangleq & fv(D) \cup fv(D') \end{array}$$

$$\begin{array}{lll} fv(x\,\langle\tilde{v}\rangle) & \triangleq & \{x\} \cup \{u \in \tilde{v}\} \\ fv(\texttt{def}\ D\ \texttt{in}\ P) & \triangleq & (fv(P) \cup fv(D)) - \mathbf{dv}(D) \\ fv(P \mid P') & \triangleq & fv(P) \cup fv(P') \end{array}$$

Figure 5.3
Received, defined, and free variables.

Let $J = ready\langle printer\rangle \mid job\langle file\rangle$, $P = printer\langle file\rangle$, and $P' = ready\langle laser\rangle \mid job\langle f1\rangle$. The free variables in the expression $\texttt{def}\ J \rhd P\ \texttt{in}\ P'$ are *laser* and *f1*. The variables *printer* and *file*, which appear free in P, are bound in $J \rhd P$, since they are received variables in J. The variables *ready* and *job*, which appear free in P', are bound by the process $\texttt{def}\ J \rhd P\ \texttt{in}\ P'$ since they are defined variables in J and therefore $J \rhd P$. Notice that any occurrence of *printer* or *file* in P' would appear free in $\texttt{def}\ J \rhd P\ \texttt{in}\ P'$. Conversely, occurrences of *ready* or *job* in P would be bound by the defined port names.

5.2 Operational Semantics

The operational semantics of the join calculus is given by a set of *heating* and *cooling* reversible rules, denoted by $\rightleftharpoons$, and by a single *reduction* rule, denoted by $\longrightarrow$, as shown in figure 5.4. These rules operate on *solutions* of the form $\mathcal{R} \vdash \mathcal{M}$, where we only display the reaction rules and molecules in the solution *in focus*, i.e., those

(*str-join*)		$\vdash$	$P \mid Q$	$\rightleftharpoons$		$\vdash$	$P \uplus Q$
(*str-and*)	$D \wedge E$	$\vdash$		$\rightleftharpoons$	$D \uplus E$	$\vdash$	
(*str-def*)		$\vdash$	$\texttt{def}\ D\ \texttt{in}\ P$	$\rightleftharpoons$	$D\sigma_d$	$\vdash$	$P\sigma_d$
(*red*)	$J \triangleright P$	$\vdash$	$J\sigma_r$	$\longrightarrow$	$J \triangleright P$	$\vdash$	$P\sigma_r$

Figure 5.4
Join calculus operational semantics.

that participate in the transition. These are taken from the multisets $\mathcal{R}$ and $\mathcal{M}$ respectively.

The first three rules are reversible, and correspond to a notion of structural equivalence, including reflection. The last rule is the only reduction rule in the join calculus.

The first two structural rules, (*str-join*) and (*str-and*), essentially say that the parallel composition operator for processes, |, and the multiset union operator for reaction rules, $\wedge$, are both commutative and associative.

The third structural rule, (*str-def*), specifies the *heating* of a defining molecule, $\texttt{def}\ D\ \texttt{in}\ P$, which changes the multiset of reaction rules, $\mathcal{R}$, by adding a new definition D. The substitution σ_d is applied to both D and P to ensure that the defined variables, $\mathbf{dv}(D)$ are *fresh*, i.e., $dom(\sigma_d) = \mathbf{dv}(D) \wedge ran(\sigma_d) \cap fv(\mathcal{R} \vdash \mathcal{M}) = \emptyset$. This substitution thus ensures that the scope of defined names is static. By applying the rule from right to left, we can also extrude the scope of defined variables, as in the π calculus (see section 3.1.2).

The reduction rule, (*red*), defines a single computation step where the join pattern J is matched by a molecule in the solution, using substitution σ_r, whose domain is the received variables $\mathbf{rv}(J)$. The molecule on the right-hand side of the reaction rule, P, is placed into the solution, once the substitution σ_r has been applied. We can think of defined variables as *ports*, received variables as *formal arguments*, and applying the substitution σ_r to P as replacing *formal arguments* by *actual arguments* according to the pattern match (actually received names).

Let us consider some sample join calculus expressions from (Fournet and Gonthier, 1996):

Example 5.1

$\texttt{def}\ x\,\langle u\rangle \triangleright y\,\langle u\rangle\ \texttt{in}\ P.$

In this join calculus expression, x is a *defined* name, bound in P, while y is a free variable. The expression takes names transmitted locally over x in P and forwards them outside the definition over y. This is illustrated by the following sequence of transition steps, assuming $P = (x\,\langle v\rangle \mid x\,\langle w\rangle)$:

$$
\begin{aligned}
&\emptyset \vdash \texttt{def}\ x\langle u\rangle \rhd y\langle u\rangle\ \texttt{in}\ (x\langle v\rangle \mid x\langle w\rangle)\\
&\quad\rightleftharpoons\ x\langle u\rangle \rhd y\langle u\rangle \vdash x\langle v\rangle \mid x\langle w\rangle\\
&\quad\rightleftharpoons\ x\langle u\rangle \rhd y\langle u\rangle \vdash x\langle v\rangle \uplus x\langle w\rangle\\
&\quad\longrightarrow\ x\langle u\rangle \rhd y\langle u\rangle \vdash y\langle v\rangle \uplus x\langle w\rangle\\
&\quad\rightleftharpoons\ \emptyset \vdash (\texttt{def}\ x\langle u\rangle \rhd y\langle u\rangle\ \texttt{in}\ x\langle w\rangle) \uplus y\langle v\rangle \qquad (5.1)\\
&\quad\rightleftharpoons\ \emptyset \vdash y\langle v\rangle \mid \texttt{def}\ x\langle u\rangle \rhd y\langle u\rangle\ \texttt{in}\ x\langle w\rangle.
\end{aligned}
$$

Notice that in the reduction step, we apply the substitution $\{v/u\}$ to the right-hand side of the reaction rule, $y\langle u\rangle$, to get the replacing atom in the solution: $y\langle v\rangle$. Also, notice that the cooling rule, (*str-def*), when applied from right to left, to get to the solution 5.1 only considers the atom $x\langle w\rangle$. This is possible because the only defined variable, x, does not appear free in the rest of the solution: the atom $y\langle v\rangle$.

Example 5.2

$\texttt{def}\ y\langle u\rangle \rhd x\langle u\rangle\ \texttt{in}\ \texttt{def}\ x\langle u\rangle \rhd y\langle u\rangle\ \texttt{in}\ P.$

In this expression, any free occurrences of x in P are bound by the second definition. However, the leftmost occurrence of x appears free. The rightmost y, as well as any free occurrences of y in P are bound by the first definition. This join calculus expression takes names communicated over the local x and in two steps forwards them to the outside over the nonlocal name x. This is illustrated by the following sequence of steps, assuming $P = (x\langle v\rangle \mid Q)$:

$$
\begin{aligned}
&\emptyset \vdash \texttt{def}\ y\langle u\rangle \rhd x\langle u\rangle\ \texttt{in}\ \texttt{def}\ x\langle u\rangle \rhd y\langle u\rangle\ \texttt{in}\ (x\langle v\rangle \mid Q)\\
&\quad\rightleftharpoons\ y\langle u\rangle \rhd x\langle u\rangle \vdash \texttt{def}\ x\langle u\rangle \rhd y\langle u\rangle\ \texttt{in}\ (x\langle v\rangle \mid Q)\\
&\quad\rightleftharpoons\ y\langle u\rangle \rhd x\langle u\rangle \uplus x'\langle u\rangle \rhd y\langle u\rangle \vdash (x'\langle v\rangle \mid Q\{x'/x\}) \qquad (5.2)\\
&\quad\rightleftharpoons\ y\langle u\rangle \rhd x\langle u\rangle \uplus \underline{x'\langle u\rangle \rhd y\langle u\rangle} \vdash \underline{x'\langle v\rangle} \uplus Q\{x'/x\}\\
&\quad\longrightarrow\ \underline{y\langle u\rangle \rhd x\langle u\rangle} \uplus x'\langle u\rangle \rhd y\langle u\rangle \vdash \underline{y\langle v\rangle} \uplus Q\{x'/x\}\\
&\quad\longrightarrow\ y\langle u\rangle \rhd x\langle u\rangle \uplus x'\langle u\rangle \rhd y\langle u\rangle \vdash x\langle v\rangle \uplus Q\{x'/x\}\\
&\quad\rightleftharpoons\ y\langle u\rangle \rhd x\langle u\rangle \vdash (\texttt{def}\ x\langle u\rangle \rhd y\langle u\rangle\ \texttt{in}\ Q) \uplus x\langle v\rangle\\
&\quad\rightleftharpoons\ \emptyset \vdash (\texttt{def}\ y\langle u\rangle \rhd x\langle u\rangle\ \texttt{in}\ \texttt{def}\ x\langle u\rangle \rhd y\langle u\rangle\ \texttt{in}\ Q) \uplus x\langle v\rangle\\
&\quad\rightleftharpoons\ \emptyset \vdash x\langle v\rangle \mid \texttt{def}\ y\langle u\rangle \rhd x\langle u\rangle\ \texttt{in}\ \texttt{def}\ x\langle u\rangle \rhd y\langle u\rangle\ \texttt{in}\ Q.
\end{aligned}
$$

Notice that to get to the solution 5.2 we apply the rule (*str-def*) from left to right. However, we cannot use for σ_d the empty substitution, since the defined variable x appears free in the multiset of rules $\mathcal{R}$, i.e., $x \in fv(y\langle u\rangle \rhd x\langle u\rangle)$. Therefore, we must use the substitution $\sigma_d = \{x'/x\}$, where we assume $x' \notin fv(Q)$. In the reduction steps, we underline the reaction rule and molecule *in focus* for readability.

Example 5.3

$\texttt{def}\ x_1\langle u\rangle \mid x_2\langle v\rangle \triangleright x\langle u,v\rangle\ \texttt{in}\ P.$

In this join calculus expression, variables x_1 and x_2 are defined and therefore bound in P, while variable x appears free. The expression's behavior is to multiplex messages on the external name x whose parts are supplied on the internal names x_1 and x_2. This is illustrated by the following sequence of transition steps, assuming $P = x_1\langle y\rangle \mid x_2\langle z\rangle$:

$$\begin{aligned}
&\emptyset \vdash \texttt{def}\ x_1\langle u\rangle \mid x_2\langle v\rangle \triangleright x\langle u,v\rangle\ \texttt{in}\ x_1\langle y\rangle \mid x_2\langle z\rangle\\
&\quad\rightleftharpoons\quad x_1\langle u\rangle \mid x_2\langle v\rangle \triangleright x\langle u,v\rangle \vdash x_1\langle y\rangle \mid x_2\langle z\rangle\\
&\quad\longrightarrow\quad x_1\langle u\rangle \mid x_2\langle v\rangle \triangleright x\langle u,v\rangle \vdash x\langle y,z\rangle\\
&\quad\rightleftharpoons\quad \emptyset \vdash (\texttt{def}\ x_1\langle u\rangle \mid x_2\langle v\rangle \triangleright x\langle u,v\rangle\ \texttt{in}\ 0) \uplus x\langle y,z\rangle\\
&\quad\rightleftharpoons\quad \emptyset \vdash x\langle y,z\rangle \mid \texttt{def}\ x_1\langle u\rangle \mid x_2\langle v\rangle \triangleright x\langle u,v\rangle\ \texttt{in}\ 0.
\end{aligned}$$

Example 5.4

$\texttt{def}\ x\langle v\rangle \mid y\langle k\rangle \triangleright k\langle v\rangle\ \texttt{in}\ P.$

In this join calculus expression, variables x and y are defined and therefore bound in P. Variables v and k are received and therefore bound in the definition, however, any occurrences of v and k in P would appear free in the whole expression. The expression's behavior is similar to a π calculus channel where values are sent over x and requests for values are sent over y. The introductory example with a *printer* and a *job* follows this communication pattern:

$$\begin{aligned}
&\emptyset \vdash \texttt{def}\ \mathit{ready}\langle \mathit{printer}\rangle \mid \mathit{job}\langle \mathit{file}\rangle \triangleright \mathit{printer}\langle \mathit{file}\rangle\ \texttt{in}\ \mathit{ready}\langle \mathit{laser}\rangle \mid \mathit{job}\langle f1\rangle\\
&\quad\rightleftharpoons\ \longrightarrow\ \rightleftharpoons\quad \emptyset \vdash \texttt{def}\ \mathit{ready}\langle \mathit{printer}\rangle \mid \mathit{job}\langle \mathit{file}\rangle \triangleright \mathit{printer}\langle \mathit{file}\rangle\ \texttt{in}\ \mathit{laser}\langle f1\rangle.
\end{aligned}$$

Example 5.5

$\texttt{def}\ s\langle\rangle \triangleright P \wedge s\langle\rangle \triangleright Q\ \texttt{in}\ s\langle\rangle.$

This join calculus expression's behavior is nondeterministic choice between P and Q, similar to the π calculus expression $P + Q$.

Example 5.6

$\texttt{def}\ \mathit{once}\langle\rangle \mid y\langle v\rangle \triangleright x\langle v\rangle\ \texttt{in}\ y\langle 1\rangle \mid y\langle 2\rangle \mid y\langle 3\rangle \mid \mathit{once}\langle\rangle.$

This join calculus expression's behavior is also nondeterministic choice between $x\,\langle 1\rangle$, $x\,\langle 2\rangle$, and $x\,\langle 3\rangle$, similar to the π calculus expression $\bar{x}1 + \bar{x}2 + \bar{x}3$.

Example 5.7

$\texttt{def}\ loop\,\langle\rangle\ \rhd\ P \mid loop\,\langle\rangle\ \texttt{in}\ loop\,\langle\rangle\ .$

This join calculus expression's behavior is to create an unbounded number of replicas of P, similarly to the π calculus expression $!P$.

5.3 Equivalence of Join Calculus Expressions

In order to treat equivalence of join calculus expressions, in section 5.3.1 we consider a reduced syntax from the one presented in section 5.1. In section 5.3.2, we define structural congruence as a syntactic equivalence, and an operational semantics using a labeled transition system. Section 5.3.3 defines observational congruence as a behavioral *may*-equivalence. We refer the reader to Fournet and Gonthier (1996) for an encoding of the full calculus into the core calculus presented here, as well as a formal proof of the equivalent expressive power of these two calculi.

5.3.1 A Core Calculus

The core join calculus is a restricted, yet fully equivalent, variant of the full join calculus, with simpler definitions, join patterns, and molecules.

P ::=		**Processes**
	$x\,\langle u\rangle$	*Atom*
	$P_1 \mid P_2$	*Molecule*
	$\texttt{def}\ x\,\langle u\rangle \mid y\,\langle v\rangle\ \rhd\ P_1\ \texttt{in}\ P_2$	*Definition.*

Notice that atoms can only contain monadic messages and there are no definition conjunctions. Also notice that we assume that all reaction rules are *inlined* into the process expression by *cooling* the full expression into a single process with definition headers. As before, the scope of u and v is restricted to P_1 whereas the scope of the defined port names x and y includes both P_1 and P_2.

5.3.2 Structural Congruence and Semantics

Structural congruence, denoted by $\equiv$, is the smallest relation such that for all processes P, Q, R, S, and for all definitions D, D' such that $\mathbf{dv}(D), \mathbf{dv}(D')$ contain only fresh names:

$$P \mid Q \equiv Q \mid P$$
$$(P \mid Q) \mid R \equiv P \mid (Q \mid R)$$
$$P \mid \texttt{def}\ D\ \texttt{in}\ Q \equiv \texttt{def}\ D\ \texttt{in}\ P \mid Q$$
$$\texttt{def}\ D\ \texttt{in}\ \texttt{def}\ D'\ \texttt{in}\ P \equiv \texttt{def}\ D'\ \texttt{in}\ \texttt{def}\ D\ \texttt{in}\ P$$

$$P \equiv_\alpha Q \implies P \equiv Q$$
$$P \equiv Q \implies P \mid R \equiv Q \mid R$$
$$R \equiv S, P \equiv Q \implies \texttt{def}\ J \triangleright R\ \texttt{in}\ P \equiv \texttt{def}\ J \triangleright S\ \texttt{in}\ Q,$$

where $\equiv_\alpha$ represents syntactic equivalence by α-renaming of bound variables.

The operational semantics of the core calculus is given by the τ-transitions of a reduction relation with transitions labeled as $\xrightarrow{\delta}$, where δ ranges over $\{D\} \cup \{\tau\}$. The transition relation is the smallest relation such that for every definition $D = x\langle u\rangle \mid y\langle v\rangle \triangleright R$,

$$x\langle s\rangle \mid y\langle t\rangle \xrightarrow{D} R\{(s,t)/(u,v)\},$$

and for every transition $P \xrightarrow{\delta} P'$,

$$P \mid Q \xrightarrow{\delta} P' \mid Q$$
$$\texttt{def}\ D\ \texttt{in}\ P \xrightarrow{\delta} \texttt{def}\ D\ \texttt{in}\ P' \qquad \text{if } fv(D) \cap \mathbf{dv}(\delta) = \emptyset$$
$$\texttt{def}\ \delta\ \texttt{in}\ P \xrightarrow{\tau} \texttt{def}\ \delta\ \texttt{in}\ P' \qquad \text{if } \delta \neq \tau$$
$$Q \xrightarrow{\delta} Q' \qquad \text{if } P \equiv Q \wedge P' \equiv Q'.$$

The relationship between the core calculus presented here and the full join calculus presented in sections 5.1 and 5.2 is formalized by the following lemma:

Lemma 5.1 The structural congruence $\equiv$ is the smallest congruence that contains all pairs of processes P, Q such that $\vdash P \rightleftharpoons^* \vdash Q$. The reduction relation $\xrightarrow{\tau}$ contains exactly the pairs of processes P, Q up to $\equiv$ such that $\vdash P \longrightarrow \vdash Q$.

5.3.3 Observational Equivalence

As discussed in section 4.3, two programs are considered to be *equivalent* if they behave the same when placed in any observing context. In the join calculus, congruence relationships are used to determine the "observing contexts," and being able to emit a value on a free name is considered "similar behavior." This is reasonable, since the only way for a join calculus process to communicate with any outside context is to export messages on its free names.

To test the ability of a process P to emit a name on variable x, we define an *asynchronous, output-only barb*, $P\downarrow_x$, as a predicate defined as follows:

$$P\downarrow_x \;\triangleq\; x \in fv(P) \wedge \exists\tilde{v}, \mathcal{R}, \mathcal{M} \;\mid\; \emptyset \vdash P \;\longrightarrow^*\; \mathcal{R} \vdash \mathcal{M}, x\langle\tilde{v}\rangle,$$

where $\longrightarrow^*$ represents any sequence of $\longrightarrow$ and $\rightleftharpoons$. This is a *may*-equivalence, since $P\downarrow_x$ tests whether P may emit outputs on x, but does not necessarily mean that under all possible reductions, P *must* emit outputs on x.

Let us consider a simple example in the full join calculus with nondeterminism:

$$P = \texttt{def}\; s\langle\rangle \rhd x\langle\rangle \wedge s\langle\rangle \rhd y\langle\rangle \;\texttt{in}\; s\langle\rangle.$$

In this case, $P\downarrow_x$ since given the following reduction:

$$\emptyset \vdash P$$

$$\rightleftharpoons^* \quad \underline{s\langle\rangle \rhd x\langle\rangle} \uplus s\langle\rangle \rhd y\langle\rangle \vdash \underline{s\langle\rangle}$$

$$\longrightarrow \quad s\langle\rangle \rhd x\langle\rangle \uplus s\langle\rangle \rhd y\langle\rangle \vdash x\langle\rangle,$$

there exist $\tilde{v} = \emptyset$, $\mathcal{R} = \{s\langle\rangle \rhd x\langle\rangle, s\langle\rangle \rhd y\langle\rangle\}$, and $\mathcal{M} = \emptyset$, such that $\emptyset \vdash P \;\longrightarrow^*\; \mathcal{R} \vdash \mathcal{M}, x\langle\tilde{v}\rangle$.

Of course, we could have a similar argument that $P\downarrow_y$, since P may also emit outputs on y.

A *may* observation relates process P to processes Q and R:

$$Q = \texttt{def}\; s\langle\rangle \rhd x\langle\rangle \;\texttt{in}\; s\langle\rangle$$

$$R = \texttt{def}\; s\langle\rangle \rhd y\langle\rangle \;\texttt{in}\; s\langle\rangle$$

as follows: $P\downarrow_x$, $P\downarrow_y$, $Q\downarrow_x$, and $R\downarrow_y$.

The observational congruence between processes is the largest equivalence relation $\approx$ that is a refinement of the output barbs $\downarrow_x$ that is weak-reduction-closed, and that is a congruence for definitions and parallel compositions: $\forall P, Q$, if $P \approx Q$, then:

1. $\forall x \in \mathcal{N}, P\downarrow_x \Longrightarrow Q\downarrow_x$
2. $P \;\longrightarrow^*\; P' \Longrightarrow \exists Q', Q \;\longrightarrow^*\; Q' \wedge P' \approx Q'$
3. $\forall D,\; \texttt{def}\; D \;\texttt{in}\; P \approx \texttt{def}\; D \;\texttt{in}\; Q$
4. $\forall R,\; R \mid P \approx R \mid Q$.

Example 5.8

$$fv(P) = \emptyset \Longrightarrow P \approx 0.$$

In this example, no process P has any barb (i.e., no process P can make any observations,) since there are no free variables in P. 0 can simulate reductions in P with no reductions.

Example 5.9

$P \equiv Q \implies P \approx Q.$

Since structural equivalence is a syntactic equivalence, two structurally equivalent expressions P and Q cannot be distinguished by any observations, they can simulate each other, and they can be embedded in definitions or parallel compositions maintaining observational equivalence.

Example 5.10

$x\langle u\rangle \not\approx y\langle u\rangle$.

In this example, $x\langle u\rangle \downarrow_x$ while it is not true that $y\langle u\rangle \downarrow_x$.

Example 5.11

$\texttt{def}\ z\langle t\rangle \triangleright t\langle u\rangle\ \texttt{in}\ z\langle x\rangle \not\approx \texttt{def}\ z\langle t\rangle \triangleright t\langle u\rangle\ \texttt{in}\ z\langle y\rangle$.

Once again, $\texttt{def}\ z\langle t\rangle \triangleright t\langle u\rangle\ \texttt{in}\ z\langle x\rangle \downarrow_x$ since $\texttt{def}\ z\langle t\rangle \triangleright t\langle u\rangle\ \texttt{in}\ z\langle x\rangle \longrightarrow^* \mathcal{R} \vdash x\langle u\rangle$ for $\mathcal{R} = \{z\langle t\rangle \triangleright t\langle u\rangle\}$ while it is not true that $\texttt{def}\ z\langle t\rangle \triangleright t\langle u\rangle\ \texttt{in}\ z\langle y\rangle \downarrow_x$.

Example 5.12

$z\langle x\rangle \not\approx z\langle y\rangle$.

These two processes cannot be distinguished without context, since both $z\langle x\rangle \downarrow_z$ and $z\langle y\rangle \downarrow_z$. However, inside a definition context, such as in example 5.11, they can be distinguished apart. Therefore, they are not observationally equivalent.

Example 5.13

$\texttt{def}\ u\langle z\rangle \triangleright v\langle z\rangle\ \texttt{in}\ x\langle u\rangle \approx x\langle v\rangle$.

In these two processes, distinct names are sent on x, namely u and v, however, their behavior is identical in every context. For example, consider:

$P_1 = \texttt{def}\ x\langle t\rangle \triangleright t\langle y\rangle\ \texttt{in def}\ u\langle z\rangle \triangleright v\langle z\rangle\ \texttt{in}\ x\langle u\rangle$

$P_2 = \texttt{def}\ x\langle t\rangle \triangleright t\langle y\rangle\ \texttt{in}\ x\langle v\rangle$.

$P_1 \downarrow_v$ since $P_1 \longrightarrow^* \mathcal{R} \vdash v\langle y\rangle$ for some $\mathcal{R}$. $P_2 \downarrow_v$ also follows since $P_2 \longrightarrow^* \mathcal{R} \vdash v\langle y\rangle$ for some $\mathcal{R}$.

5.4 Common Examples

5.4.1 Reference Cell in the Join Calculus

A reference cell, described in section 1.4.1, can be defined in the join calculus as follows:

$$\texttt{def}\; mkcell\langle v_0, k_0\rangle \triangleright \left(\begin{array}{lll} \texttt{def} & get\langle k\rangle \mid s\langle v\rangle & \triangleright\; k\langle v\rangle \mid s\langle v\rangle \\ \wedge & set\langle u,k\rangle \mid s\langle v\rangle & \triangleright\; k\langle\rangle \mid s\langle u\rangle \\ \texttt{in} & s\langle v_0\rangle \mid k_0\langle get, set\rangle & \end{array}\right) \;\texttt{in}\; P. \tag{5.3}$$

Each application of the *mkcell* definition creates a new definition (with fresh names *get*, *set*, and *s*), exports two of these newly defined names (*get* and *set*) over the outside name k_0, and keeps the name *s* internally with the invariant of holding the current state of the cell, initially v_0.

Similarly to π calculus channels, requests on the *get* name read the current value of the cell from the *s* name and reply on the received *k* name, maintaining the cell's invariant by producing an $s\langle v\rangle$ atom. Likewise, requests on the *set* name with a new cell's value *u* and an acknowledgement channel *k*, read the current cell's value from *s*, and replace the contents to *u* by producing an $s\langle u\rangle$ atom as well as acknowledging the set operation with a signal $k\langle\rangle$.

The following is an example cell client join calculus expression:

$$P = \texttt{def}\; c\langle g, s\rangle \triangleright s\langle w_1, k\rangle \;\texttt{in}\; mkcell\langle w_0, c\rangle.$$

When the atom $k\langle\rangle$ appears in the solution, the cell whose interface is $\langle g, s\rangle$ will have the value w_1.

5.4.2 Mutual Exclusion in the Join Calculus

We can try to solve the mutual exclusion problem, described in section 1.4.2, by using a *semaphore*, as follows:

$$\texttt{def}\; s\langle\rangle \triangleright P \mid s\langle\rangle \quad \wedge \quad s\langle\rangle \triangleright Q \mid s\langle\rangle \;\texttt{in}\; s\langle\rangle\,. \tag{5.4}$$

But actually the join calculus expression 5.4 is equivalent to the π calculus expression $!(P+Q)$, which does not exactly guarantee mutual exclusion, since $!(P+Q) \equiv^* (P+Q) \mid (P+Q) \mid !(P+Q) \xrightarrow{\tau}{}^{*} P \mid Q \mid !(P+Q)$.

We can, however, slightly modify the definition to ensure mutual exclusion as follows:

$$\texttt{def}\left(\begin{array}{llll} & s\langle\rangle & \triangleright & \texttt{def}\; J_P \triangleright s\langle\rangle \;\texttt{in}\; J_P \\ \wedge & s\langle\rangle & \triangleright & \texttt{def}\; J_Q \triangleright s\langle\rangle \;\texttt{in}\; J_Q \end{array}\right) \texttt{in}\; s\langle\rangle\,. \tag{5.5}$$

Notice that J_P follows the syntax of a join pattern, but is also used as a process in the solution. This definition essentially ensures that when J_P is chosen to execute, the reaction rule that can potentially trigger J_Q is not enabled until J_P has completed execution, and vice versa. For example, let $J_P = a\langle\rangle$ and let $J_Q = b\langle\rangle$, then it will never be the case that the solution has both atoms $a\langle\rangle$ and $b\langle\rangle$, which was not the case with definition 5.4.

Notice that the join calculus does not specify any *fairness* constraints, that is, even though J_P and J_Q can both make progress, there is no guarantee that both eventually will. In theory, an *unfair* execution where J_P is always chosen over J_Q or vice versa, is admissible.

5.4.3 Dining Philosophers in the Join Calculus

The dining philosophers problem, described in section 1.4.3, can be encoded in the join calculus as follows:

$$\texttt{def}\left(\begin{array}{lll} & \mathit{phil}\langle i,l,r\rangle & \triangleright\ \ \texttt{def}\ l\langle\rangle \mid r\langle\rangle\ \triangleright\ \mathit{eat}\langle i\rangle \mid l\langle\rangle \mid r\langle\rangle\ \texttt{in}\ 0 \\ \wedge & \mathit{chopstick}\langle c\rangle & \triangleright\ \ c\langle\rangle \end{array}\right)\texttt{in}\ P. \tag{5.6}$$

An advantage of the join calculus is that steps 1 and 2 (picking up the left and right chopsticks) can be modeled as a single join pattern matching step, thereby eliminating any potential for deadlock.

A table with two philosophers and two chopsticks can be modeled as follows:

$$P = \mathit{phil}\langle 0, c_0, c_1\rangle \mid \mathit{phil}\langle 1, c_1, c_0\rangle \mid \mathit{chopstick}\langle c_0\rangle \mid \mathit{chopstick}\langle c_1\rangle.$$

Notice that each chopstick is modeled as an atom ($c\langle\rangle$) that is in the solution when it is available. Each philosopher is thus in a continuous loop picking up the left and right chopsticks atomically ($l\langle\rangle\ |r\langle\rangle$,) then eating ($\mathit{eat}\langle i\rangle$) and releasing both chopsticks back into the solution.

A table with n philosophers can be modeled as follows[1]:

$$P = \prod_{0\leq i<n} (\mathit{phil}\langle i, c_i, c_{(i+1)\bmod n}\rangle \mid \mathit{chopstick}\langle c_i\rangle).$$

5.5 Discussion and Further Reading

The join calculus is a reflective model of concurrent computation that constrains communication to happen under lexically scoped definitions, which can be thought of as *sites*. It extends Berry and Boudol's Chemical Abstract Machine (Berry and Boudol, 1990) by adding reflection and imposing locality in communication. The join calculus combines the restriction, reception, and replication operators found in the π calculus into a single (joint) receptor definition. Its semantics enables the atomic replacement of a multiset of *molecules* in a higher-order solution by another multiset of *molecules*. The join calculus, like the π calculus, and unlike the actor model of computation, does not enforce fair execution paths, which limits reasoning about composability, in particular, considering *must*-equivalences, as opposed to *may*-equivalences.

Chapter 5 followed the join calculus syntax, semantics, and several examples from the presentation by Fournet and Gonthier (1996). Fournet and Gonthier further present a fully abstract encoding of the full join calculus presented in section 5.1 into the core join calculus presented in section 5.3.1, thereby proving that these two models have the same expressive power up to observational equivalence. They further present fully abstract encodings between the summation-free asynchronous π calculus and the join calculus, proving these calculi have the same expressive power, up to their weak output-only barbed congruences.

Chapter 10 will consider programming using join patterns in JoCaml, a programming language following the concurrency model of the join calculus.

5.6 Exercises

1. Compute the sets of received, defined, free, and bound variables in the join calculus expression 5.3.
2. Compute the sets of received, defined, free, and bound variables in the join calculus expression 5.6.
3. Using the operational semantics, reduce the following join calculus expression:

$\texttt{def}\ a\langle\rangle \triangleright b\langle\rangle \wedge b\langle\rangle \triangleright a\langle\rangle\ \texttt{in}\ a\langle\rangle.$

4. Consider the join calculus expression 5.2, where we apply the substitution $\sigma_d = \{x'/x\}$ to *heat* the defining molecule in the previous expression, since variable x appears free in the multiset of rules $\mathcal{R}$. What happens if we use the empty substitution instead? Continue the join calculus reduction using the empty substitution and discuss what is wrong about it.
5. What is the difference between the following two join calculus expressions:

(a)

$\texttt{def}\ s\langle\rangle \triangleright P \wedge s\langle\rangle \triangleright Q\ \texttt{in}\ s\langle\rangle.$

(b)

$\texttt{def}\ s\langle\rangle \triangleright P\ \texttt{in}\ \texttt{def}\ s\langle\rangle \triangleright Q\ \texttt{in}\ s\langle\rangle.$

6. The core join calculus specified in section 5.3.1, does not consider polyadic messages as part of its syntax. How would you encode the behavior of the following full join calculus expression in the core join calculus:

$\texttt{def}\ s\langle x, y\rangle \triangleright t\langle x, y\rangle\ \texttt{in}\ s\langle u, v\rangle.$

7. The core join calculus specified in section 5.3.1, does not consider multiple definitions as part of its syntax. How would you encode the nondeterministic behavior of the following full join calculus expression in the core join calculus:

$\texttt{def}\ s\langle\rangle \triangleright x\langle\rangle \wedge s\langle\rangle \triangleright y\langle\rangle\ \texttt{in}\ s\langle\rangle.$

8. Using the operational semantics of the core join calculus described in section 5.3.2, prove:

$\texttt{def}\ \mathit{ready}\langle \mathit{printer}\rangle \mid \mathit{job}\langle \mathit{file}\rangle \triangleright \mathit{printer}\langle \mathit{file}\rangle\ \texttt{in}\ \mathit{ready}\langle \mathit{laser}\rangle \mid \mathit{job}\langle \mathit{f1}\rangle$

$\xrightarrow{\tau} \texttt{def}\ \mathit{ready}\langle \mathit{printer}\rangle \mid \mathit{job}\langle \mathit{file}\rangle \triangleright \mathit{printer}\langle \mathit{file}\rangle\ \texttt{in}\ \mathit{laser}\langle \mathit{f1}\rangle.$

9. In the operational semantics of the core join calculus described in section 5.3.2, why is the side condition $fv(D) \cap \mathbf{dv}(\delta) = \emptyset$ significant in the operational semantics rule:

$$\texttt{def}\ D\ \texttt{in}\ P \xrightarrow{\delta} \texttt{def}\ D\ \texttt{in}\ P' \qquad \text{if } fv(D) \cap \mathbf{dv}(\delta) = \emptyset.$$

Give an example, where a reduction would be incorrect if the side condition were not enforced.

10. Example 5.8 assumes that reductions of an arbitrary process P with no free names (in the λ calculus, termed *combinators*) cannot possibly create a new expression with free names. Prove this assumption. That is, prove:

$$fv(P) = \emptyset \quad \wedge \quad P \quad \longrightarrow^* \quad P' \quad \Longrightarrow \quad fv(P') = \emptyset$$

11. Reduce the join calculus expression 5.3, where

$P = \texttt{def}\ c\langle g, s\rangle \triangleright s\langle w_1, k\rangle\ \texttt{in}\ \mathit{mkcell}\langle w_0, c\rangle.$

12. The dining philosophers example given in join calculus expression 5.6 cannot end up in deadlock, since a philosopher atomically chooses both chopsticks or none. Modify the example to allow the potential for deadlock to arise.

Note

1. We use the product notation for parallel process composition, i.e., $\prod_{0\leq i<n} P_i \triangleq P_0 \mid P_1 \mid \ldots \mid P_{n-1}$.

6 Ambient Calculus

Mobile ambients model concurrency and communication in processes and devices that can *move* about administrative boundaries (Cardelli and Gordon, 2000).

Movement of *ambients* (along with contained ambients and communicating processes) and destruction of ambient boundaries are synchronous primitives. Interprocess communication is asynchronous and can occur only among processes in the same ambient. Mobile ambients do not have a unique identity for communication, but instead use the ambient itself as a shared communication medium. Security is modeled as the ability or inability to cross ambient boundaries.

Mobile ambients explicitly model boundaries that exist in physical systems—for example, communication between computers inside a firewall and computers outside the firewall are typically restricted or disallowed. Ambients also model hierarchies of processes and subjective movement; as when a person goes from one room to another with a laptop or a smart phone, any computing processes inside the laptop or the phone continue to execute and communicate internally without necessarily being affected by the person's movement. Similarly, if two people move about inside a train, they may be able to communicate if they are in the same wagon, but their communication ability is independent of the train movement. Ambients also model mobile code, where the capability to communicate with other processes is directly affected by the ability to co-locate with them.

In the following sections, we will introduce the ambient calculus syntax, its semantics, a technique called *contextual equivalence* to prove equivalence of ambient programs, and common examples illustrating the usage of the ambient calculus. Finally, we will refer the interested reader to literature describing further developments of the mobile ambients theory.

6.1 Syntax

Concurrent mobile computation is modeled in the ambient calculus as processes communicating within mobile ambients. Process variables are denoted by uppercase letters such as P, Q, R, whereas ambient names are denoted by lowercase letters such as k, m, n, p. The ambient calculus syntax is shown in figure 6.1.

A simple interaction between two processes can be written as follows in the ambient calculus:

$m[p[\texttt{out}\ m.\texttt{in}\ n.\langle M\rangle]] \mid n[\texttt{open}\ p.(x).Q]$.

In this expression, ambients m and n can be regarded as modelling two machines in a network, ambient p can be regarded as a network packet moving from machine m to machine n. Following the movement and opening of ambient p, inter-process communication occurs inside ambient n.

Notice that ambients can contain other ambients forming a hierarchical structure. Also notice that ambient movement (i.e., `in` n, `out` m) and destruction (i.e., `open` p) primitives are *synchronous*. In this example, the process `out` m.`in` $n.\langle M\rangle$ (inside ambient p) cannot proceed until the `out` m capability has been exercised. That can happen only when the enclosing ambient (p) is inside—and therefore able to exit—an ambient named m. Likewise, the process `open` $p.(x).Q$ cannot proceed until the `open` p capability has been exercised. That can happen only if there is an ambient at the same level (inside ambient n) named p. Therefore, the only way that this ambient calculus expression can proceed is by moving ambient p outside of ambient m, resulting in the following expression:

$m[] \mid n[\texttt{open}\ p.(x).Q] \mid p[\texttt{in}\ n.\langle M\rangle]$.

M	::=	x	Variable x
		`in` n	Enter ambient n
		`out` n	Exit ambient n
		`open` n	Open ambient n
		$M.M$	Capabilities path
P, Q	::=	0	Empty process
		$P \mid Q$	Concurrent composition of P and Q
		$!P$	Replication of P
		$(\nu n)P$	New name n, scope restricted to P
		$M[P]$	Ambient creation
		$M.P$	Synchronous action
		$\langle M\rangle$	Asynchronous output: write M
		$(x).P$	Synchronous input: read x

Figure 6.1
Ambient calculus syntax.

Once again, the only applicable primitive is $\texttt{in}\ n$ in $\texttt{in}\ n.\langle M\rangle$, which requires an ambient named n as a sibling of its enclosing ambient (p.) After moving ambient p inside ambient n, the resulting ambient calculus expression is

$m[] \mid n[\texttt{open}\ p.(x).Q \mid p[\langle M\rangle]]$.

Now, the $\texttt{open}\ p$ capability in process $\texttt{open}\ p.(x).Q$ has become enabled and can be exercised resulting in the ambient calculus expression

$m[] \mid n[(x).Q \mid \langle M\rangle]$.

It is only after the movement (and destruction) of p that the two processes $(x).Q$ and $\langle M\rangle$ can interact. After interaction, all free occurrences of x in expression Q must be replaced by M, resulting in the final expression

$m[] \mid n[Q\{M/x\}]$,

where $Q\{M/x\}$ denotes applying the substitution $\{M/x\}$ to process expression Q, i.e., all free occurrences of x in Q are replaced by M. We can illustrate this ambient interaction pictorially as in figure 6.2. For example, if $M = \texttt{out}\ n.\texttt{in}\ m$ and $Q = q[x.0]$, then $Q\{M/x\} = q[\texttt{out}\ n.\texttt{in}\ m.0]$ and the complete ambient calculus expression evolves as $m[q[]] \mid n[]$, where ambient q may represent a network packet from machine n into machine m acknowledging receipt of original packet p.

When parentheses are not specified, we assume that unary operators have precedence over binary operators. For example, $(\nu n)P \mid Q$ should be read as $((\nu n)P) \mid Q$, not as $(\nu n)(P \mid Q)$.

6.1.1 Free and Bound Variables

The only two operators that *bind* variables (which we do not distinguish from ambient names) are synchronous input and restriction. That is, $(x).P$ *binds* x in P, and $(\nu n)P$ also *binds* n in P. All other variables are said to occur *free* in an ambient calculus expression. We denote the *bound* and *free* variables in an expression e, as $bv(e)$ and $fv(e)$ respectively.

Notice that the ambient calculus syntax admits nonsensical expressions, such as $n.P$ and $\texttt{in}\ n[P]$. A practical implementation of the ambient calculus could rule these invalid expressions out using a type system.

6.1.2 Structural Congruence

Two ambient calculus expressions P and Q are said to be *structurally congruent,* denoted as $P \equiv Q$, if they represent the same process, although they may be syntactically different. $P \equiv Q$, under any of the conditions represented in figure 6.3.

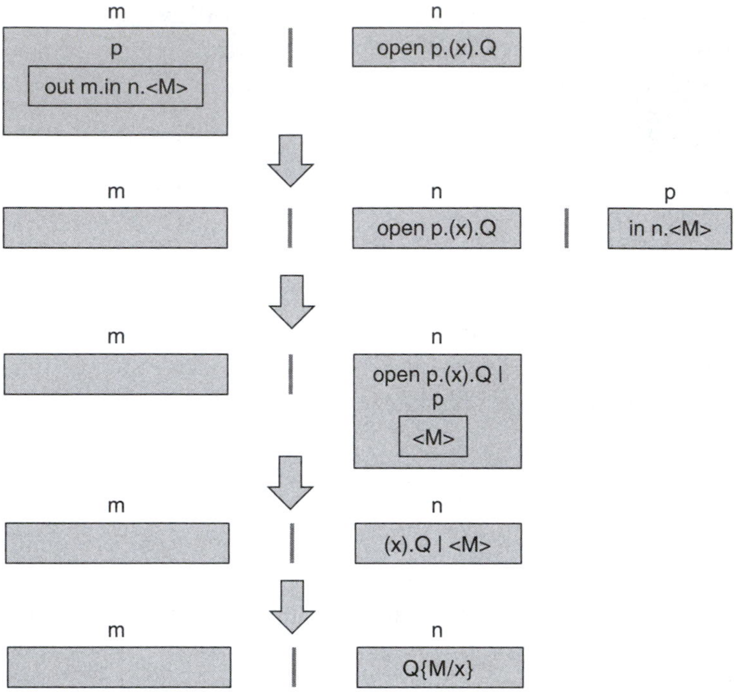

Figure 6.2
A pictorial representation of ambient and process interaction in the ambient calculus.

6.2 Operational Semantics

The ambient calculus operational semantics is expressed in terms of a reduction relation, $\longrightarrow$, as shown in figure 6.4.

The first three rules specify the behavior of ambient mobility and opening, the fourth rule specifies interprocess communication. The subsequent three rules specify that progress can be made by a process in the context of a concurrent composition, a restricted scope, and an ambient, respectively. The last rule formalizes the intuition that structural congruence is a syntactic form of equivalence.

Notice that movement of ambients is *subjective*: the process that triggers ambient movement is *inside* the ambient that is being moved. On the other hand, opening of ambients is *objective*: the process that triggers ambient opening is *outside* the ambient that is being opened.

P and Q are structurally congruent, $P \equiv Q$, in any of the following cases:

1. P and Q are variants of α-conversion.
2. P, Q, and R are related by reflexive, symmetric, or transitive laws (structural congruence is an equivalence):
$$P \equiv P$$
$$P \equiv Q \implies Q \equiv P$$
$$P \equiv Q, Q \equiv R \implies P \equiv R$$
3. P and Q are related by the Abelian monoid laws for $|$:
$$\begin{aligned} P \mid Q &\equiv Q \mid P \\ (P \mid Q) \mid R &\equiv P \mid (Q \mid R) \\ P \mid 0 &\equiv P \end{aligned}$$
4. P and Q are related by scope extension laws:
$$\begin{aligned} (\nu n)0 &\equiv 0 & \\ (\nu n)(P \mid Q) &\equiv P \mid (\nu n)Q & \text{if } n \notin fv(P). \\ (\nu n)(m[P]) &\equiv m[(\nu n)P] & \text{if } n \neq m. \\ (\nu n)(\nu m)P &\equiv (\nu m)(\nu n)P & \end{aligned}$$
5. P and Q are related by syntactic contextual equivalence:
$$\begin{aligned} P \equiv Q &\implies P \mid R \equiv Q \mid R \\ P \equiv Q &\implies !P \equiv !Q \\ P \equiv Q &\implies (\nu n)P \equiv (\nu n)Q \\ P \equiv Q &\implies n[P] \equiv n[Q] \\ P \equiv Q &\implies M.P \equiv M.Q \\ P \equiv Q &\implies (x).P \equiv (x).Q \end{aligned}$$
6. P and Q are related by the replication laws:
$$\begin{aligned} !P &\equiv P \mid !P \\ !0 &\equiv 0 \end{aligned}$$

Figure 6.3
Structural congruence.

$$\begin{aligned} n[\texttt{in }\ m.P \mid Q] \mid m[R] &\longrightarrow m[n[P \mid Q] \mid R] \\ m[n[\texttt{out }\ m.P \mid Q] \mid R] &\longrightarrow n[P \mid Q] \mid m[R] \\ \texttt{open }\ n.P \mid n[Q] &\longrightarrow P \mid Q \\ (x).P \mid \langle M \rangle &\longrightarrow P\{M/x\} \end{aligned}$$

$$\begin{aligned} P \longrightarrow Q &\implies P \mid R \longrightarrow Q \mid R \\ P \longrightarrow Q &\implies (\nu n)P \longrightarrow (\nu n)Q \\ P \longrightarrow Q &\implies n[P] \longrightarrow n[Q] \end{aligned}$$

$$P \equiv P', P \longrightarrow Q, Q \equiv Q' \implies P' \longrightarrow Q'$$

Figure 6.4
Ambient calculus operational semantics.

Entry Capability

The rule for exercising the `in` m capability moves the *enclosing* ambient n inside another ambient with name m, which must be at the same level as n. The reduction rule

$$n[\texttt{in}\ m.P \mid Q] \mid m[R] \quad \longrightarrow \quad m[n[P \mid Q] \mid R]$$

can be pictorially depicted as:

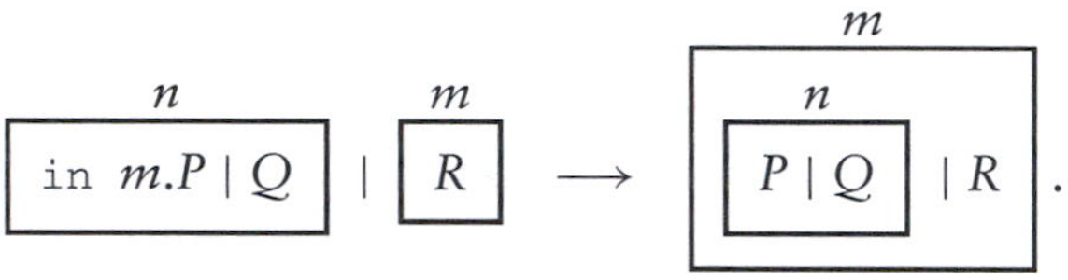

Notice that the ambient movement includes all processes (and ambients) inside the ambient, in this case Q. Notice also that the hierarchical structure changes from having two top-level ambients (m and n) to having only one (m.) The ambient n effectively becomes contained by the ambient m after successful application of this rule. Notice also that there may be competing processes trying to move ambient n, for example, in expression $n[\texttt{in}\ m.P \mid \texttt{in}\ o.Q] \mid m[] \mid o[]$ in which case computation progress is nondeterministic. Notice also that there may be competing ambients with the same name, as in expression $n[\texttt{in}\ m.P] \mid m[Q] \mid m[R]$, where again, computation is nondeterministic.

Exit Capability

The rule for exercising the `out` m capability moves the *enclosing* ambient n outside its parent ambient, which must be named m. The reduction rule

$$m[n[\texttt{out}\ m.P \mid Q] \mid R] \quad \longrightarrow \quad n[P \mid Q] \mid m[R]$$

can be pictorially depicted as

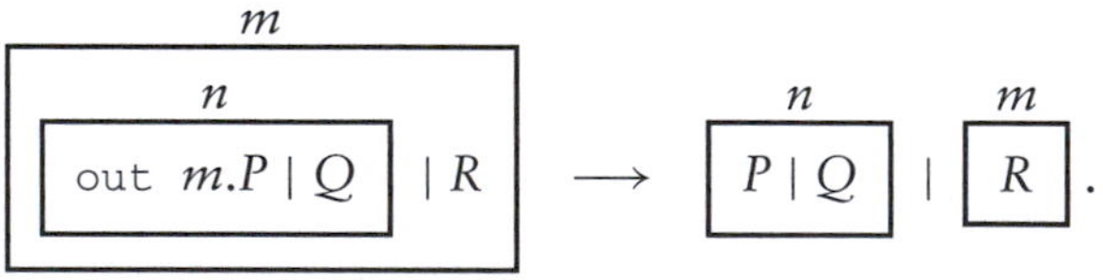

Notice that the ambient movement includes all processes (and ambients) inside the ambient, in this case Q. Notice also that the hierarchical structure changes from having one top-level ambient (m) to having two (m and n). The ambient n effectively becomes a sibling of the ambient m after successful application of this rule. Notice also that if the parent ambient is not named m, the process P remains blocked until such a situation arises.

Open Capability

The rule for exercising the $\mathtt{open}\ n$ capability opens the ambient n, which must be at the same level as the acting process. The reduction rule

$$\mathtt{open}\ n.P \mid n[Q] \quad \longrightarrow \quad P \mid Q$$

can be pictorially depicted as

$\mathtt{open}\ n.P \mid$ 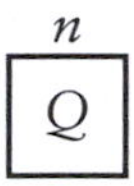 $\longrightarrow \quad P \mid Q.$

Notice that opening an ambient n, removes the boundary enclosing processes (and other ambients) inside the ambient, in this case Q. Notice also that if there is no ambient named n at the same level as the opening process, the process P remains blocked until such a situation arises. Nondeterministic behavior can occur if there are multiple ambients with the same name at the same level, as in expression $\mathtt{open}\ n.P \mid n[Q] \mid n[R]$.

Objective versus Subjective Primitives

The movement of ambients in the calculus is *subjective*, that is, it is started by a process sitting *inside* the ambient. An alternative definition of movement would be *objective*, that is, started by a process *outside* the ambient, as follows:

$$\mathtt{mv\ in}\ n.P \mid n[Q] \quad \longrightarrow \quad n[P \mid Q]$$
$$n[\mathtt{mv\ out}\ n.P \mid Q] \quad \longrightarrow \quad P \mid n[Q].$$

One problem with this alternative definition is that objective moves do not move active ambients (potentially containing active processes and other ambients.) Instead, objective moves move only processes, limiting the dynamicity of the hierarchical structure formed by ambients afforded by the subjective movement primitives.

The opening of ambients is *objective*, that is, triggered by a process *outside* the ambient. An alternative definition of opening would be *subjective*, that is, started by a process *inside* the ambient, as follows:

$$n[\mathtt{acid}\ n.P \mid Q] \quad \longrightarrow \quad P \mid Q.$$

The main argument against a subjective primitive for opening ambients is the ease of entrapment of an ambient, as demonstrated by the following definition and reduction:

$$\mathit{entrap}\ m \quad \triangleq \quad (\nu k)(k[] \mid (\nu q)q[\mathtt{in}\ m.\mathtt{acid}\ q.\mathtt{in}\ k.0]) \qquad (6.1)$$
$$\mathit{entrap}\ m \mid m[P] \quad \longrightarrow^* \quad (\nu k)k[m[P]].$$

In particular, the only capability needed by *entrap m* is the input capability, $\texttt{in}\ m$.

With the objective primitive for opening ambients, it is possible to create a restricted version of subjective ambient dissolution, to be used with an opening capability, as follows:

$$acid\ n.P \quad \triangleq \quad acid[\texttt{out}\ n.\texttt{open}\ n.P]$$

$$n[acid\ n.P \mid Q] \mid \texttt{open}\ acid \quad \longrightarrow^* \quad P \mid Q.$$

However, in this case, it is necessary to have two capabilities associated with ambient n, the exit capability $\texttt{out}\ n$ and the opening capability $\texttt{open}\ n$. Furthermore, it must be possible to locate the *helper process*, $\texttt{open}\ acid$, at the same level as ambient n.

Similarly, with the subjective primitives for moving ambients, it is possible to create restricted versions of objective ambient movement:

$$\begin{array}{lcl}
allow\ n & \triangleq & !\texttt{open}\ n \\
mv\ in\ n.P & \triangleq & (\nu k)k[\texttt{in}\ n.enter[\texttt{out}\ k.\texttt{open}\ k.P]] \\
mv\ out\ n.P & \triangleq & (\nu k)k[\texttt{out}\ n.exit[\texttt{out}\ k.\texttt{open}\ k.P]] \\
n^{\downarrow}[P] & \triangleq & n[P \mid allow\ enter] \\
n^{\uparrow}[P] & \triangleq & n[P] \mid allow\ exit \\
n^{\downarrow\uparrow}[P] & \triangleq & n[P \mid allow\ enter] \mid allow\ exit.
\end{array}$$

These definitions assume that k, *enter* and *exit* are *fresh* variables, i.e., $\{k, enter, exit\} \notin fv(P)$. They are to be used as follows:

$$mv\ in\ n.P \mid n^{\downarrow\uparrow}[Q] \quad \longrightarrow^* \quad n^{\downarrow\uparrow}[P \mid Q]$$

$$n^{\downarrow\uparrow}[mv\ out\ n.P \mid Q] \quad \longrightarrow^* \quad P \mid n^{\downarrow\uparrow}[Q].$$

For example, consider the following reduction, assuming that k is *fresh*, that is, $k \notin fv(P) \cup fv(Q)$, where we sometimes underline the subexpression that we are currently considering for pedagogical purposes:

$$mv\ in\ n.P \mid n^{\downarrow}[Q]$$

$$\begin{array}{l}
\triangleq \quad (\nu k)k[\texttt{in}\ n.enter[\texttt{out}\ k.\texttt{open}\ k.P]] \mid n[Q \mid !\texttt{open}\ enter] \\
\equiv (\nu k)(k[\underline{\texttt{in}\ n.}enter[\texttt{out}\ k.\texttt{open}\ k.P]] \mid n[Q \mid !\texttt{open}\ enter]) \\
\longrightarrow (\nu k)n[k[enter[\underline{\texttt{out}\ k.}\texttt{open}\ k.P]] \mid Q \mid !\texttt{open}\ enter] \\
\longrightarrow (\nu k)n[k[] \mid enter[\texttt{open}\ k.P] \mid Q \mid \underline{!\texttt{open}\ enter}] \\
\equiv (\nu k)n[k[] \mid enter[\texttt{open}\ k.P] \mid Q \mid \underline{\texttt{open}\ enter} \mid !\texttt{open}\ enter]
\end{array}$$

$$\longrightarrow (\nu k)n[k[] \mid \underline{\texttt{open}\ k.P} \mid Q \mid !\texttt{open}\ \ enter]$$

$$\longrightarrow (\nu k)n[P \mid Q \mid !\texttt{open}\ \ enter]$$

$$\equiv^* n[P \mid Q \mid !\texttt{open}\ \ enter]$$

$$\triangleq \quad n^{\downarrow}[P \mid Q].$$

The step $\equiv^*$ removing (νk) is justified by the following steps, where we assume that $k \notin fv(P)$:

$$(\nu k)P \equiv (\nu k)(P \mid 0) \equiv P \mid (\nu k)0 \equiv P \mid 0 \equiv P.$$

6.3 Equivalence of Ambient Calculus Expressions

In this section, we study a notion of equivalence of ambient calculus expressions. Particularly, we consider *contextual equivalence*, a kind of observational equivalence, in which two expressions are said to be contextually equivalent if and only if they admit the *same elementary observations* when placed inside an arbitrary enclosing process.

6.3.1 Contextual Equivalence

In the ambient calculus, we formulate contextual equivalence in terms of *the potential* for observing the presence of top-level ambients, whose names are not restricted.

We say that an ambient calculus expression P *exhibits a name* n, denoted as $P \downarrow n$, if that process P contains a top-level ambient named n, which is not restricted. More formally,

$$P \downarrow n \quad \triangleq \quad \exists (P', P'', \vec{m} \mid n \notin \{\vec{m}\}) : P \equiv (\nu \vec{m})(n[P'] \mid P'').$$

We say that an ambient calculus expression P *converges to a name* n, denoted as $P \Downarrow n$, if P may exhibit n after zero or more reductions. More formally,

$$P \Downarrow n \quad \triangleq \quad \exists Q : P \longrightarrow^* Q \ \wedge \ Q \downarrow n.$$

We define a *context*, C, as an ambient calculus expression with one or more *holes*, denoted as $()$. When filling a context hole with an expression P, denoted as $C(P)$, free variables and names in P may become bound. For example, if $C = (x).(\nu n)()$ and $P = n[\langle x \rangle]$, then n and x become bound in $C(P) = (x).(\nu n)n[\langle x \rangle]$. If there are no free variables, except for ambient names, in an expression, we say it is *closed*. So, for example, $n[]$ is closed, but $\langle x \rangle$ is not.

Two ambient calculus expressions, P and Q, are considered *contextually equivalent*, denoted as $P \simeq Q$, if for all closing contexts C and names n, the expression resulting from filling the context's holes with P converges to n if and only if the expression resulting from filling the context's holes with Q also converges to n. More formally,

$$P \simeq Q \quad \triangleq \quad \forall (C, n \mid C(P), C(Q) \text{ closed}) : C(P) \Downarrow n \iff C(Q) \Downarrow n.$$

Notice that to prove two ambient calculus expressions *not* contextually equivalent, it suffices to show *one* context C and *one* name n that distinguishes the expressions apart.

Example 6.1

$n[] \not\simeq (\nu n)n[]$.

Proof Let $C = ()$, then $C(n[]) = n[]$. By definition, $C(n[]) \downarrow n$, for $\overrightarrow{m} = \emptyset, P' = P'' = 0$. Therefore $C(n[]) \Downarrow n$. Furthermore, $C((\nu n)n[]) = (\nu n)n[]$. However, since no reductions apply to this expression, and by definition, it does not exhibit n, we cannot derive $C((\nu n)n[]) \Downarrow n$.

Example 6.2

$n[] \mid \texttt{open}\ n.0 \not\simeq 0$.

Proof Let $C = ()$, then $C(n[] \mid \texttt{open}\ n.0) = n[] \mid \texttt{open}\ n.0$. By definition, $C(n[] \mid \texttt{open}\ n.0) \downarrow n$, for $\overrightarrow{m} = \emptyset, P' = 0, P'' = \texttt{open}\ n.0$. Therefore $C(n[] \mid \texttt{open}\ n.0) \Downarrow n$. Furthermore, $C(0) = 0$. However, since no reductions apply to this expression, and by definition, it does not exhibit n, we cannot derive $C(0) \Downarrow n$.

So, in general, we can say that $P \longrightarrow Q$ does not imply $P \simeq Q$.

Contextual equivalence is a *may*-equivalence, since two expressions are considered equivalent if they both *may* make the observation. Please refer to section 4.3 for alternative definitions of equivalence that arise with nondeterminism: *testing*-equivalence and *must*-equivalence.

From a practical perspective, contextual equivalence is too weak, since it does not distinguish between a deterministic process in which an observation can *always* be made, and a nondeterministic process, in which the observation is *sometimes* made. In practical systems, these so-called *race conditions* are very difficult to debug.

Example 6.3

$(\nu m)(\texttt{open}\ m \mid m[n[]] \mid m[]) \simeq (\nu m)(\texttt{open}\ m \mid m[n[]])$.

Consider the following two ambient calculus expressions

$e_1 = (\nu m)(\texttt{open}\ m \mid m[n[]] \mid m[])$

$e_2 = (\nu m)(\texttt{open}\ m \mid m[n[]])$.

Consider the context $C = ()$, so $C(e_1) = e_1$, and $C(e_2) = e_2$.
Expression e_2 will *always* exhibit n, after one reduction as follows:

$(\nu m)(\texttt{open}\ m \mid m[n[]]) \longrightarrow (\nu m)n[]$.

Since $(\nu m)n[] \downarrow n$, we can conclude $C(e_2) \Downarrow n$.
Expression e_1 *may* also exhibit n as in the following possible reduction:

$(\nu m)(\texttt{open}\ m \mid m[n[]] \mid m[]) \longrightarrow (\nu m)(n[] \mid m[])$.

Since $(\nu m)(n[] \mid m[]) \downarrow n$, we can conclude $C(e_1) \Downarrow n$.
However, e_1 also *may not* exhibit n as in the following alternative reduction:

$(\nu m)(\texttt{open}\ m \mid m[n[]] \mid m[]) \longrightarrow (\nu m)(m[n[]])$.

$(\nu m)(m[n[]])$ does *not* exhibit n.

Nonetheless, contextual equivalence, as a *may*-equivalence, makes e_1 and e_2 equivalent, $e_1 \simeq e_2$, since $C(e_1) \Downarrow n \iff C(e_2) \Downarrow n$ for all C and n. We have considered only the empty context, without loss of generality, since any additional context cannot interact with e_1 or e_2's m ambient because of the restriction operator.

In order to show that two expressions are contextually equivalent, it must be shown that for *any* context they converge to the same names. Gordon and Cardelli (2003) developed some techniques that allow proving contextual equivalence of ambient calculus expressions by only considering a limited form of contexts, as opposed to arbitrary contexts.

6.4 Common Examples

6.4.1 Reference Cell in the Ambient Calculus

A reference cell, described in section 1.4.1, can be defined in the ambient calculus as follows:

$$\begin{aligned} \mathit{cell}\ c\ w &\triangleq c^{\downarrow\uparrow}[\langle w\rangle], \\ \mathit{get}\ c\ (x).P &\triangleq \mathit{mv\ in}\ c.(x).(\langle x\rangle \mid \mathit{mv\ out}\ c.P), \\ \mathit{set}\ c\ \langle w\rangle\ .P &\triangleq \mathit{mv\ in}\ c.(x).(\langle w\rangle \mid \mathit{mv\ out}\ c.P). \end{aligned}$$

The cell is modeled as an ambient named c that allows objective move operations. The cell's invariant is to keep the current value of the cell as the unique output inside the ambient. Initially, the value w is written.

The *get* operation is modeled as a process that enters the cell (the ambient c), reads the current value (in subexpression (x)), and concurrently writes the same value to the cell (to keep the invariant) and exits the cell c. Notice that process P's free occurrences of variable x will become bound to the cell's content.

The *set* operation is similar to the *get* operation, except that the new value w is written into the cell. Notice that x should be chosen *fresh*, i.e., $x \notin fv(P)$, otherwise, the *set* definition binds free occurrences of x in P to the old value of the cell, reminiscent of an atomic *get-and-set* primitive.

6.4.2 Mutual Exclusion in the Ambient Calculus

The mutual exclusion problem, described in section 1.4.2, can be solved by using a *semaphore*, as follows:

$$\begin{aligned} \mathit{semaphore}\ s &\triangleq s[\,], \\ \mathit{acquire}\ s.P &\triangleq \texttt{open}\ s.P, \\ \mathit{release}\ s &\triangleq s[\,]. \end{aligned}$$

Processes P and Q can mutually exclude each other, assuming that s is *fresh*, that is, $s \notin fv(P) \cup fv(Q)$, as follows:

$$(\nu s)(\mathit{semaphore}\ s \mid !\mathit{acquire}\ s.P.\mathit{release}\ s \mid !\mathit{acquire}\ s.Q.\mathit{release}\ s) \mid R.$$

Notice that the ambient calculus does not specify any *fairness* constraints, that is, even though P and Q can both make progress, there is no guarantee that both eventually will. For example, suppose $P = \mathit{get}\ c\ (x).\mathit{set}\ c\,\langle \texttt{open}\ n.x\rangle$, $Q = \mathit{get}\ c\ (x).\mathit{set}\ c\ \langle \texttt{open}\ m.x\rangle$, and $R = \mathit{cell}\ c\ \texttt{open}\ n$. The semaphore ensures that the *get* and *set* operations in P happen without interference from those in Q. However, there is no guarantee that the content of the cell c will be different from a capability that only refers to ambient n, and never to ambient m. In other words, a computation path in which Q never gets to execute—that is, an *unfair* computation path—is admissible.

6.4.3 Dining Philosophers in the Ambient Calculus

The dining philosophers problem, described in Section 1.4.3, can be encoded in the ambient calculus as follows:

$$\begin{aligned} \mathit{philosopher}\ l\ r &\triangleq\ !\mathit{acquire}\ l.\mathit{acquire}\ r.(\mathit{release}\ l \mid \mathit{release}\ r), \\ \mathit{chopstick}\ c &\triangleq \mathit{semaphore}\ c. \end{aligned}$$

A table with two philosophers and two chopsticks can be modeled as follows:

$$\textit{philosopher}\ c_0\ c_1 \mid \textit{philosopher}\ c_1\ c_0 \mid \textit{chopstick}\ c_0 \mid \textit{chopstick}\ c_1.$$

Notice that each chopstick is modeled as a semaphore (c) that is acquired when it is picked up (*acquire* c). Each philosopher is thus in a continuous loop (denoted by the !) picking up the left chopstick (l), then the right chopstick (r), and then releasing both chopsticks concurrently (*release* l | *release* r).

A table with n philosophers can be modeled as follows:[1]

$$\prod_{0 \le i < n} (\textit{philosopher}\ c_i\ c_{(i+1)\bmod n} \mid \textit{chopstick}\ c_i).$$

6.5 Discussion and Further Reading

The ambient calculus models mobility of processes and mobility of devices. It was created by Luca Cardelli and Andrew Gordon in 1998 (Cardelli and Gordon, 2000). Its roots can be traced to the π calculus and other concurrent process algebras. The key difference between the π calculus and the ambient calculus is the latter's ability to model hierarchical process boundaries, movement of *active* ambients across those boundaries, and the restricted interprocess communication to inside an ambient boundary. The last characteristic is similar to the join calculus' modeling of local-only communication. Movement and destruction of ambients is subjective and objective, respectively, and it is restricted by capabilities that can be communicated.

This chapter has mostly followed the presentation in Cardelli and Gordon's papers on mobile ambients (Cardelli and Gordon, 2000; Gordon and Cardelli, 2003). We have not explicitly distinguished the sorts of names and variables to make our presentation clearer and more consistent with the π calculus presentation. We also consider expressions which are α-equivalent (reducible to each other by α-renaming bound variables) to be structurally congruent, as opposed to *equal*. Finally, we introduce the ambient calculus with process communication, whereas Cardelli and Gordon first introduce a variant of the calculus without communication, which they show to be Turing-complete.

As Gordon and Cardelli (2003) point out, there have been additional works on equivalences of ambient calculus expressions, and their induced equational theories. We refer the reader to this paper and its citations for further study on proving contextual equivalence of ambient calculus expressions, and the theory of ambient calculi in general.

6.6 Exercises

1. Reduce the following ambient calculus expressions using the definitions provided in section 6.2:

(a) $n[acid\ n.P \mid Q] \mid \texttt{open}\ acid$

(b) $n^{\upharpoonleft}[mv\ out\ n.P \mid Q]$

2. Consider the following definitions of a firewall and an agent:

$$firewall \triangleq (\nu w)w[k[\texttt{out}\ w.\texttt{in}\ k'.\texttt{in}\ w] \mid \texttt{open}\ k'.\texttt{open}\ k''.P]$$

$$agent \triangleq k'[\texttt{open}\ k.k''[Q]]$$

Assuming that $w \notin fv(Q)$ and $k, k', k'' \notin (fv(P) \cup fv(Q))$, reduce the following expression:

$agent \mid firewall$

3. Using the definition 6.1, reduce the following ambient calculus expression:

$entrap\ m \mid m[P]$

4. Define a representation of natural numbers in the ambient calculus. Define *increment* and *decrement* operations.

5. Create an ambient calculus expression that exhibits nondeterminism using the $\texttt{out}\ n$ primitive.

6. The *set* operation in the reference cell definition in section 6.4.1 needs to use a *fresh* variable x, i.e., $x \notin fv(P)$, otherwise, it binds free occurrences of x in P to the old value of the reference cell. Modify the definition of the *set* operation so that a fresh variable is not needed. *Hint*: Create an expression so that free occurrences of x in P are not captured by the input operation.

7. Consider the following expressions:

$$e_1 \triangleq !(\nu n)P$$

$$e_2 \triangleq (\nu n)!P.$$

Are expressions e_1 and e_2 contextually equivalent? Justify your answer.

8. Consider the following expressions:

$$e_1 \triangleq n[P] \mid n[Q]$$

$$e_2 \triangleq n[P \mid Q].$$

Are expressions e_1 and e_2 contextually equivalent? Justify your answer.

9. Assuming $m \neq n$, prove the following:

(a) $m[] \not\simeq n[]$.

(b) $\texttt{open}\ m \not\simeq \texttt{open}\ n$.

(c) $\texttt{in}\ m \not\simeq \texttt{in}\ n$.

(d) $\texttt{out}\ m \not\simeq \texttt{out}\ n$.

10. Prove that structural congruence implies contextual equivalence. That is, $P \equiv Q \implies P \simeq Q$.

Note

1. We use the notation $\prod_{0 \leq i < n} P_i \quad \triangleq \quad P_0 \mid P_1 \mid \ldots \mid P_{n-1}$.

7 Formalizing Concurrency, Distribution, and Mobility

In this chapter, concluding part I, we provide a comprehensive comparison between the four theoretical models we have presented. We will discuss and compare properties of the π calculus, the actor model, the join calculus, and mobile ambients, side by side, such as their expressive power, synchronous vs. asynchronous communication, shared vs. distributed memory, fairness, model of concurrency, model of distribution, model of mobility, and reasoning techniques. An open research direction is investigating whether it is possible to create a uniform framework to model concurrency, distribution, and mobility with the expressive qualities and reasoning capabilities of all these formal models.

Section 7.1 discusses ontological commitments in the models including synchrony of communication and state encapsulation. Section 7.2 illustrates the expressiveness of the models by showing corresponding encodings of Turing-complete languages. Section 7.3 considers key semantic properties of the models including composability, fairness, and explicit support for distribution and mobility. Section 7.4 discusses theories developed to support reasoning about programs expressed in these models. Finally, section 7.5 refers to additional literature for formal proofs and further reading.

7.1 Ontological Commitments

7.1.1 Synchronous or Asynchronous Communication

Communication between concurrency units—such as processes, actors, or join calculus atoms—can be *synchronous*, where multiple concurrency units evolve simultaneously in a single time step, or *asynchronous*, where the *output* action can happen in a time step and the *input* action can happen at a later time in a separate time step.

The π calculus uses *synchronous* communication as its most fundamental means of interprocess communication. For example, in the expression

$$\bar{a}x.P \mid a(y).Q,$$

the process expressions corresponding to P and Q are *guarded* by their respective output and input actions. The expression evolves in a single time step according to the π calculus operational semantics as

$P \mid Q\{x/y\}$,

where $\{x/y\}$ represents the substitution of free occurrences of y in Q for x, after α-renaming if necessary to prevent capturing free variables. We say that P and Q are guarded because neither P nor Q could have proceeded in the absence of a concurrent process reading or writing over channel a respectively.

The actor model, on the other hand, uses *asynchronous* communication as its most fundamental means of inter-actor communication. For example, an actor whose behavior is

$\texttt{seq}(\texttt{send}(a, c), \texttt{ready}(b))$

can immediately evolve according to the actor model's operational semantics as

$\texttt{ready}(b)$

with the message $\langle a \Leftarrow c\rangle$ modeled as becoming "en route" to its target actor a. Notice that this communication can occur independently of the state of the target actor, that is, whether a is ready to receive the message or not, the sender can still proceed with its computation $\texttt{ready}(b)$. The message reception occurs at a later time, when actor a's behavior becomes

$\texttt{ready}(b')$,

which, according to the actor model's operational semantics, can then evolve in the presence of message $\langle a \Leftarrow c\rangle$ in the network, as

$b'(c)$,

that is, a's behavior b', a lambda abstraction, is applied to the message content c. Notice that the message sending and message reception events are two separate transitions that can occur at very different times, which is why we call the communication *asynchronous*.

The join calculus uses *synchronous* communication as its most fundamental means of interprocess communication. For example, the join calculus expression

$\texttt{def}\ a\langle x\rangle \mid b\langle x\rangle \triangleright c\langle x\rangle\ \texttt{in}\ a\langle y\rangle \mid b\langle y\rangle$

can evolve as

$\texttt{def}\ a\langle x\rangle \mid b\langle x\rangle \triangleright c\langle x\rangle\ \texttt{in}\ c\langle y\rangle$

in a single time step according to the join calculus operational semantics. Notice that the expression $c\langle x\rangle$ cannot be exhibited until both $a\langle x\rangle$ and $b\langle x\rangle$ can be matched in the multiset of molecules of the underlying chemical abstract machine. The substitution $\sigma_r = \{y/x\}$ was applied to the join pattern to match the initial molecule and to the consequent of the reaction rule to produce the final atom $c\langle y\rangle$. Notice that even though the atoms $a\langle y\rangle$ and $b\langle y\rangle$ may have been produced at different earlier times, it is only when both are present in the multiset of molecules that the pattern $a\langle x\rangle \mid b\langle x\rangle$ can be matched enabling a synchronization step. The join pattern matching process can then be regarded as a *synchronous* communication between the different molecules.

The ambient calculus uses *asynchronous* intra-ambient interprocess communication. That is, communication can occur only between processes within the same ambient. For example, the ambient calculus expression

$$m[\langle x\rangle \mid (y).P]$$

can evolve according to the ambient calculus operational semantics as

$$m[P\{x/y\}]$$

in a single time step. Notice that process P is *guarded* by the input action (y); thus, it cannot execute until another process writes inside its containing ambient—in this case, m. However, the output action $\langle x\rangle$ cannot guard any processes according to the syntax of the ambient calculus; therefore, we say that the model has *asynchronous output*. It is worth mentioning that primitives for ambient movement and opening (but not process communication) are synchronous. For example,

$$n[\texttt{in}\ m \mid \langle x\rangle] \mid m[\texttt{open}\ n.Q \mid (y).P]$$

can evolve as

$$m[n[\langle x\rangle] \mid \texttt{open}\ n.Q \mid (y).P]$$

only because there is an ambient named m at the same level as ambient n which contains the process exercising the capability `in` m. Notice, in particular, that capability `open` n is *guarding* process Q, which cannot proceed until the capability can be exercised, that is, until an ambient named n is at the same level. Since in the resulting expression, we have an ambient named n inside m, the computation can proceed as

$$m[\langle x\rangle \mid Q \mid (y).P],$$

which can finally evolve as

$$m[Q \mid P\{x/y\}].$$

7.1.2 Shared or Distributed Memory

Memory or state in concurrency units—such as processes, actors, or join calculus atoms—can be *shared*, where multiple concurrency units have the capability to read it and update it, or *distributed* where only one concurrency unit owns it and can read it, update it, or communicate its content to other units.

The π calculus has a *shared memory* model, where multiple processes can read from a shared channel or write to a shared channel. For example, the expression

$$a(x).P \mid a(y).Q \mid \bar{a}b.R \mid \bar{a}c.S \tag{7.1}$$

can evolve according to the π calculus operational semantics in several different ways, since all four concurrent processes are sharing channel a. Two of the ways it could evolve include

$$P\{b/x\} \mid Q\{c/y\} \mid R \mid S$$

and

$$P\{c/x\} \mid Q\{b/y\} \mid R \mid S.$$

For a pictorial representation, see figure 7.1.

If $R = \bar{a}d.R'$, expression 7.1 could also evolve as

$$P\{b/x\} \mid Q\{d/y\} \mid R' \mid \bar{a}c.S,$$

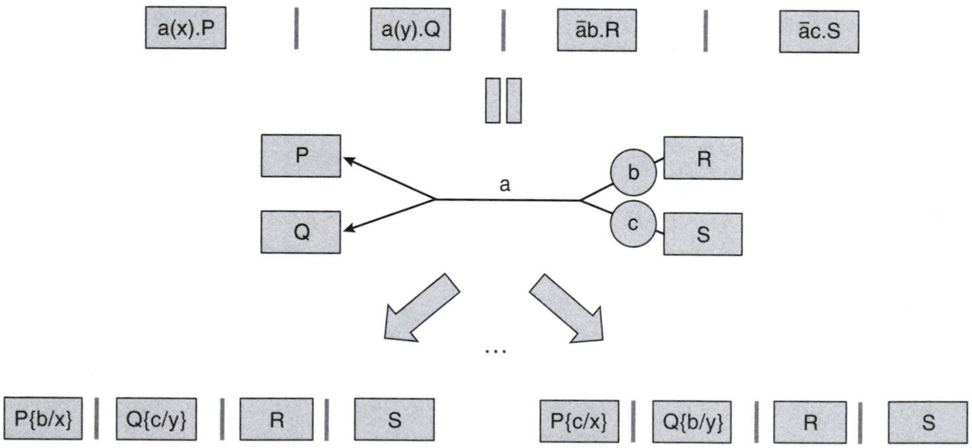

Figure 7.1
A pictorial representation of shared memory in the π calculus.

and if $P = a(z).P'$, expression 7.1 could also evolve as

$$P'\{(b,c)/(x,z)\} \mid a(y).Q \mid R \mid S.$$

Essentially, all co-bound (free) channel names represent shared memory and thus have the potential for process interaction. A simple, yet powerful means to restrict access to shared memory, is to use the restriction operator ν. For example,

$$(\nu a)(a(x).P \mid \bar{a}b.R) \mid (\nu a)(a(y).Q \mid \bar{a}c.S)$$

ensures that this expression can only evolve as

$$(\nu a)(P\{b/x\} \mid R) \mid (\nu a)(Q\{c/y\} \mid S).$$

However, when a restricted channel name is sent to a process outside its original scope, the scope is *extruded* to include the receiving process; for example,

$$b(x).Q \mid (\nu a)\bar{b}a.P$$

is structurally congruent to

$$(\nu a)(b(x).Q \mid \bar{b}a.P),$$

assuming that $a \notin \mathbf{fn}(Q)$. This expression can then evolve to

$$(\nu a)(P \mid Q\{a/x\}).$$

Therefore, channel name restriction alone cannot guarantee exclusive access to memory. If a channel is restricted and its name is never sent over another channel, we can guarantee its scope is limited and access is therefore restricted. For example, see channel l in the reference cell example in section 3.4.1.

The actor model, on the other hand, follows a *distributed* memory model, where state is fully encapsulated within an actor and cannot be seen or modified by other actors directly. For example, consider the reference cell from section 4.4.1:

```
cell = rec( λb.λc.λm.
          if( get?(m),
              seq( send(cust(m), c),
                   ready(b(c))),
              if( set?(m),
                  ready(b(contents(m))),
                  ready(b(c)))))
```

The internal state c cannot be seen by other actors because of lexical scoping rules. It can be communicated in messages as in send(*cust*(m), c) and it can be changed by the actor in response to a message as in *ready*(b(*contents*(m))), but there is no way for other actors to access it or update it directly. In general, behaviors in the actor language can be written as

$$\texttt{rec(}\ \lambda b.\lambda s_1.\ldots.\lambda s_n.\lambda m.\ \ldots\texttt{ready}(b(s_1')\ldots(s_n'))\ldots)$$

where state variables $s_1, \ldots, s_n$ are fully encapsulated and can only be changed by the owner actor by using $\texttt{ready}(b(s_1')\ldots(s_n'))$. Actors can send acquaintance references (names) to other actors in messages, but the only action that those other actors can take with these names is to send them messages. For example, the code

$$\texttt{let}\ a = \texttt{new}(cell(0))\ \texttt{in seq(}\ \texttt{send}(b, a),\ \texttt{send}(c, a),\ \texttt{send}(d, a))$$

will allow actors b, c, and d to have access to actor a, the reference cell. However, this access is limited to sending it messages and sending its name to other known actors, but never to accessing its internal state directly.

The join calculus models state as a multiset of reaction rules and a multiset of molecules and therefore follows a *shared* memory model. For example, the join calculus expression

$$\texttt{def}\ a\langle x\rangle \triangleright b\langle x\rangle \wedge a\langle x\rangle \triangleright c\langle x\rangle\ \texttt{in}\ a\langle y\rangle \mid a\langle z\rangle$$

can evolve according to the join calculus operational semantics in several different ways, since the defined port name a is shared by multiple reaction rules and molecules. Let $D = a\langle x\rangle \triangleright b\langle x\rangle \wedge a\langle x\rangle \triangleright c\langle x\rangle$, the expression could evolve as

$$\texttt{def}\ D\ \texttt{in}\ b\langle y\rangle \mid c\langle z\rangle$$

or

$$\texttt{def}\ D\ \texttt{in}\ c\langle y\rangle \mid b\langle z\rangle$$

or

$$\texttt{def}\ D\ \texttt{in}\ b\langle y\rangle \mid b\langle z\rangle$$

or

$$\texttt{def}\ D\ \texttt{in}\ c\langle y\rangle \mid c\langle z\rangle$$

depending on the (nondeterministic) order of reaction rule selection and pattern matching. A simple, yet powerful means to restrict interaction in the join calculus is to use scoping rules. For example,

$$\texttt{def}\ a\langle x\rangle \triangleright b\langle x\rangle\ \texttt{in}\ a\langle y\rangle \mid \texttt{def}\ a\langle x\rangle \triangleright c\langle x\rangle\ \texttt{in}\ a\langle z\rangle$$

ensures that this expression can evolve only as

$$\texttt{def}\ a\langle x\rangle \triangleright b\langle x\rangle\ \texttt{in}\ b\langle y\rangle \mid \texttt{def}\ a\langle x\rangle \triangleright c\langle x\rangle\ \texttt{in}\ c\langle z\rangle\,.$$

Observing the full derivation following the join calculus structural congruence and operational semantics rules in figure 5.4:

$$\begin{aligned}
&\emptyset \vdash \texttt{def}\ a\langle x\rangle \triangleright b\langle x\rangle\ \texttt{in}\ a\langle y\rangle \mid \texttt{def}\ a\langle x\rangle \triangleright c\langle x\rangle\ \texttt{in}\ a\langle z\rangle \\
&\rightleftharpoons\ a'\langle x\rangle \triangleright b\langle x\rangle \vdash a'\langle y\rangle \mid \texttt{def}\ a\langle x\rangle \triangleright c\langle x\rangle\ \texttt{in}\ a\langle z\rangle \qquad (7.2)\\
&\rightleftharpoons\ a'\langle x\rangle \triangleright b\langle x\rangle \wedge a''\langle x\rangle \triangleright c\langle x\rangle \vdash a'\langle y\rangle \mid a''\langle z\rangle \qquad (7.3)\\
&\longrightarrow\ a'\langle x\rangle \triangleright b\langle x\rangle \wedge a''\langle x\rangle \triangleright c\langle x\rangle \vdash b\langle y\rangle \mid a''\langle z\rangle\\
&\longrightarrow\ a'\langle x\rangle \triangleright b\langle x\rangle \wedge a''\langle x\rangle \triangleright c\langle x\rangle \vdash b\langle y\rangle \mid c\langle z\rangle\\
&\rightleftharpoons\ a'\langle x\rangle \triangleright b\langle x\rangle \vdash b\langle y\rangle \mid \texttt{def}\ a\langle x\rangle \triangleright c\langle x\rangle\ \texttt{in}\ c\langle z\rangle\\
&\rightleftharpoons\ \emptyset \vdash \texttt{def}\ a\langle x\rangle \triangleright b\langle x\rangle\ \texttt{in}\ b\langle y\rangle \mid \texttt{def}\ a\langle x\rangle \triangleright c\langle x\rangle\ \texttt{in}\ c\langle z\rangle,
\end{aligned}$$

we see that the substitutions $\sigma_{d'} = \{a'/a\}$ used to get expression 7.2 and $\sigma_{d''} = \{a''/a\}$ used to get expression 7.3 are critical to prevent unintended interactions that would produce atoms $b\langle z\rangle$ or $c\langle y\rangle$. Static scoping provides a means to control undesired interference but similarly to the π calculus, the scope of a defined name can be *extruded* to enable interaction with other molecules. For example, consider the following expression:

$$\texttt{def}\ c\langle x\rangle \triangleright P\ \texttt{in}\ \texttt{def}\ a\langle\rangle \triangleright b\langle\rangle\ \texttt{in}\ c\langle a\rangle\,,$$

which, assuming $a \notin \mathbf{fn}(P)$, can evolve to

$$\texttt{def}\ c\langle x\rangle \triangleright P\ \texttt{in}\ \texttt{def}\ a\langle\rangle \triangleright b\langle\rangle\ \texttt{in}\ P\{a/x\},$$

where the scope of defined port a has been extruded to expression P. Let us consider the reduction process:

$$\begin{aligned}
&\emptyset \vdash \texttt{def}\ c\langle x\rangle \triangleright P\ \texttt{in}\ \texttt{def}\ a\langle\rangle \triangleright b\langle\rangle\ \texttt{in}\ c\langle a\rangle\\
&\rightleftharpoons\ c\langle x\rangle \triangleright P \vdash \texttt{def}\ a\langle\rangle \triangleright b\langle\rangle\ \texttt{in}\ c\langle a\rangle\\
&\rightleftharpoons\ c\langle x\rangle \triangleright P \wedge a\langle\rangle \triangleright b\langle\rangle \vdash c\langle a\rangle \qquad (7.4)\\
&\longrightarrow\ c\langle x\rangle \triangleright P \wedge a\langle\rangle \triangleright b\langle\rangle \vdash P\{a/x\}\\
&\rightleftharpoons\ c\langle x\rangle \triangleright P \vdash \texttt{def}\ a\langle\rangle \triangleright b\langle\rangle\ \texttt{in}\ P\{a/x\}\\
&\rightleftharpoons\ \emptyset \vdash \texttt{def}\ c\langle x\rangle \triangleright P\ \texttt{in}\ \texttt{def}\ a\langle\rangle \triangleright b\langle\rangle\ \texttt{in}\ P\{a/x\},
\end{aligned}$$

where the key step to get expression 7.4 requires $a \notin \mathbf{fn}(P)$. Therefore, the scope of defined names in reaction rules alone, like in the π calculus, does not guarantee restricted access. If a defined port name is never sent over another port, we can guarantee its scope is limited and access restricted. For example, see defined port s in the reference cell example in section 5.4.1.

The ambient calculus uses a *shared* memory model whereby ambient names represent the state of a computation and can be shared. For example, consider the expression

$$\texttt{open}\ n \mid n[\langle a\rangle] \mid n[\langle b\rangle] \mid (x).P,$$

which can evolve as

$$P\{a/x\} \mid n[\langle b\rangle]$$

or

$$P\{b/x\} \mid n[\langle a\rangle].$$

Similarly, the expression

$$m[\texttt{in}\ n.P] \mid n[Q] \mid n[R]$$

can evolve as

$$n[m[P] \mid Q] \mid n[R]$$

or

$$n[Q] \mid n[m[P] \mid R].$$

In the ambient calculus, like in the π calculus and the join calculus, a restriction operator, ν, allows to restrict the scope of ambient names to prevent undesired interactions; but also a structural congruence rule for scope extrusion enables to potentially expose names that should be restricted. For example, the expression

$$(\nu n)(\texttt{open}\ n \mid n[\langle a\rangle] \mid (x).P) \mid n[\langle b\rangle]$$

can evolve only as

$$(\nu n)P\{a/x\} \mid n[\langle b\rangle],$$

but the expression

$$(\nu n)(\langle n\rangle \mid n[Q]) \mid (x).P,$$

assuming $n \notin \mathbf{fn}(P)$, is structurally equivalent to

$$(\nu n)(\langle n\rangle \mid n[Q] \mid (x).P),$$

which can evolve as

$$(\nu n)(n[Q] \mid P\{n/x\}).$$

If $P = \texttt{open}\ x.P'$, then this expression evolves as

$$(\nu n)(Q \mid P'\{n/x\}),$$

where the ambient n, whose scope was originally restricted, has been opened by the process P, which was originally outside its scope. Therefore, ambient name restriction alone, like in the π calculus and the join calculus, cannot guarantee exclusive access to state. If an ambient name is restricted and its name is never sent out either by itself—as in $\langle n\rangle$—or as part of a capability—as in $\langle\texttt{open}\ n\rangle$, then we can guarantee that its scope is limited and access is therefore restricted. The reference cell example given in section 6.4.1 does not protect the internal cell state, since a process given the cell's name can enter the cell's ambient and break its invariant, for example, as follows:

$$mget\ c\ (x).P \quad \triangleq \quad mv\ in\ c.(x).mv\ out\ c.P.$$

This malicious *mget* operation enters the reference cell's ambient, reads the cell's value, and does not put it back, breaking the cell's invariant.

7.1.3 Summary

Figure 7.2 summarizes the fundamental means of communication and memory models of the different concurrency models we have studied in this part of the book.

Model	Primitive Communication	Memory Model
π calculus	Synchronous	Shared
Actors	Asynchronous	Distributed
Join calculus	Synchronous	Shared
Mobile ambients	Asynchronous	Shared

Figure 7.2
Most fundamental communication and memory models in different concurrency models.

7.2 Expressive Power

Since the different models of concurrent computation we have studied make different ontological commitments with respect to synchronous or asynchronous communication and shared or distributed memory, their relative expressive power is an open question.

All the formal models of concurrency that we have studied are Turing-complete. That is, we can use each model to simulate a Turing machine, and therefore, any computable function can be expressed in these models.

One way to demonstrate Turing-completeness is to emulate a Turing machine "mechanically", as Cardelli and Gordon (2000) demonstrates for the mobile ambient subcalculus without communication. Another strategy is to be able to translate a Turing-complete language in the formalism. For example, the λ calculus is translated into the π calculus (Milner, 1990), actors (Agha et al., 1997) and the join calculus (Fournet and Gonthier, 1996), and the π calculus is translated into the ambient calculus (Cardelli and Gordon, 2000). In the following sections, we show several of these encodings to illustrate the expressive power of the different models.

7.2.1 Encoding of the λ Calculus in the π Calculus

Milner (1990) described two translations of the λ calculus in a subset of the π calculus, which includes replication, but excludes summation, match, and the silent guard τ. We will describe the translation of the λ calculus that uses normal order evaluation, that is, leftmost redex first. We refer the reader to Milner (1990) for a translation of the call-by-value λ calculus, as well as for proofs of correctness of both translations.

Recall that the syntax for the λ calculus is:

$$
\begin{array}{rll}
e ::= & x & \text{– variable} \\
| & \lambda x.e & \text{– functional abstraction} \\
| & (e \quad e) & \text{– function application.}
\end{array}
$$

The translation into the π calculus follows:

$$
\begin{array}{rcll}
[\![x]\!]_u & \triangleq & \bar{x}u & \\
[\![\lambda x.e]\!]_u & \triangleq & u(x,v).[\![e]\!]_v & \\
[\![(e_1 \quad e_2)]\!]_u & \triangleq & (\nu v)([\![e_1]\!]_v \mid (\nu x)\bar{v}\langle x,u\rangle.[\![x := e_2]\!]) & \text{assuming } x \notin \mathbf{fn}(e_2). \\
[\![x := e]\!] & \triangleq & !x(w).[\![e]\!]_w. &
\end{array}
$$

The difficulty in translating the λ calculus lies in the fact that β reduction uses a relatively complex primitive operation, namely substitution of terms for names. The intuition of the translation is that a λ calculus expression e is represented by a π calculus process $[\![e]\!]_u$, where u is the name of the link along which e "receives" its arguments. $[\![x := e]\!]$ represents an *environment* where x is bound to e, which is represented by a process that continuously receives requests for a channel w over channel x and sends e's representation after evaluation convergence over w. This effectively emulates substitutions as agents. A lambda abstraction $\lambda x.e$ is represented by a π calculus process $[\![\lambda x.e]\!]_u$ that receives two channels over u, the name of the variable that is bound, x, and the name of a channel v where the rest will be transmitted, followed by the abstraction body representation $[\![e]\!]_v$. Finally, function application $(e_1 \quad e_2)$ is encoded as the parallel composition of the representation of the functional abstraction $[\![e_1]\!]_v$ with a process that writes on v the two channels x and u—representing the abstraction variable name and the channel where the final evaluation result is to be sent respectively—followed by an environment where x is bound to the expression e_2.

Let us consider an example of β reduction in the λ calculus:

$$(\lambda x.x \quad y) \overset{\beta}{\rightarrow} y.$$

The π calculus translation follows:

$$\begin{aligned}
&[\![(\lambda x.x \quad y)]\!]_u \\
&\quad \triangleq \quad (\nu v)([\![\lambda x.x]\!]_v \mid (\nu x)\bar{v}\langle x,u\rangle.[\![x := y]\!]) \\
&\quad \triangleq \quad (\nu v)(v(x,w).[\![x]\!]_w \mid (\nu x)\bar{v}\langle x,u\rangle.!x(w).[\![y]\!]_w) \\
&\quad \triangleq \quad (\nu v)(v(x,w).\bar{x}w \mid (\nu x)\bar{v}\langle x,u\rangle.!x(w).\bar{y}w) \\
&\quad \equiv (\nu v)(\nu x)(v(x,w).\bar{x}w \mid \bar{v}\langle x,u\rangle.!x(w).\bar{y}w) \\
&\quad \overset{\tau}{\longrightarrow}{}^{*} (\nu v)(\nu x)(\bar{x}u \mid !x(w).\bar{y}w) \\
&\quad \equiv (\nu x)(\bar{x}u \mid x(w).\bar{y}w \mid !x(w).\bar{y}w) \\
&\quad \overset{\tau}{\longrightarrow} (\nu x)(\bar{y}u \mid !x(w).\bar{y}w) \\
&\quad \equiv \bar{y}u \mid (\nu x)(!x(w).\bar{y}w) \qquad (7.5) \\
&\quad \sim \bar{y}u \\
&\quad \triangleq \quad [\![y]\!]_u.
\end{aligned}$$

The first three steps (and the last step) unfold (and fold) the definitions. We use structural congruence and operational semantics rules of the π calculus to derive expression 7.5. The step to reach expression $\bar{y}u$ uses congruence, since $(\nu x)(!x(w).\bar{y}w) \sim 0$. For this particular example, we did not need the replication operator (!). Milner notices that replication in the π calculus is needed for emulating nonlinear lambda calculus terms, such as the Y combinator, where variables appear more than once in their scope, and therefore the finite subcalculus (π calculus without replication) does not have the full expressive power of the λ calculus, only the linear λ calculus.

7.2.2 Encoding of the λ Calculus in the Actor Model

The actor model extends the λ calculus (Agha et al., 1997) and is therefore Turing-complete by construction.

A simple translation of the λ calculus in the actor language creates an actor configuration with one sink actor per free variable and an empty network, as follows:

$$[\![e]\!]_{\{v_0,\ldots,v_n\}} \quad \triangleq \quad \emptyset, [e]_a, [sink]_{v_0}, \ldots, [sink]_{v_n} \ \| \ \emptyset,$$

where a is *fresh* (*i.e.*, $a \notin \{v_0, \ldots, v_n\} \cup fv(e)$,) and $sink = \texttt{rec}(\lambda b.\lambda m.\texttt{ready}(b))$.

The existence of the sink actors is necessary to ensure the syntactic restriction of free variables in actor configurations (see section 4.2.1.)

We can then translate a λ calculus expression e into the actor language as $[\![e]\!]_{fv(e)}$.

Let us consider the sample derivation $(\lambda x.x \quad y) \xrightarrow{\beta} y$:

$$\begin{aligned}
&[\![(\lambda x.x \quad y)]\!]_{\{y\}} \\
&\triangleq \quad \emptyset, [(\lambda x.x \quad y)]_a, [sink]_y \ \| \ \emptyset \\
&\xrightarrow{[\mathbf{fun}:a]} \quad \emptyset, [y]_a, [sink]_y \ \| \ \emptyset \\
&\triangleq \quad [\![y]\!]_{\{y\}}.
\end{aligned}$$

Since the transition relation $\xrightarrow{[\mathbf{fun}:a]}$ subsumes $\rightarrow_\lambda$, which itself subsumes λ calculus β reduction, the proof of correctness of this translation is straightforward.

7.2.3 Encoding of the λ Calculus in the Join Calculus

As with the π calculus, we will provide a translation that uses normal order reduction (Fournet and Gonthier, 1996). That is, evaluation is leftmost redex first. The translation follows:

$$\begin{aligned}
[\![x]\!]_v \quad &\triangleq \quad x\,\langle v\rangle \\
[\![\lambda x.e]\!]_v \quad &\triangleq \quad \texttt{def}\ k\,\langle x, w\rangle \triangleright [\![e]\!]_w\ \texttt{in}\ v\,\langle k\rangle \\
[\![(e_1 \quad e_2)]\!]_v \quad &\triangleq \quad \texttt{def}\ x\,\langle u\rangle \triangleright [\![e_2]\!]_u\ \texttt{in}\ \texttt{def}\ w\,\langle k\rangle \triangleright k\,\langle x, v\rangle\ \texttt{in}\ [\![e_1]\!]_w.
\end{aligned}$$

The intuition is that λ calculus abstractions export a channel k that serves evaluation requests by providing two names: x to send requests for the value of the argument, and w to eventually return a value when evaluation converges.

Let us consider an example of β reduction in the λ calculus:

$$(\lambda x.x \quad y) \xrightarrow{\beta} y.$$

The join calculus translation is as follows:

$$\begin{aligned}
&[\![(\lambda x.x \quad y)]\!]_v \\
&\triangleq \quad \texttt{def}\ x\langle u\rangle \triangleright [\![y]\!]_u\ \texttt{in def}\ w\langle k\rangle \triangleright k\langle x,v\rangle\ \texttt{in}\ [\![\lambda x.x]\!]_w \\
&\triangleq \quad \texttt{def}\ x\langle u\rangle \triangleright y\langle u\rangle\ \texttt{in def}\ w\langle k\rangle \triangleright k\langle x,v\rangle\ \texttt{in}\ [\![\lambda x.x]\!]_w \\
&\triangleq \quad \texttt{def}\ x\langle u\rangle \triangleright y\langle u\rangle\ \texttt{in def}\ w\langle k\rangle \triangleright k\langle x,v\rangle\ \texttt{in def}\ k\langle x,w'\rangle \triangleright [\![x]\!]_{w'}\ \texttt{in}\ w\langle k\rangle \\
&\triangleq \quad \texttt{def}\ x\langle u\rangle \triangleright y\langle u\rangle\ \texttt{in def}\ w\langle k\rangle \triangleright k\langle x,v\rangle\ \texttt{in def}\ k\langle x,w'\rangle \triangleright x\langle w'\rangle\ \texttt{in}\ w\langle k\rangle.
\end{aligned}$$

This join calculus expression can evolve according to the join calculus operational semantics as follows:

$$\begin{aligned}
&\emptyset \vdash \texttt{def}\ x\langle u\rangle \triangleright y\langle u\rangle\ \texttt{in def}\ w\langle k\rangle \triangleright k\langle x,v\rangle\ \texttt{in def}\ k\langle x,w'\rangle \triangleright x\langle w'\rangle\ \texttt{in}\ w\langle k\rangle \\
&\rightleftharpoons \quad x\langle u\rangle \triangleright y\langle u\rangle \vdash \texttt{def}\ w\langle k\rangle \triangleright k\langle x,v\rangle\ \texttt{in def}\ k\langle x,w'\rangle \triangleright x\langle w'\rangle\ \texttt{in}\ w\langle k\rangle \\
&\rightleftharpoons \quad x\langle u\rangle \triangleright y\langle u\rangle, w\langle k\rangle \triangleright k\langle x,v\rangle \vdash \texttt{def}\ k\langle x,w'\rangle \triangleright x\langle w'\rangle\ \texttt{in}\ w\langle k\rangle \\
&\rightleftharpoons \quad x\langle u\rangle \triangleright y\langle u\rangle, \underline{w\langle k\rangle \triangleright k\langle x,v\rangle}, k\langle x,w'\rangle \triangleright x\langle w'\rangle \vdash \underline{w\langle k\rangle} \\
&\longrightarrow \quad x\langle u\rangle \triangleright y\langle u\rangle, w\langle k\rangle \triangleright k\langle x,v\rangle, \underline{k\langle x,w'\rangle \triangleright x\langle w'\rangle} \vdash \underline{k\langle x,v\rangle} \\
&\longrightarrow \quad \underline{x\langle u\rangle \triangleright y\langle u\rangle}, w\langle k\rangle \triangleright k\langle x,v\rangle, k\langle x,w'\rangle \triangleright x\langle w'\rangle \vdash \underline{x\langle v\rangle} \\
&\longrightarrow \quad x\langle u\rangle \triangleright y\langle u\rangle, w\langle k\rangle \triangleright k\langle x,v\rangle, k\langle x,w'\rangle \triangleright x\langle w'\rangle \vdash y\langle v\rangle \\
&\triangleq \quad [\![y]\!]_v.
\end{aligned}$$

Notice that in the last step, we have ignored reaction rules that define variables x, w, and k, since these do not appear in the solution $y\langle v\rangle$.

7.2.4 Encoding the Asynchronous π Calculus in the Ambient Calculus

To encode the asynchronous π calculus, a restricted version of the calculus that we presented in chapter 3, the key challenge is to encode channel names and interprocess communication.

The encoding will represent each channel by an ambient. For a process to communicate over a channel, it will have to enter the ambient representing the channel before communication takes place and exit the channel after communication. The restriction that communication has to be localized to an ambient is similar to the local communication advocated by the join calculus, presented in chapter 5. All processes, as well as ambients representing channels, will be assumed to coexist at the top level of the ambient hierarchy.

Following is a possible encoding:

$$\begin{aligned} \mathit{channel}\ c &\triangleq c^{\downarrow\uparrow}[\,] \\ c(x).P &\triangleq \mathit{mv\ in}\ c.(x).\mathit{mv\ out}\ c.P \\ \bar{c}a &\triangleq \mathit{mv\ in}\ c.\langle a\rangle\,. \end{aligned}$$

These definitions satisfy the expected π calculus reduction $c(x).P \mid \bar{c}a \xrightarrow{\tau} P\{a/x\}$, assuming the presence of a channel c as follows:

$$\begin{aligned} & c(x).P \mid \bar{c}a \mid \mathit{channel}\ c \\ &\triangleq\ \mathit{mv\ in}\ c.(x).\mathit{mv\ out}\ c.P \mid \mathit{mv\ in}\ c.\langle a\rangle \mid c^{\downarrow\uparrow}[\,] \\ &\longrightarrow^{*} c^{\downarrow\uparrow}[(x).\mathit{mv\ out}\ c.P \mid \langle a\rangle] \\ &\longrightarrow c^{\downarrow\uparrow}[\mathit{mv\ out}\ c.P\{a/x\}] \\ &\longrightarrow^{*} P\{a/x\} \mid c^{\downarrow\uparrow}[\,] \\ &\triangleq\ P\{a/x\} \mid \mathit{channel}\ c. \end{aligned}$$

The new channel operator in the π calculus, $(\nu c)P$, has to restrict the scope of the channel name c to P. This can be accomplished with the restriction operator in the ambient calculus as follows:

$$[\![(\nu c)P]\!] \triangleq (\nu c)(c^{\downarrow\uparrow}[\,] \mid [\![P]\!]).$$

We do not need to create ambients representing input-bound variables in the π calculus, such as x in the preceding example, since variable substitution during communication eliminates all free occurrences of these variables, so they cannot be directly used for communication, as in $P\{a/x\}$ in the example. Furthermore, we already create an ambient for restriction-bound variables during translation from π calculus to ambient calculus, as shown in the definition of the restriction operator. Therefore, since variables in the π calculus can be bound only by the new channel and the input primitives, we only need to consider free variables in a π calculus expression, in order to create appropriate channels for communication.

Following is the full asynchronous π calculus encoding, where a π calculus expression P is translated as $[\![P]\!]_{fv(P)}$:

$$
\begin{aligned}
[\![P]\!]_S &\triangleq [\![S]\!] \mid [\![P]\!] \\
[\![\{c_1, \ldots, c_n\}]\!] &\triangleq c_1^{\downharpoonleft\upharpoonleft}[] \mid \ldots \mid c_n^{\downharpoonleft\upharpoonleft}[] \\
[\![(\nu c)P]\!] &\triangleq (\nu c)(c^{\downharpoonleft\upharpoonleft}[] \mid [\![P]\!]) \\
[\![0]\!] &\triangleq 0 \\
[\![P \mid Q]\!] &\triangleq [\![P]\!] \mid [\![Q]\!] \\
[\![!P]\!] &\triangleq ![\![P]\!] \\
[\![c(x).P]\!] &\triangleq mv\ in\ c.(x).mv\ out\ c.[\![P]\!] \\
[\![\bar{c}a]\!] &\triangleq mv\ in\ c.\langle a \rangle\,.
\end{aligned}
$$

Since it is possible to encode the choice-free synchronous π calculus and the λ calculus in the asynchronous π calculus, then these calculi can also be indirectly encoded by the ambient calculus (Cardelli and Gordon, 2000).

7.2.5 Summary

Figure 7.3 summarizes the minimum demonstrated expressive power of the different concurrency models we have studied in this part of the book.

7.3 Semantic Properties

In this section, we will study semantic properties of the different models of concurrent, distributed, and mobile computation. In particular, we will comparatively look at unbounded concurrency, composability, fairness, distribution, and mobility.

Model	Illustrated Expressive Power
π calculus	λ calculus
Actors	λ calculus
Join Calculus	λ calculus
Mobile Ambients	π calculus

Figure 7.3
Expressive power of different concurrency models.

7.3.1 Unbounded Concurrency

One of the key differences between earlier models of concurrency—such as Petri nets, calculus of communicating systems (CCS), or communicating sequential processes (CSP)—and more recent ones is the latter's ability to model unbounded concurrency. As discussed in section 7.2.1, unbounded concurrency is a prerequisite to model nonlinear lambda calculus expressions, including recursive computation.

The π calculus provides unbounded concurrency through the replication operator, !. For example, the expression:

$$!\bar{c}x$$

represents a process that can write infinitely often name x over channel c.

The actor model uses the `new` primitive to create new concurrency units. Combined with recursion in the λ calculus, it can create infinitely many actors. For example, the actor program

```
let r = rec( λb.λm.
             seq( send(new(b), m),
                  ready(b)))
 in   send(new(r), nil)
```

lets r represent a *reproductive* program that upon message reception creates another reproductive actor and forwards the message indefinitely.

The join calculus allows for unbounded concurrency by using recursive reaction rules. For example, the expression

$$\texttt{def}\ r\langle\rangle \triangleright c\langle x\rangle \mid r\langle\rangle\ \texttt{in}\ r\langle\rangle$$

creates infinitely many replicas of the atom $c\langle x\rangle$ in the multiset of molecules of the corresponding chemical abstract machine.

The ambient calculus, similarly to the π calculus, supports unbounded concurrency through a replication operator, !. For example, the expression

$$!n[]$$

creates infinitely many ambients named n.

Figure 7.4 summarizes the key operators for unbounded concurrency in the different concurrency models we have studied in this part of the book.

7.3.2 Composability

Composability is the ability to compose larger more complex systems from smaller simpler ones. A key desirable aspect is that reasoning be *modular*, that is, properties

Model	Operator	Example
π calculus	!	$!\bar{c}x$
Actors	rec, new	rec($\lambda b.\lambda m.$seq(send(new(b), m), ready(b)))
Join calculus	$\triangleright$	def $r\,\langle\rangle \triangleright c\,\langle x\rangle \mid r\,\langle\rangle$ in $r\,\langle\rangle$
Mobile ambients	!	$!n[]$

Figure 7.4
Unbounded concurrency operators in different concurrency models.

of the smaller systems should continue to hold after composition. How the smaller systems *interact* with each other is also of paramount importance.

In the π calculus, composability is supported directly by using the process composition operator $\mid$. For example, the expression

$$\bar{c}x.P \mid d(y).Q$$

represents the concurrent composition of two otherwise independent processes, assuming that their free name sets are disjoint, i.e., $\mathbf{fn}(P) \cap \mathbf{fn}(Q) = \emptyset$.

More interestingly, though, we can compose systems that can then communicate through channels whose names are free. For example, the composition

$$\bar{c}x.P \mid c(y).Q$$

generally enables the interaction

$$\xrightarrow{\tau} P \mid Q\{x/y\}.$$

However, α renaming has to be used when composing systems that can lead to name collisions. For example, consider $P = 0$ and $Q = c(x).\bar{x}y$; then

$$\bar{c}x \mid c(y).c(x).\bar{x}y$$

cannot evolve to

$$c(x).\bar{x}x$$

because the precondition $\mathbf{bn}(\alpha) \cap \mathbf{fn}(Q) = \emptyset$ of the PAR rule in the π calculus operational semantics would not be satisfied (see figure 3.6). Therefore, we must first α-rename Q to get $c(x').\bar{x}'y$, and we can then proceed with the derivation:

$$\bar{c}x \mid c(y).c(x').\bar{x}'y$$

$$\xrightarrow{\tau} c(x').\bar{x}'x,$$

where the x in the original first process component remains free.

In the actor model presented in chapter 4, we chose not to present support for composability of actor configurations. However, Agha, Mason, Smith, and Talcott present a model for *open* distributed systems (Agha et al., 1997), where actor configurations explicitly model the interface with their environment as a set of names for *receptionists*, ρ, and a set of names for *external actors*, χ, as follows:

$$\langle \alpha \mid \mu \rangle^{\rho}_{\chi},$$

with the following syntactic restrictions:

1. $\rho \subseteq dom(\alpha)$, $dom(\alpha) \cap \chi = \emptyset$.
2. If $a \in dom(\alpha)$, then $fv(\alpha(a)) \subseteq dom(\alpha) \cup \chi$.
3. If $\langle a \Leftarrow v \rangle \in \mu$, then $fv(a) \cup fv(v) \subseteq dom(\alpha) \cup \chi$.

The actor operational semantics (in figure 4.6) is extended with two rules for interaction with the environment:

$$\frac{a \in \chi}{\langle \alpha \mid \{\langle a \Leftarrow v \rangle\} \uplus \mu \rangle^{\rho}_{\chi} \xrightarrow{[\mathbf{out}:a,v]} \langle \alpha \mid \mu \rangle^{\rho \cup (fv(v) \cap dom(\alpha))}_{\chi}}$$

$$\frac{a \in \rho \quad fv(v) \cap dom(\alpha) \subseteq \rho}{\langle \alpha \mid \mu \rangle^{\rho}_{\chi} \xrightarrow{[\mathbf{in}:a,v]} \langle \alpha \mid \{\langle a \Leftarrow v \rangle\} \uplus \mu \rangle^{\rho}_{\chi \cup (fv(v) - dom(\alpha))}}.$$

Two actor configurations

$$\kappa = \langle \alpha \mid \mu \rangle^{\rho}_{\chi}$$

and

$$\kappa' = \langle \alpha' \mid \mu' \rangle^{\rho'}_{\chi'}$$

are *composable* only if:

1. $dom(\alpha) \cap dom(\alpha') = \emptyset$,
2. $\chi \cap dom(\alpha') \subseteq \rho'$, and
3. $\chi' \cap dom(\alpha) \subseteq \rho$.

The actor configuration composition $\kappa || \kappa'$ is defined as

$$\langle \alpha \cup \alpha' \mid \mu \uplus \mu' \rangle^{\rho \cup \rho'}_{(\chi \cup \chi') - (\rho \cup \rho')}.$$

Agha, Mason, Smith, and Talcott show that actor configuration composition is associative and commutative with $\kappa_{\emptyset} = \langle \emptyset \mid \emptyset \rangle^{\emptyset}_{\emptyset}$ as the identity configuration:

Model	Composability	Interface
π calculus	$P\|Q$	Free names (α-renaming if collisions)
Actors	$\kappa\|\|\kappa'$	Actor names (receptionists) —no collisions allowed
Join Calculus	$P\|Q$	Free names (α-renaming if collisions)
Mobile Ambients	$P\|Q$	Free names (α-renaming if collisions)

Figure 7.5
Composability properties in different concurrency models.

$$\kappa \mid\mid \kappa_{\emptyset} = \kappa$$

$$\kappa \mid\mid \kappa' = \kappa' \mid\mid \kappa$$

$$(\kappa \mid\mid \kappa') \mid\mid \kappa'' = \kappa \mid\mid (\kappa' \mid\mid \kappa'').$$

Furthermore, actor configuration composition preserves computation paths and fair computation paths:

$$\tau(\kappa \mid\mid \kappa') = \tau(\kappa) \mid\mid \tau(\kappa')$$

$$\mathcal{F}(\kappa \mid\mid \kappa') = \mathcal{F}(\kappa) \mid\mid \mathcal{F}(\kappa').$$

Composability in the join calculus and the ambient calculus is supported through the composition operator | similarly to the π calculus.

Figure 7.5 summarizes the fundamental composability properties of the different concurrency models we have studied in this part of the book.

7.3.3 Fairness

Fairness is a semantic property that ensures that valid (infinite) computation paths do not consistently ignore one of the possible ways in which a computation may evolve.

Fairness is critical when reasoning about composed systems. In particular, a correct system can become incorrect due to composition with an infinitely running program: the computation path that never allows the otherwise correct program to make progress is still valid in the absence of fairness. For example in the π calculus, consider the reference cell from section 3.4.1 composed with a nonterminating process as follows:

$$\texttt{Ref}(g, s, i) \mid \bar{s}\langle c, v\rangle \mid !\bar{c}x \mid !c(y).$$

A valid computation path follows:

Model	Fairness
π calculus	None
Actors	Only fair computation paths are valid
Join Calculus	None
Mobile Ambients	None

Figure 7.6
Fairness requirement in different concurrency models.

$$
\begin{aligned}
&\texttt{Ref}(g,s,i) \mid \bar{s}\langle c,v\rangle \mid !\bar{c}x \mid !c(y)\\
&\quad \equiv \texttt{Ref}(g,s,i) \mid \bar{s}\langle c,v\rangle \mid !\bar{c}x \mid !c(y) \mid \bar{c}x \mid c(y)\\
&\quad \xrightarrow{\tau} \texttt{Ref}(g,s,i) \mid \bar{s}\langle c,v\rangle \mid !\bar{c}x \mid !c(y)\\
&\quad \equiv \texttt{Ref}(g,s,i) \mid \bar{s}\langle c,v\rangle \mid !\bar{c}x \mid !c(y) \mid \bar{c}x \mid c(y)\\
&\quad \xrightarrow{\tau} \texttt{Ref}(g,s,i) \mid \bar{s}\langle c,v\rangle \mid !\bar{c}x \mid !c(y)\\
&\quad \ldots
\end{aligned}
$$

namely, a path in which the reference cell never gets a change to receive the *set* request over channel s.

The only model that explicitly supports fairness is the actor model. Section 4.2.4 described how the actor operational semantics restricts valid computation paths to only those which are *fair*. A system composed of an actor representing a reference cell such as the one presented in section 4.4.1, a client of the reference cell, and an actor representing an infinite computation such as the reproductive actor presented in section 7.3.1 will preserve the correctness of the reference cell because of fairness.

Neither the join calculus nor the ambient calculus explicitly address fairness.

Figure 7.6 summarizes the fairness properties of the different concurrency models we have studied in this part of the book.

7.3.4 Distribution

Distributed computing is inherently concurrent. However, distribution aspects go far beyond concurrency. Of particular importance from a modeling perspective is the capability to reason about the location (and potential co-location) of concurrent computations, the heterogeneous cost of interaction, the security aspects of interaction across multiple locations, and the potential for partial failures.

The concurrent computing models that we have studied offer diverse levels of abstraction and therefore support reasoning about distributed computation to different degrees.

In the π calculus, there is no explicit representation of locations. Processes can arbitrarily and uniformly interact with any other processes, as long as they share a channel name. Therefore, from a modeling perspective, it is not directly possible to distinguish between the interaction of two processes in the same processor and the interaction of two processes in two computers across two different continents. Therefore, in an executable realization of the π calculus, a channel abstraction may be implemented as a single machine register in the simplest case, or it may require a network socket implementation requiring the coordination of multiple servers for interprocess communication. Since channels are first-class communicable entities and process communication topology is thus dynamic, this so-called process "mobility" may require significantly expensive channel implementation strategies. Furthermore, truly synchronous communication is impossible to implement among processors in geographically distant computers.

In the actor model, sequential computation is modeled using the λ calculus, making the distributed interaction between actors explicit through a network, modeled as a multiset of messages en route. The state encapsulation and asynchronous communication aspects of the actor model (see section 7.1) make it better suited to model and implement distributed computing systems. However, there is no explicit notion of actor location, and therefore, communication between actors in the same processor and actors across the planet is uniformly modeled.

The join calculus models distributed computing by conceptually separating places and rules of interaction between processes. However, the "heating/cooling" structural congruence rules enable different reaction rules and processes to come together in the same multiset, albeit after applying name substitutions to ensure that rules defining the same port names do not conflict with each other. As a calculus, the interaction between "distributed" processes is therefore restricted, but in practice, the join calculus does not explicitly model heterogeneous network communication either.

The ambient calculus explicitly models boundaries of interaction and capabilities to cross and break these boundaries. Mobile ambients very naturally model separate locations and while the model does not enable direct communication across distributed processes, distributed interaction can be indirectly modeled as inter-ambient process movement and intra-ambient process communication.

7.3.5 Mobility

Mobility takes distributed computing from a relatively static paradigm to a much more dynamic paradigm where concurrent units of computation can move about the system enabling dynamically reconfigurable distributed software systems. An important application of mobility is *elastic* computation—that is, computing that can shrink and grow with demand and resources—which forms the basis of new distributed computing paradigms such as *cloud computing*. Another important application of mobility is *soft fault tolerance*, where partial network and geographically distributed machines down-times and failures can be masked by distributed system migrations.

Because of the different levels of abstraction afforded by the concurrent computing models that we have studied, support for reasoning about and implementation of mobile distributed systems is diverse.

The π calculus was originally described by Milner as a "calculus of *mobile* processes." However, the calculus does not explicitly model different locations, and therefore, neither process distribution nor process mobility are directly modeled. The calculus allows channel names to be exchanged, thereby, supporting a dynamic topology of process interconnection, which is what Milner described as a form of process mobility, since earlier theories of concurrent computation allowed only a static topology of communication, for example, Petri nets or CSP. Nonetheless, mobility as described earlier in this section, is not directly supported by the π calculus.

The actor model, like the π calculus, does not have an explicit representation of locations, and is therefore unable to directly model mobility. However, just as we discussed for distributed computing, the semantic features of asynchronous communication and state encapsulation enable relatively easy implementations of actor migration protocols (see chapter 9).

The join calculus models mobility relatively indirectly by structural congruence rules that allow rules of interaction to move back and forth from the multiset of reaction rules to the multiset of molecules, thereby enabling and disabling interaction between processes. As discussed earlier in the context of support for distributed computing, name substitutions ensure that rules defining identical port names do not conflict with each other.

Mobile ambients model *mobility* in a first-class manner; indeed, the ambient subcalculus that includes only mobility primitives (and has no explicit interprocess communication primitives) is shown to be Turing-complete. Mobile ambients explicitly account for the possibility of ambients moving, while contained ambients and processes continue to interact and make progress. This could, for example, model the mobility of a laptop or a cellular phone from one network domain to another while programs continue to run and communicate over the device's operating system. The ambient calculus is best at explicitly modeling mobile code, data, devices, and users.

7.4 Reasoning about Programs

Formal models of computation, including concurrent computation, have multiple purposes. A very important one is being able to reason about programs following these models. Reasoning requires abstraction: being able to focus on essential components while disregarding nonessential ones. Arguably, the simpler the model, the easier it is to formally prove properties about programs in the model. Hence, the λ calculus and the π calculus strive to achieve minimality and lend themselves well to theories of reasoning about programs. Formal models of computation also serve another important purpose: to help programming language designers and distributed application developers to organize complex systems into manageable components that are easier to reason about, to prove correct, to implement, and to integrate. The actor model, the join calculus, and mobile ambients are closer to real-world distributed systems, and arguably they better serve this second purpose. Nonetheless, the closer the model to the real world, the more complex its elements, and thus, the harder it becomes to reason about programs in the model.

In this section, we review some of the most important theoretical developments of the π calculus, the actor model, the join calculus, and mobile ambients. In particular, we highlight the essence of these theories and give an example of the reasoning capability they enable.

In sequential computing, an important result is the *halting theorem*, which states that determining whether an arbitrary sequential program *halts*—or stops execution—is undecidable. The theoretical models of concurrent computation that we have discussed try to prove another property: whether two programs (expressed using the language of expressions in the model) are *equivalent*.

The π calculus develops an algebraic theory of equivalence based on *bisimilarity*, where two process expressions are said to be *bisimilar* if they can indefinitely mimic—or *simulate* the transitions of—each other. Strong congruence relates processes more strongly than (strong) bisimilarity by requiring all name substitutions to preserve bisimilarity. This is to account for arbitrary input from an arbitrary environment. Axiomatizations of the finite subcalculus—i.e., the π calculus without recursion and replication—have been developed (Parrow, 2001). An example of an equivalence that we can prove using the π calculus follows:

$$a \mid \bar{b} \quad = \quad a.\bar{b} + \bar{b}.a + \texttt{if } a = b \texttt{ then } \tau,$$

that is, the parallel composition of a process that reads a signal on channel a with a process that writes a signal on channel b is *semantically equivalent* to the nondeterministic choice among three processes: (1) one that *sequentially* reads a signal over a and then writes a signal over b, (2) one that *sequentially* writes a signal over b followed by reading a signal over a, and (3) one that checks whether a is the same channel as b and in such case, it performs no action.

The actor model considers three notions of *observational equivalence*: *testing*, *may*, and *must* observational equivalences. Given the nondeterministic execution of concurrent programs, an actor program e may observe an event in *all* possible computation paths (called a *success* observation), only in *some* computation paths (called a *success/failure* observation), or in *no* computation paths (called a *failure* observation). *Testing* equivalence makes another actor program e' equivalent to e when all observations are the same under all possible execution contexts. The weaker *must* and *may* equivalences, make e' equivalent to e, even if only successful observations or only failure observations are the same for all observing contexts. Agha et al. prove that *testing* and *must* equivalences collapse into one under the assumption of fairness (Agha et al., 1997). An example of an equivalence that can be proved using the actor model theory follows:

$$\texttt{seq}(\texttt{send}(a,1),\texttt{send}(a,2)) \quad = \quad \texttt{seq}(\texttt{send}(a,2),\texttt{send}(a,1)),$$

that is, the order of message sending is not relevant, since messaging in the actor model is *asynchronous*.

The join calculus theory uses the notion of *barbs*, logical predicates that test the ability of a process to *exhibit* a free port name—that is, to emit over that port name. A *may* observational equivalence is then defined as a refinement of the barbs relationship for all names that is closed under reduction, and that is a congruence for definitions and parallel composition (Fournet and Gonthier, 1996) (for more details, see section 5.3.3). An example of a join calculus expression equivalence follows:

$$\texttt{def}\; u\,\langle z\rangle \;\rhd\; v\,\langle z\rangle \;\; \texttt{in}\, x\,\langle u\rangle \;\approx\; x\,\langle v\rangle\,,$$

which equates a process that emits v on port name x to a process that emits u on x inside the context of a process definition. The key is that these two process expressions cannot be distinguished from each other by any context in the monoadic join calculus.

Mobile ambients use a similar notion of observational *may* equivalence termed *contextual equivalence*. Two ambient calculus expressions are defined to be equivalent if they both *converge* to the same names under all *closing* contexts. Converging to a name means eventually exhibiting the name, i.e., containing an ambient at the top level with a free name after zero or more reductions. A closing context is one such that when filling the context's hole with the expression, free variables may only be ambient names (see section 6.3.) For example, the ambient calculus theory allows to prove the following semantic equivalence (Gordon and Cardelli, 2003):

$$(\nu n)n[P] \simeq 0 \quad \text{assuming } n \notin \mathbf{fn}(P),$$

which means that if an ambient name n is restricted, and there are no capabilities associated to n in processes inside the ambient, it is equivalent to the null process.

Figure 7.7 summarizes the reasoning theories developed for the different concurrency models we have studied in this part of the book.

Model	Reasoning Theory
π calculus	Bisimulation, equational theory
Actors	Testing, may, and must observational equivalences
Join Calculus	May observational equivalence
Mobile Ambients	Contextual may observational equivalence

Figure 7.7
Reasoning theory in different concurrency models.

7.5 Discussion and Further Reading

In this chapter, we compared and contrasted four modern models of concurrent computation: the π calculus (Milner et al., 1992), the actor model (Hewitt, 1977; Agha, 1986; Agha et al., 1997), the join calculus (Fournet and Gonthier, 1996), and mobile ambients (Cardelli and Gordon, 2000).

First, we analyzed ontological commitments in the different models, in particular, the choice of synchronous or asynchronous communication and the state encapsulation properties leading to a shared or a distributed memory model. These are fundamental aspects to consider if trying to unify the models into a single framework.

Second, we considered the expressive power of the different models, in particular, we presented abstract encodings of a Turing-complete language in each model, demonstrating that the four models are Turing-complete. We showed an encoding of the λ calculus in the π calculus following Milner (1990). Subsequently, we gave a relatively straightforward encoding of the λ calculus in the actor language defined in Agha et al. (1997). The encoding of the λ calculus in the join calculus followed the call-by-name encoding presented in Fournet and Gonthier (1996), which also presents a parallel call-by-value encoding, as well as encodings of the π calculus into the join calculus and of the join calculus in the π calculus, thereby demonstrating that the π calculus and the join calculus are equivalent. Finally, we presented an encoding of the π calculus in the ambient calculus following Cardelli and Gordon (2000), which implies the ambient calculus can also encode the λ calculus and the join calculus. Agha and Thati (2004) created $A\pi$, an encoding of the actor model as a typed asynchronous variant of the π calculus.

In the third section, we evaluated semantic properties of the models including: (1) *unbounded concurrency,* which fundamentally makes modern models depart from earlier concurrency models such as Petri nets (Reisig, 1983), CCS (Milner, 1980), and CSP (Hoare, 1985); (2) *composability*, the ability to compose complex systems from simpler ones, which is supported directly at the level of process expressions in the π calculus, the join calculus and the ambient calculus, but rather at a more abstract level in the actor model in terms of actor configurations (Agha et al.,

1997); (3) *fairness*, the ability to disallow unfair computations, which is critical to modular reasoning, since in its absence, correctness of a system is lost when composing it with another one, which is only considered in the actor model; and finally the different models' support for explicit (4) *distribution* and (5) *mobility* aspects. Talcott has considered composability in actor systems beyond the notion of actor configurations explained in this chapter, aiming to raise the level of abstraction while allowing modular reasoning about open distributed systems. In particular, Talcott (1998) has introduced *open event diagrams*, *interaction diagrams*, and *interaction paths* as semantic models in order of lower to higher level of abstraction.

Finally, we illustrated the theories developed to reason about programs using the different concurrency models, by describing examples of simple programs proved to be semantically equivalent using these theories (Parrow, 2001; Agha et al., 1997; Fournet and Gonthier, 1996; Gordon and Cardelli, 2003).

7.6 Exercises

1. The asynchronous π calculus restricts syntactically the π calculus so that no processes can follow an output action. Detail the difference between the following π calculus expressions:

$\bar{a}x.P$

$\bar{a}x \mid P.$

Write a process expression P for which these two expressions are *not* equivalent.

2. Section 4.1.1 illustrated a *join continuation* actor, which serves the purpose of synchronizing the actions of two actors—the one computing the product of the left branch of the tree and the one computing the product of the right branch. What semantic conditions need to be imposed on this *joincont* actor for the synchronization to be successful?

3. In the join calculus scope extrusion example, we required that $a \notin \mathbf{fn}(P)$ to get to expression 7.4. Create an expression where the condition does not hold, and argue why scope extrusion would fail in this case, and what expression would be reached instead.

4. Rewrite the ambient calculus reference cell example in section 6.4.1 so that the internal cell state is protected. *Hint*: Use a restricted ambient name and export different names for getting and setting the cell's state.

5. Prove that the ambient calculus encoding of the asynchronous π calculus described in section 7.2.4 is correct, modulo garbage ambients. That is, prove $P \xrightarrow{\tau} Q \implies [\![P]\!]_{fv(P)} \longrightarrow^{*} [\![Q]\!]_{fv(Q)} \mid R$, where $R \simeq 0$.

6. The join calculus and the π calculus have been proven equivalent in Fournet and Gonthier (1996). What would be the difficulties involved in proving equivalence of the actor model and the π calculus or the join calculus?
7. The join calculus and the π calculus have been proven equivalent in Fournet and Gonthier (1996). What would be the difficulties involved in proving equivalence of the mobile ambients model and the π calculus or the join calculus?
8. Using the join calculus, create a system composed out of simpler ones, paying special attention to the *interface* between components. Comment on restrictions in terms of naming free and defined variables.
9. Using the ambient calculus, create a system composed out of simpler ones, paying special attention to the *interface* between components. Comment on restrictions in terms of naming ambients.
10. Discuss guaranteed message delivery as a semantic property of the actor model. Is this property required to ensure fair computations?
11. Create a join calculus expression that behaves correctly in isolation, but that when composed with another nonterminating join calculus expression fails to make progress in the absence of fairness.
12. Create an ambient calculus expression that behaves correctly in isolation, but that when composed with another nonterminating ambient calculus expression fails to make progress in the absence of fairness.

II Programming Languages for Distributed and Mobile Computing

II.1 Languages for Distributed Computing

In this part of the book, we will introduce well-founded programming languages for concurrent computation, including their support (or lack thereof) for developing distributed and mobile systems. The objective is twofold: first, to bridge the gap between the theory and the practice of programming concurrent systems; and second, to illustrate the challenges that real-world distributed computing imposes on going from purely theoretical models to practical programming languages and systems.

To help bridge the gap between theory and practice, we will consider programming languages that closely follow the concurrency models studied in the first part of this book. Pict is a programming language that uses the π calculus as its foundation. Nomadic Pict is an extension to the Pict language to support distribution and mobility aspects. SALSA is a programming language that implements the actor model of computation, including support for distribution and mobility. JoCaml is a programming language implementing the join calculus, as well as the distributed join calculus, an extension with distribution and mobility primitives.

Chapters 8, 9, and 10 will each cover Pict, SALSA, and JoCaml, that is, the programming language associated to the π calculus, the actor model, and the (distributed) join calculus, respectively. Each chapter will first describe the language's syntax, including its constructs for concurrency, distribution, and mobility. The syntax will be followed by the language's operational semantics, where we try to follow the corresponding model's operational semantics as much as possible. After the syntax and semantics, we illustrate higher-level concurrent programming abstractions and patterns advocated by each language.

In contrast to concurrency models that can afford very high levels of abstraction, programming languages have to specify "real-world" system issues, such as interaction with humans or other programs via standard input and output interfaces, a richer type system with complex values being passed in messages, and message patterns for easier expression of varied behaviors. Distribution and mobility issues, which are sometimes abstracted by concurrency models and "left to the infrastructure," need to also be specified as formally as possible. As a consequence, a programming language's operational semantics is often more complex than the operational semantics of its corresponding model introduced in part I of this book. In this presentation, we strive for conciseness, and focus on the semantic aspects critical to concurrency, distribution, and mobility.

We will use the same common examples described in section 1.4 to illustrate how to write these simple concurrent programs in each language. This will allow the student/reader to execute these specifications on a computer and "play with" them to obtain different behaviors and further her/his understanding of the theoretical concurrency models, as well as their programming language instantiations. We also add a new example: a *mobile reference cell*, which illustrates *strong mobility*, that is, mobile stateful computation. This is in contrast to *weak mobility*, where code can move from a computer to another, but needs to start from a new state after movement.

Finally, in chapter 11, we illustrate the development of a more complete distributed system, capturing the essence of social networking applications: a *publish-subscribe* system with information flow constraints. This example is implemented in each of the programming language introduced in this part, so that the student/reader can contrast their prototypical design patterns and richness of data structures and concurrency, distribution, and mobility abstractions.

II.2 Other Approaches to Concurrent Programming

Given the book's goal of connecting theory and practice, we selected Pict, SALSA, and JoCaml as the languages to illustrate examples and design patterns. We do not explicitly cover programming languages that support concurrency via libraries; nor other approaches to concurrent programming, such as dataflow concurrency, or concurrent logic or object oriented programming languages.

Nonetheless, here we will briefly discuss the challenge of combining stateful computation and concurrency, illustrating why safety and liveness can be easily compromised using simple examples.

Consider the Java code in figure II.1 (from Varela and Agha, 1998). This example illustrates a problem that results from having two different programming language abstractions for handling state and for handling concurrency, namely *objects* and *threads:* An object abstracts over a unit of state management, whereas a thread abstracts over a unit of concurrency. The best that an object of class `A` can do is to use the `synchronized` keyword to prevent multiple threads from entering its `m` method simultaneously, requiring them to first obtain a reentrant lock associated to the object. The same is true for class `B` and its `n` method. In this example, however, a possible

```
class A implements Runnable{
  B b;
  synchronized void m() {...b.n();...}
  public void run() { m(); }
}

class B implements Runnable{
  A a;
  synchronized void n() {...a.m();...}
  public void run() { n(); }
}

class Deadlock {
  public static void main(String[] args){
    A a = new A();  B b = new B();
    a.b = b;  b.a = a;
    Thread t1 = new Thread(a).start();
    Thread t2 = new Thread(b).start();
  }
}
```

Figure II.1
Java code illustrating the potential for deadlock in complex concurrent object interactions.

race condition arises if thread `t1` enters object `a`'s `m` method (obtaining `a`'s lock in the process) while thread `t2` enters object `b`'s `n` method (also obtaining `b`'s lock in the process) and then both threads hang: `t1` waiting for `t2` to release `b`'s lock in order to enter `b`'s `n` method and thread `t2` waiting for `t1` to release `a`'s lock in order to enter `a`'s `m` method.

Since not using the `synchronized` keyword would lead to safety problems—that is, inconsistent views of (or modifications to) an object's state,—these race conditions, often leading to deadlocks, are a very common problem with concurrent programs written in concurrent object-oriented programming languages.

Let us finally consider another example in the Oz multiparadigm programming language (Roy and Haridi, 2004):

```
local X Y in
   {Browse X}
   thread {Delay 1000} Y = 10 end
   X = Y + 100
end
```

This example illustrates two dataflow variables, namely `X` and `Y`. The value of `X` depends on the value of `Y`, which is to be assigned to in a separate child thread, which in this example suspends for a second to simulate an expensive computation. The main (parent) thread may therefore reach the expression requiring a value for `Y` before a value has been produced. Different programming languages behave differently in this scenario: the C programming language with threads, for example, would use whatever value appears in `Y`'s memory location at the time of reaching the expression needing its value. The Java programming language would assign a *default* value to the `Y` variable according to its type at initialization time, for example, 0 for integers, which would be used by the thread requiring `Y`'s value. The Prolog programming language would raise an error dynamically stating that the value of `Y` has not been initialized—a natural behavior in a nonconcurrent programming language. The Oz programming language, on the other hand, has the behavior to *suspend* the computation of `X` until such time as the value for `Y` is produced by another thread. In this particular example, Oz's behavior gives us *deterministic concurrency*: independently of the thread scheduling of the parent and child threads, the value of the dataflow variable `X` will always be the same: 110.

Unfortunately, this deterministic concurrent behavior arises only if there is *exactly one* binder for each *single-assignment* dataflow variable.

For example, the Oz code:

```
local X Y in
   {Browse X}
   thread Y = 10 end
   thread Y = 20 end
   X = Y + 100
end
```

will nondeterministically assign either 10 or 20 to `Y` and will cause an *incompatible assignment* exception to be thrown in the other thread.

Likewise, the Oz code

```
local X Y in
   {Browse X}
   thread if false then Y = 10 end end
   X = Y + 100
end
```

will silently hang waiting for another thread to assign a value to `Y`, which will never occur.

II.3 Distribution and Mobility Aspects

While all the programming languages that we present in this part of the book support concurrent systems programming using different abstractions, explicit support for distribution and mobility varies significantly.

Pict was designed as an attempt to "program with the π calculus," yet in order to make it expressive enough, significant higher-level abstractions were built atop the "pure π calculus" to make it look and feel more like a functional programming language. First and foremost, the *synchronous* communication primitive of the π calculus, was eliminated: Pict supports only asynchronous output. This, in effect, is actually good for distributed and mobile computing, since truly synchronous communication is impossible to implement in geographically distributed and mobile systems. Second, sources of nondeterminism were eliminated when possible: e.g., $P + Q$, nondeterministic choice, is not directly supported. Also, replication was restricted to replicated input and *recursive definitions* were introduced to ensure that some channels have only one receiver process, effectively disallowing expressions such as $a(x).P \mid a(x).Q \mid \bar{a}y$ that lead to nondeterministic execution of P or Q. Most likely, these deviations from the π calculus were taken to be able to generate efficient code. However, it seems unclear whether the "pure π calculus" is suitable or not as a starting point for designing a concurrent programming language, in particular, one supporting process distribution and mobility.

Pict itself does not support distribution and mobility of processes. Instead, there is a language extension, called Nomadic Pict, that extends Pict with the notion of *sites* and *agents*. Communication channels belong to agents, which can migrate between sites. Nomadic Pict has constructs for location-independent communication, which can be specified atop lower-level location-dependent communication primitives. The distinct abstraction for mobile processes (that is, named agents) implies that there are two kinds of processes, *stationary* and *mobile*, which creates a dichotomy that makes programming distributed systems in Nomadic Pict harder than it needs to be. Channels can refer to a stationary process or to a mobile agent, for instance, and it is not clear what happens when an agent containing a channel pointing to a stationary process moves to a different site.

SALSA is an extension to the Java object-oriented programming language to support the actor model of concurrent and distributed computation. While the actor model described in chapter 4 does not explicitly support the notions of location and mobility, SALSA adds the notion of *universal actors* that have unique names and enable transparent actor migration and location-independent communication using Internet-based protocols. A *naming service* ensures uniqueness of universal actor names over the Internet relying on computer name uniqueness using the Domain

Name Service (DNS.) A *theater* run-time system is a Java virtual machine with support for remote actor creation, actor migration, remote message sending, and access to local *environment* actors. Actor migration is easy to implement: in response to a `migrate` message, we serialize the actor's internal state and its mailbox of pending messages, and restart its execution in the new theater. The naming service is then informed of the actor's new location.

Other actor programming languages have extended a functional sequential core, among them Erlang and Scala. However, Erlang does not support actor mobility, and Scala does not support actor distribution or mobility. Other actor languages that lack support for distribution or mobility include E and Kilim.

JoCaml is an extension of the Objective Caml programming language to support the join calculus and the distributed join calculus. The distributed join calculus extends the join calculus described in chapter 5 with additional primitives for distribution, mobility, and failure detection. Communication is location-independent. The JoCaml run-time system adds the notions of a *name server* and *sites* to support distribution.[1] Locations are organized in JoCaml hierarchically and move with all its contained locations and processes, which resembles mobile ambients. JoCaml's notion of *location* also uses subjective mobility, like mobile ambients (see section 6.2). Locations can fail (failing all its nested locations) and a failure detection primitive allows us to detect when a location or any of its parent locations has failed.

Note

1. The last known release of JoCaml (v3.11) does not yet support mobility; however, earlier versions (such as the beta release of January 2001) did.

8 Programming with Processes

Programming with the abstractions of processes and channels found in the π calculus, can be done in the Pict programming language (Pierce and Turner, 2000), which incorporates types, records, and pattern matching into an asynchronous choice-free variant of the π calculus.

The most significant semantic differences between Pict and the π calculus as presented in chapter 3, are the following:

- *Asynchrony* Pict only allows asynchronous output: this is equivalent to restricting "continuations" of output actions to the empty process 0.
- *No choice* Pict does not support the nondeterministic choice operator $P + Q$.
- *Restricted replication* Pict restricts replication of processes to replicated input expressions $!x(y).P$.
- *No matching* Pict does not support the match and mismatch operators in the π calculus: `if` $x = y$ `then` P, `if` $x \neq y$ `then` P. It supports booleans and more general conditional expressions.
- *Typed channels* Pict statically typechecks programs to ensure that channels carry the correct data type at run-time.
- *Tuples and records* Pict supports the polyadic π calculus (see section 3.1.3) generalizing tuples of channels to tuples of tuples, etc. Pict also supports records (tuples with labeled elements) and pattern matching to bind input variables.

Distributed and mobile systems programming with π calculus abstractions can be done in the Nomadic Pict programming language (Sewell et al., 2010). Nomadic Pict extends Pict with the notion of mobile agents supporting *lower-level* (location-dependent) and *higher-level* (location-independent) communication.

In section 8.1, we cover the syntax of Pict for concurrent systems and the Nomadic Pict syntax for distributed and mobile systems. Section 8.2 specifies the operational semantics of Pict and Nomadic Pict, using a structural congruence and a reduction relation, as in the π calculus. Section 8.3 covers programming idioms and patterns used in Pict and Nomadic Pict programs, including functional and sequential programming styles. Section 8.4 goes over concurrent programming examples in Pict and a mobile reference cell example in Nomadic Pict. Sections 8.5 and 8.6 conclude with a discussion and exercises.

8.1 Pict Programming Language Syntax

8.1.1 Concurrent Systems Programming

A summary of the asynchronous choice-free π calculus primitives and the equivalent Pict programming language syntax is given in figure 8.1.

As most high-level programming languages, Pict provides special syntax for primitive types: booleans, characters, integers, and strings. All these can be encoded as processes in the π calculus, similarly to their encoding in the λ calculus presented in section 2.9. Pict also provides special primitive channels for built-in operations (e.g., `+`, `*`) and interaction with the environment (e.g., a `print` channel to write to standard output). Pict also supports records and pattern matching.

Figure 8.2 specifies Pict's core language syntax. *Values* represent elements that can be passed among processes through channels. They include variables, record fields, records, and primitive type constants. *Types* specify valid data items that can pass over channels. These include primitive types, records with specific internal structure, and channel names. The empty record, and its corresponding type are both denoted by []. *Patterns* specify generalizations of data inputs that can be received by channels: If the data sent over a channel does not match the pattern that is expected, no communication happens. If the pattern is matched, variables in the pattern become bound to the values which are communicated. A wildcard pattern matches any input data with no variables becoming bound in the process, while a layered pattern binds a variable for all the input data as well as any variables in its internal pattern. *Declarations* enable creation of scoped channel names, mutually recursive channel definitions, and type abbreviations. *Processes* represent π calculus process expressions including asynchronous output, synchronous input, replicated input,

π Calculus	Pict	
0	`()`	Empty process
$\bar{c}x.0$	`c!x`	Write x on channel c asynchronously
$c(x).P$	`c?x = p`	Read x on channel c
$P \mid Q$	`(p | q)`	Concurrent composition of P and Q
$(\nu c)P$	`(new c p)`	New channel c, scope restricted to P
$!c(x).P$	`c?*x = p`	Replicated input x on channel c

Figure 8.1
π calculus and equivalent Pict syntax.

```
Label    ::=  [Id =]                                Optional label
Path     ::=  Id{.Id}*                              Var/record field path
OType    ::=  [: Type]                              Optional type

Val      ::=                                        Values
              Path                                  Var/record field path
          |   [ Label Val ...Label Val ]            Record
          |   Bool | Char | Int | String            Primitive type constant

Type     ::=                                        Types
              ^Type                                 Input/output channel
          |   [ Label Type...Label Type ]           Record type
          |   Bool | Char | Int | String            Primitive types

Pat      ::=                                        Patterns
              Id OType                              Variable pattern
          |   [ Label Pat ...Label Pat ]            Record pattern
          |   _ OType                               Wildcard pattern
          |   Id OType @ Pat                        Layered pattern

Dec      ::=                                        Declarations
              new Id : Type                         Channel creation
          |   def Id_1 Abs_1 and ...and Id_n Abs_n  Recursive definition
          |   type Id = Type                        Type abbreviation

Proc     ::=                                        Processes
              Val ! Val                             Output atom
          |   Val ? Abs                             Input prefix
          |   Val ?* Abs                            Replicated input prefix
          |   ()                                    Empty process
          |   ( Proc | Proc )                       Parallel composition
          |   ( Dec Proc )                          Local declaration
          |   if Val then Proc else Proc            Conditional

Abs      ::=  Pat = Proc                            Process abstractions

Program  ::=  run Proc                              Programs
```

Figure 8.2
Pict programming language syntax.

parallel composition, channel creation with restricted scope, and conditional execution. *Process abstractions* specify a pattern that must be matched before a process is executed. Abstractions are used to define the behavior of processes on input communications, as well as in recursive channel definitions. Finally, a *program* is any process prefixed by the keyword `run`.

Let us consider the π calculus expression:

$\bar{c}a.P \mid c(x).Q.$

Since Pict only supports asynchronous output, we can only express

$\bar{c}a.0 \mid c(x).Q.$

A similar expression can be written in Pict as follows:

```
run (c!a | c?x=print!"done!").
```

The program, to be executable using Pict, also needs to define types for the variables *a* and *c*. If we are only going to send a *signal* on channel *c*, we can use the empty record value and type. The whole program would then look as follows:

```
run (new a:[]
      (new c:^[]
        (c!a | c?x=print!"done!")))
```

A shorter version could simply use the constant value `[]` instead of variable *a*, as follows:

```
run (new c:^[]
      (c![] | c?x=print!"done!"))
```

Another example can be an encoding of booleans, similar to the one used in the λ calculus (see section 2.9). We encode a boolean as a channel that receives two channels, a *true* and a *false* channel, and if it represents `true` it replies with a signal over the first channel, otherwise, it sends a signal over the second channel. In Pict, booleans could be encoded as follows:

```
b?[t f] = t![]   {- represents true -}
b?[t f] = f![]   {- represents false -}
```

A process that wants to test the value of the boolean can be written as follows:

```
(b![t f]
|(t?[] = print!"True"
 |f?[] = print!"False"))
```

Once again, we need to assign types to the different channels in the program, namely *b*, *t*, and *f*. So, the full executable program in Pict would read as follows:

```
run (new b:^[^[] ^[]]
      (b?[t f] = f![]  {- represents false -}
      |(new t:^[]
         (new f:^[]
           (b![t f]
           |(t?[] = print!"True"
            |f?[] = print!"False"))))))
```

We can declare a new `Boolean` type using the `type` keyword. Furthermore, Pict allows for more than two declarations to preceed a process: (Dec_1 Dec_2 *Proc*) is translated to (Dec_1 (Dec_2 *Proc*)). Likewise, composition of processes can apply to more than two processes: ($Proc_1$ | $Proc_2$ | $Proc_3$) is translated to ($Proc_1$ | ($Proc_2$ | $Proc_3$)). So the preceding example could have been written as follows:

```
run (type Boolean = ^[^[] ^[]]
     new b:Boolean
     (b?[t f] = f![]  {- represents false -}
     |(new t:^[]
       new f:^[]
        (b![t f]
        |t?[] = print!"True"
        |f?[] = print!"False"))))
```

The channel `b` that represents false in this program is an arbitrary choice (any other channel name could have been used). Process definitions in Pict allow to abstract over these channel names, and represent the same as process declarations in the π calculus. We can declare:

```
def tt[b:Boolean] = b?[t f] = t![]
and ff[b:Boolean] = b?[t f] = f![]
```

The parameters of a definition must be explicitly annotated with a type. Declarations are implemented as a creation of a new channel with replicated input on it. That way, process invocation is the same as writing over the process declaration channel. For example, the preceding definition is translated into:

```
new tt:^[Boolean]
new ff:^[Boolean]
(tt?*[b:Boolean] = b?[t f] = t![]
|ff?*[b:Boolean] = b?[t f] = f![])
```

`tt![b]` can then be used as an abbreviation for the expression `b?[t f] = t![]`. One more refinement in the above definition is that `f` is not used in `tt` and `t` is not used in `ff`, so we can use a wildcard pattern, as follows:

```
def tt[b:Boolean] = b?[t _] = t![]
and ff[b:Boolean] = b?[_ f] = f![]
```

Finally, declarations can be written without enclosing parentheses, and in such cases, any declared variables are bound in all the remaining clauses of the program. That is, $Dec_1 \ldots Dec_n$ `run` *Proc* is translated into `run` ($Dec_1 \ldots Dec_n$ *Proc*).

Thus, the full Pict program after defining a testing procedure follows:

```
type Boolean = ^[^[] ^[]]

def tt[b:Boolean] = b?[t _] = t![]
and ff[b:Boolean] = b?[_ f] = f![]

def test[b:Boolean] =
    (new t:^[] new f:^[]
      (b![t f]
      |t?[] = print!"True"
      |f?[] = print!"False"))

new b:Boolean
run (ff![b]
    |test![b])
```

8.1.2 Distributed and Mobile Systems Programming

While Pict can be used to encode concurrent programs, it cannot directly be used to encode distributed or mobile processes, since the implementation of processes and their composition is not distributed. We use the Nomadic Pict programming language, an extension of Pict, to illustrate distributed and mobile systems programming with the π calculus. Nomadic Pict incorporates two main abstractions: *sites* and *agents*. Sites denote locations where agents execute. Agents can migrate between sites and an agent's execution is modeled as a Pict process. Channels belong to specific agents.

Nomadic Pict is designed with two levels of communication: location-dependent and location-independent. Higher-level location-independent communication can be translated into lower-level location-dependent communication in many ways obtaining different properties in terms of performance and fault tolerance.

```
Proc  ::=  ...                                                  Processes
        |  Ag                                                   Agent

Ag    ::=                                                       Agents
           agent Id1 = Proc1 and ... and Idn = Procn in Proc    Create
        |  migrate to  Val Proc                                 Migrate
        |  iflocal <Val > Val ! Val then Proc else Proc         Send
        |  wait Val ? Abs timeout Val -> Proc                   Receive
        |  terminate                                            Kill
```

Figure 8.3
Nomadic Pict syntax extension.

```
<a>c!v     ≜  iflocal <a>c!v then () else ()
<a@s>c!v   ≜  agent _ = migrate to s <a>c!v in ()

c@a!v      ≜  location-independent output to channel c at agent a
```

Figure 8.4
Nomadic Pict lower-level and higher-level communication.

Figure 8.3 illustrates the syntax of the low-level language. Processes are extended to include *agents* which can be created locally and referred to by a name, as well as migrated to sites. Communication with a local agent is modeled by sending a value over a channel of the agent. Local communication can be tried, and alternative processes may execute if it is successful or if it fails. Waiting for an input on a channel may time out, after which a separate process may execute. Syntactic sugar may be used for local and remote communication as illustrated in figure 8.4. Notice that the first two forms fail silently if the agent `a` is not located in the expected local site or site `s` respectively. A higher-level location-independent communication is used to encode communication irrespective of the current location or migration patterns of an agent.

Example 8.1 An applet server can be encoded in Nomadic Pict as follows:

```
getApplet ?* [a s] =
  agent b =
    migrate to s
    ( ack@a!b | ... )
  in ()
```

The applet server receives a requesting agent `a` and its site `s`, representing a web client and its location respectively. For each request, it creates the applet, which is a new agent named `b`, whose behavior is to migrate to the site `s`, acknowledge its presence by sending its name to the requesting agent `a`, and in parallel execute its code (denoted as "...").

8.2 Pict Programming Language Operational Semantics

To formally specify the behavior of Pict programs, we first describe a *structural congruence* that equates processes based on their syntactic structure: for example, the order of evaluation of the processes in a parallel composition is not significant. Then, we define a *reduction relation* that models how computation evolves.

8.2.1 Structural Congruence

Even though defining a structural congruence is not absolutely necessary, it simplifies the reduction relation by allowing to consider only one rule for expressions which are syntactically equivalent. For example, both `(c!a | c?x=print"done!")` and `(c?x=print!"done!" | c!a)` behave the same. Since they are structurally congruent, only the reduction rule for one of the two must be specified.

$$\texttt{((}e_1 \mid e_2\texttt{)} \mid e_3\texttt{)} \equiv \texttt{(}e_1 \mid \texttt{(}e_2 \mid e_3\texttt{))} \qquad \texttt{(STR-ASSOC)}$$

$$\texttt{(}e_1 \mid e_2\texttt{)} \equiv \texttt{(}e_2 \mid e_1\texttt{)} \qquad \texttt{(STR-COMM)}$$

$$\texttt{(}e \mid \texttt{())} \equiv e \qquad \texttt{(STR-NULL)}$$

$$\frac{bv(d) \cap fv(e_2) = \emptyset}{\texttt{((}d\ e_1\texttt{)} \mid e_2\texttt{)} \equiv \texttt{(}d\ \texttt{(}e_1 \mid e_2\texttt{))}} \qquad \texttt{(STR-EXTRUDE)}$$

$$\frac{bv(d_1) \cap fv(d_2) = \emptyset \qquad bv(d_2) \cap fv(d_1) = \emptyset}{\texttt{(}d_1\ \texttt{(}d_2\ e\texttt{))} \equiv \texttt{(}d_2\ \texttt{(}d_1\ e\texttt{))}} \qquad \texttt{(STR-SWAPDEC)}$$

$$\texttt{(STR-COALESCE)}$$

$$\frac{\begin{array}{c}\{x_1, \ldots, x_m\} \cap \{x_{m+1}, \ldots, x_n\} = \emptyset \\ (fv(a_1) \cup \ldots \cup fv(a_m)) \cap \{x_{m+1}, \ldots, x_n\} = \emptyset\end{array}}{\begin{array}{c}\texttt{(def}\ x_1\ a_1 \ldots\ \texttt{and}\ x_m\ a_m\ \texttt{(def}\ x_{m+1}\ a_{m+1} \ldots\ \texttt{and}\ x_n\ a_n\ e\texttt{))} \equiv \\ \texttt{(def}\ x_1\ a_1 \ldots\ \texttt{and}\ x_m\ a_m\ \texttt{and}\ x_{m+1}\ a_{m+1} \ldots\ \texttt{and}\ x_n\ a_n\ e\texttt{)}\end{array}}$$

Figure 8.5
Pict structural congruence rules.

Figure 8.5 shows the structural congruence rules for Pict. The first three rules specify that parallel composition is associative, commutative, and its identity is the empty process `()`. The `(STR-EXTRUDE)` rule specifies scope extrusion. This allows for a channel name to exit its scope if written on an outside channel. An example follows:

```
((new c:^[] a!c) | a?x = print!"done")).
```

Because of structural congruence, this expression is equivalent to:

```
(new c:^[] (a!c | a?x = print!"done")),
```

which can then evolve after a communication over channel `a`. We say that the scope of channel `c` has been extruded to include the process `a?x = print!"done"`.

Finally, the rules `(STR-SWAPDEC)` and `(STR-COALESCE)` enable the swapping and the merging of adjacent declarations, as long as naming conflicts are first resolved. Pict uses α-renaming of bound variables introduced in new declarations to ensure that names are always different.

8.2.2 Operational Semantics of Concurrent Execution

Pattern Matching When a pattern `p` is matched by a value `v`, the result is a substitution $\sigma = \{\mathtt{v}/\mathtt{p}\}$, defined as follows:

$$
\begin{aligned}
\{\mathtt{v}/\mathtt{x}\mathtt{:T}\} &= \{\mathtt{v}/\mathtt{x}\}\\
\{\mathtt{v}/\_\mathtt{:T}\} &= \{\}\\
\{\mathtt{v}/(\mathtt{x}\mathtt{:T@p})\} &= \{\mathtt{v}/\mathtt{x}\} \cup \{\mathtt{v}/\mathtt{p}\}\\
\{[\mathtt{l}_1\ \mathtt{v}_1 \ldots \mathtt{l}_n\ \mathtt{v}_n \ldots]/[\mathtt{l}_1\ \mathtt{p}_1 \ldots \mathtt{l}_n\ \mathtt{p}_n]\} &= \{\mathtt{v}_1/\mathtt{p}_1\} \cup \ldots \cup \{\mathtt{v}_n/\mathtt{p}_n\}.
\end{aligned}
$$

If `v` and `p` do not have the same structure, then σ is undefined.

Reduction Relation Figure 8.6 specifies the reduction relation that enables Pict expressions to evolve. The notation $\mathtt{e} \rightarrow \mathtt{e}'$ denotes that `e` can evolve as $\mathtt{e}'$. The `(RED-COMM)` rule specifies interprocess communication over channel `x` where the output value `v` matches the input pattern `p`. The process evolves as the expression `e` where any occurrences of `p` are substituted by `v`. The `(RED-DEF)` rule specifies process definition invocation, where the value `v` is sent over the defined channel $\mathtt{x}_i$ whose input pattern $\mathtt{p}_i$ matches `v`. The process invocation expression $\mathtt{x}_i\mathtt{!v}$ is substituted for the definition body $\mathtt{e}_i$ with the appropriate substitution $\sigma = \{\mathtt{v}/\mathtt{p}_i\}$ applied. The rules `(RED-IF-T/F)` specify the behavior of the conditional statement. The rules `(RED-DEC)` and `(RED-PRL)` enable reductions under declarations or parallel

$$\frac{\{\mathtt{v/p}\}\ \textit{defined}}{(\mathtt{x!v} \mid \mathtt{x?p = e})} \rightarrow \mathtt{e}\{\mathtt{v/p}\} \qquad \text{(RED-COMM)}$$

$$\frac{\{\mathtt{v/p}_i\}\ \textit{defined}}{\begin{array}{l}(\mathtt{def\ x_1\ p_1 = e_1 \ldots\ and\ x_n\ p_n = e_n\ (x_i!v \mid e))} \rightarrow \\ (\mathtt{def\ x_1\ p_1 = e_1 \ldots\ and\ x_n\ p_n = e_n\ (e_i\{v/p_i\} \mid e))}\end{array}} \qquad \text{(RED-DEF)}$$

$$\mathtt{if\ true\ then\ e_1\ else\ e_2} \rightarrow \mathtt{e_1} \qquad \text{(RED-IF-T)}$$

$$\mathtt{if\ false\ then\ e_1\ else\ e_2} \rightarrow \mathtt{e_2} \qquad \text{(RED-IF-F)}$$

$$\frac{\mathtt{e} \rightarrow \mathtt{e'}}{(\mathtt{d\ e}) \rightarrow (\mathtt{d\ e'})} \qquad \text{(RED-DEC)}$$

$$\frac{\mathtt{e_1} \rightarrow \mathtt{e_1'}}{(\mathtt{e_1} \mid \mathtt{e_2}) \rightarrow (\mathtt{e_1'} \mid \mathtt{e_2})} \qquad \text{(RED-PRL)}$$

$$\frac{\mathtt{e_1} \equiv \mathtt{e_1'} \qquad \mathtt{e_1} \rightarrow \mathtt{e_2} \qquad \mathtt{e_2} \equiv \mathtt{e_2'}}{\mathtt{e_1'} \rightarrow \mathtt{e_2'}} \qquad \text{(RED-STR)}$$

Figure 8.6
Pict operational semantics.

compositions. Finally, the rule (RED-STR) formalizes the intuition that structurally congruent processes are equivalent from an operational semantics perspective.

8.2.3 Operational Semantics of Distribution and Mobility

The operational semantics for Nomadic Pict extends the reduction relation of the Pict operational semantics by considering *configurations* of the form $\Gamma \Vdash \mathcal{LP}$, where Γ represents a typing context, and $\mathcal{LP}$ represents a located process. A located process $@_a\mathtt{e}$ denotes that process e is executing at agent a. The judgement $\Gamma \vdash a@s$ means that agent a is located at site s according to the type context Γ.

The agent expressions are given a reduction semantics as illustrated in figure 8.7. The (RED-AGNT) rule specifies the creation of a new agent named b at the same site s as the creating agent a. Agent a executes $\mathtt{e_2}$ while agent b executes $\mathtt{e_1}$. The name b is bound both in $\mathtt{e_1}$ and $\mathtt{e_2}$. The (RED-MIGR) rule specifies the migration of agent a to site s and its subsequent execution of expression e. The (RED-PICT) rule specifies internal computation within an agent a. It subsumes the concurrent execution of processes for Pict specified in figure 8.6. In particular, interprocess communication via a channel ((RED-COMM) rule) can only occur if the writing and reading processes are located *at the same agent* a. The last two rules, (RED-SNDS) and (RED-SNDF), respectively specify local communication when both agents a and b are co-located, case in which it is successful, and when they are not, case in which it fails. Sewell et al. (2010) does not specify formally a semantics for the wait and terminate primitives.

$$\frac{\Gamma \vdash a@s}{\Gamma \Vdash @_a\texttt{agent b = e}_1\texttt{ in e}_2 \rightarrow \Gamma \oplus b \mapsto s \Vdash @_b\texttt{e}_1 \mid @_a\texttt{e}_2} \qquad \texttt{(RED-AGNT)}$$

$$\frac{}{\Gamma \Vdash @_a\texttt{migrate to s e} \rightarrow \Gamma \oplus a \mapsto s \Vdash @_a\texttt{e}} \qquad \texttt{(RED-MIGR)}$$

$$\frac{\texttt{e} \rightarrow \texttt{e}'}{\Gamma \Vdash @_a\texttt{e} \rightarrow \Gamma \Vdash @_a\texttt{e}'} \qquad \texttt{(RED-PICT)}$$

$$\frac{\Gamma \vdash a@s \quad \wedge \quad \Gamma \vdash b@s}{\Gamma \Vdash @_a\texttt{iflocal <b>c!v then e}_1\texttt{ else e}_2 \rightarrow \Gamma \Vdash @_a\texttt{e}_1 \mid @_b\texttt{c!v}} \qquad \texttt{(RED-SNDS)}$$

$$\frac{\Gamma \vdash a@s \quad \wedge \quad \Gamma \vdash b@s' \quad \wedge \quad s \neq s'}{\Gamma \Vdash @_a\texttt{iflocal <b>c!v then e}_1\texttt{ else e}_2 \rightarrow \Gamma \Vdash @_a\texttt{e}_2} \qquad \texttt{(RED-SNDF)}$$

Figure 8.7
Nomadic Pict operational semantics.

8.3 Pict Programming Patterns

8.3.1 Functional Programming

Pict offers convenient derived forms that enable viewing processes as functions, and therefore allow to program in Pict as if it were a functional programming language.

The convention in Pict is that a process definition that uses its last parameter for output can be thought of as a function, and syntactic sugar is provided so that it can be written as if it were a function definition:

$$\texttt{def f(a}_1\texttt{:T}_1\texttt{...a}_n\texttt{:T}_n\texttt{):T = v} \quad \triangleq \quad \texttt{def f [a}_1\texttt{:T}_1\texttt{...a}_n\texttt{:T}_n\texttt{ r:/T] = r!v.}$$

The type `/T` is used for channels that communicate values of type `T`, except that these channels have been created using a process definition. This ensures that it is the same receiver process that always responds to inputs over the channel.

For example, `+` is a built-in channel that receives two numbers and returns the addition in the third argument. Its type is therefore `/[Int Int /Int]`. We could use it as follows:

```
run (def r x:Int = printi!x  +![2 3 r]).
```

However, since the process reading on the channel `+` follows the convention of functions, we can also simply make the channel `r` implicit and write `(+ 2 3)` as if it were a value:

```
run (printi!(+ 2 3)).
```

Similarly, we can define a `double` process as:

```
def double[x:Int r:/Int] = +![x x r],
```

or we can use the equivalent *functional* style:

```
def double(x:Int):Int = (+ x x).
```

Furthermore, there is syntactic support for anonymous abstractions:

```
\a  ≜  (def x a  x).
```

For example,

```
def applyTwice (f x) = (f (f x))
printi!(applyTwice double 3)
```

can also be written as:

```
def applyTwice (f x) = (f (f x))
printi!(applyTwice \(x) = (+ x x)  3)
```

or as:

```
printi!(\(f x) = (f (f x))  \(x) = (+ x x)  3).
```

8.3.2 Value Declarations and Sequencing

One common programming pattern is to ensure that an operation has ended before starting another one. Pict offers blocking value declarations as well as signaling that enable processes to synchronize and execute sequentially.

For example, suppose two process write "hello" and "world" respectively to standard output:

```
run (print!"hello"
    |print!"world")
```

Since $(e_1|e_2) \equiv (e_2|e_1)$, this program could print these words in any order: `helloworld` or `worldhello`.

The most obvious way to synchronize between two processes is to communicate a value over a shared channel. For example:

```
run (new c:^[]
      (pr!["hello" (rchan c)]
      |c?[] = print!"world"))
```

In this example, we create a channel `c` which is used by the first process to signal completion to the second process. This ensures that "hello" is printed before "world." We have used a primitive called `pr` that prints to the standard output stream (like `print`) but also receives a *responsive channel* where it can send a completion signal to indicate that it has finished its work. A *responsive channel* is a type of channel that gets created by process definitions: it ensures that inputs to that channel are always received and processed by the same process. For example, the following code would also have achieved the same effect:

```
run (def c[] = print!"world"
     pr!["hello" c])
```

The type of `c` is `/[]`. There is a global definition for this common type of channels carrying completion signals:

```
type Sig = /[].
```

This "continuation-passing style" of communication is so common that there is syntactic sugar for it:[1]

```
(val p = v   e)    ≜    new c (c?p = e | c!v).
```

Notice that in the translation of a `(val p = v e)` expression, the body `e` is guarded by an input over the continuation channel. That means that the behavior of the expression is to *block* until a value `v` has been computed and pattern matched against `p`.

Using this syntactic sugar, the example could be written as follows:

```
run (val [] = (pr "hello")
     (pr "world"))
```

The pattern "invoke an operation, wait for a signal, and continue" is so common that Pict offers syntactic sugar for it:

```
v;    ≜    val [] = v.
```

As a consequence, the same example can be written as follows:

```
run((pr "hello");
    (pr "world"))
```

8.4 Common Examples

8.4.1 Reference Cell in Pict

A reference cell in Pict can be written as follows:

```
def refInt [res: /[/[/Int] /[Int Sig]]] =
(new contents:^Int
 run contents!0
 def get [res:!Int]
      = contents?v = ( contents!v | res!v )
 def set [v:Int c:Sig]
      = contents?_ = ( contents!v | c![] )
 res![get set]
)
```

This definition returns a tuple with the get and set servers. Therefore, a client of the reference cell can be coded as follows:

```
val [g1 s1] = (refInt)
val [g2 s2] = (refInt)

run ((s2 5);
     (prNL (int.toString (g1)));
     (prNL (int.toString (g2))))
```

The `prNL` function prints a string and moves the cursor to the next line. The `int.toString` function takes an integer argument and returns its string representation. Executing the code will print 0 and 5.

Another way to write the reference cell is to separately define the type and to return a record with both servers labeled `get` and `set` respectively, as follows:

```
type RefInt = [
  get=/[/Int]
  set=/[Int Sig]
]

def refInt () : RefInt =
(new contents:^Int
 run contents!0
 [
   get = \[res:!Int]
          = contents?v = ( contents!v | res!v )
```

```
   set = \[v:Int c:Sig]
          = contents?_ = ( contents!v | c![] )
 ])
```

The new definition would be used as follows:

```
val c1 = (refInt)
val c2 = (refInt)

run ((c2.set 5);
     (prNL (int.toString (c1.get)));
     (prNL (int.toString (c2.get))))
```

Notice that using a record to return the different "operation servers" on an encapsulated state starts to resemble *object-based* programming.

8.4.2 Mutual Exclusion in Pict

We can define two processes that mutually exclude each other by using a semaphore. The semaphore is a channel that sends a signal (`[]`) when a process can proceed, and otherwise does not send anything. Releasing the semaphore can be done by sending a signal over the same channel.

```
def sem[s:^[]] = s![]

new s:^[]

run (sem![s]
    |s?[] = pr!["hello world" (rchan s)]
    |s?[] = pr!["hi there" (rchan s)]
    )
```

Notice that we use sequencing, since we do not want to release the semaphore until we have finished processing the `pr` printing message. If printing were implemented by sending one character or one word at a time to the console, this code would ensure that the "hello world" and "hi there" phrases do not get intermixed.

8.4.3 Dining Philosophers in Pict

The dining philosophers problem can be encoded in Pict as follows:

```
type Chopstick = ^[]

def phil[l:Chopstick r:Chopstick]
    = l?[] = r?[] = ( l![] | r![] | phil![l r])
```

```
and chopstick[c:Chopstick] = c![]

new c0:Chopstick
new c1:Chopstick

run (chopstick![c0] | chopstick![c1]
    |phil![c0 c1]   | phil![c1 c0])
```

This definition closely follows the π calculus definition in section 3.4.3. A chopstick is represented as a channel that has an output signal (`[]`) on it to denote that the chopstick is available, and otherwise has no output. A philosopher is modeled as a process that takes two channels representing the left and right chopsticks respectively, and continuously (1) reads a signal from the left chopstick denoting picking it up, (2) reads a signal from the right chopstick denoting picking it up, and (3) releases both chopsticks concurrently by sending a signal over their respective channels.

A more complete definition could include names for philosophers and print "eating" and "thinking" messages when both chopsticks have been obtained and released respectively. It could also accept an arbitrary number of philosophers. And finally, it could avoid starvation by ensuring that philosophers do not enter a *deadlock* by all picking up the left chopsticks and waiting for their right chopsticks to become available. These are all left as exercises to the reader.

8.4.4 Mobile Reference Cell in Nomadic Pict

A mobile reference cell can be written in Nomadic Pict (see figure 8.8) as an agent that exports three channels: a `get` channel to receive query requests, a `set` channel to receive update requests, and a `migrate` channel to receive migration requests.

A mobile reference cell `c` can be created at site `s1`, and an agent `a` can use it and migrate it to another site `s2` as follows:

```
val c = (mobRefInt s1)

agent a =
(
 (c.set a 5);
 (prNL (int.toString (c.get a)));
 (c.mig a s2);
 (c.set a 3);
 (prNL (int.toString (c.get a)))
)
```

```
type MobRefInt =
[
  get=/[Agent /Int]
  set=/[Agent Int Sig]
  mig=/[Agent Site Sig]
]

def mobRefInt (s:Site) : MobRefInt =
(
  new get:^[Agent /Int]
  new set:^[Agent Int Sig]
  new mig:^[Agent Site Sig]

  agent refIntAg =
  (
    new contents:^Int
    run contents!0
    migrate to s
    ( get?*[a:Agent res:/Int] =
           contents?v = (contents!v | res@a!v)
    | set?*[a:Agent v:Int c:Sig] =
           contents?_ = (contents!v | c@a![])
    | mig?*[a:Agent s:Site c:Sig] =
           migrate to s  c@a![])
  ) in
  [
    get = \[a:Agent res:/Int]      = get@refIntAg![a res]
    set = \[a:Agent v:Int c:Sig]   = set@refIntAg![a v c]
    mig = \[a:Agent s:Site c:Sig] = mig@refIntAg![a s c]
  ]
)
```

Figure 8.8
Mobile reference cell in Nomadic Pict.

8.5 Discussion and Further Reading

The Pict programming language (Pierce and Turner, 2000) is the result of exploring the design space of concurrent programming languages based on the π calculus, in an analogous way to sequential functional programming languages, such as ML and Haskell, which are based on the λ calculus. Pict was created by Benjamin Pierce and David Turner in 1992.

The Nomadic Pict extension, designed by Pawel Wojciechowski, Peter Sewell, and Benjamin Pierce (Sewell et al., 1998, 2010), extends Pict with the notion of mobile agents, to explore distributed and mobile systems programming with the π calculus. Nomadic Pict uses a two-level communication architecture to differentiate between location-independent and location-dependent communication.

Chapter 8 has followed to a great extent presentations and examples provided in published research articles and tutorials (Pierce and Turner, 2000; Pierce, 1998; Sewell et al., 2010; Wojciechowski, 2000). Since our focus in this book is on how Pict and Nomadic Pict support concurrent, distributed, and mobile systems programming with the π calculus as their basis, we have not treated in detail topics such as types, polymorphism, standard libraries, and program compilation and execution instructions. For detailed treatments of these topics, we refer the interested reader to Pierce (1998) and Wojciechowski (2000).

8.6 Exercises

1. Pict does not directly support the nondeterministic choice operator in the π calculus: $P + Q$. How could you get the same behavior using Pict's operators? *Hint*: $P + Q$ can be encoded as $(\nu c)(\bar{c} \mid c.P \mid c.Q)$ for a *fresh* c.
2. Pict does not support synchronous output in the π calculus: $\bar{c}x.P$. How could you get that behavior in Pict? Given the following encoding into the asynchronous polyadic π calculus, where $a \notin fv(P) \cup fv(Q)$:

$$\begin{array}{lcl} \bar{c}x.P & \triangleq & (\nu a)(\bar{c}\langle x, a\rangle \mid a.P) \\ c(x).Q & \triangleq & c(x,a).(\bar{a} \mid Q). \end{array}$$

(a) Represent it in Pict.
(b) Comment on its correctness. Is the behavior the same as what is expected in the synchronous π calculus?

3. Pict only supports replicated input expressions in the π calculus: $!x(y).P$ How could you represent replicated output, e.g., $!\bar{x}y$?
4. Write an abstract data type for a *list* in Pict.

5. In Pict, define a `compose` abstraction as a higher-order function that takes two functions and returns the function representing their composition. Use it to compose a `double` function (that multiplies a number by 2) with an `increment` function (that adds 1 to a number). Use it with two anonymous abstractions representing functions.
6. Modify the dining philosophers example in Pict (see section 8.4.3) to:
(a) print "thinking" and "eating" messages.
(b) receive `n` as an argument and create a table with *n* philosophers.
(c) eliminate the possibility of deadlock.

7. How would you encode location-independent communication in terms of the location-dependent communication primitives? (Refer to figure 8.4 for the location-dependent communication primitives in Nomadic Pict.)
8. In Nomadic Pict, channels are associated to agents, so interprocess communication can only happen within an agent. Write a Nomadic Pict program where two agents share the same channel (after scope extrusion) yet cannot communicate over the channel since the writing process is on an agent and the reading process is on a different agent.
9. Write an abstract data type for a *distributed list* in Nomadic Pict. Different elements in the list can be in different sites.
10. Create a *nomad dining philosophers* example in Nomadic Pict. Philosophers eat in a *dining room* and think in a *thinking room*, assuming different rooms are in different sites.

Note

1. The semantics of continuation-passing style needs to consider more complex values, but for pedagogical reasons in this explanation we consider that values are simple. We refer the reader to Pierce and Turner (2000) for a more complete explanation of complex values.

9 Programming with Actors

Programming with the abstraction of *actors* can be done in several modern high level programming languages, including the SALSA programming language (Varela and Agha, 2001), Erlang (Armstrong et al., 1996), and Scala (Odersky, 2006). While Erlang and Scala extend a functional programming language core and focus on programming concurrent systems, SALSA extends an object-oriented programming language core and focuses on programming distributed and mobile systems (see figure 9.1).

The most significant semantic differences between SALSA and the actor language presented in chapter 4, are the following:

- *Object-oriented core* Agha, Mason, Smith, and Talcott's language (from now on, AMST) uses the λ calculus to model sequential computation within an actor. SALSA instead uses a sequential non-shared-memory subset of Java to model internal state and computation within an actor.
- *Classes as behaviors, methods as messages* AMST uses a lambda abstraction to model an actor's behavior: receiving a message is modeled as applying the abstraction to the incoming message content. SALSA uses classes (in object-oriented terms) to model actor behaviors: individual actors are objects (instances of behavior classes) that conceptually encapsulate an independent thread of execution, and messages are modeled as potential asynchronous method invocations on these instances. Since method return values are produced asynchronously, we introduce *tokens* to represent the future values to be returned by messages (see figure 9.2.)
- *Static behaviors* AMST enables actors to completely change their behavior when becoming *ready* to receive new messages. SALSA's actors always have the same static *behavior*, however, this behavior may depend on the internal state of the actor, which can change between message receptions.

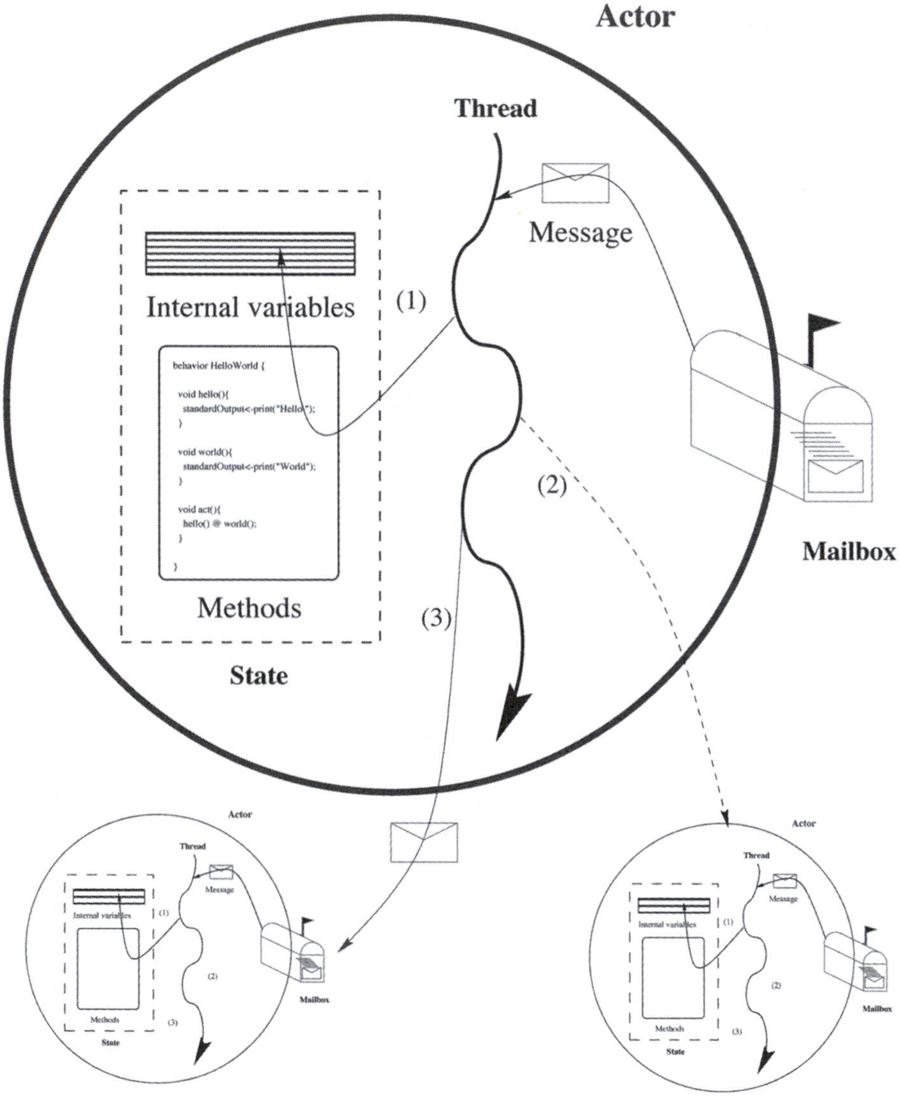

Figure 9.1
In response to a message, an actor can: (1) modify its local state, (2) create new actors, and/or (3) send messages to acquaintances.

Actor-oriented programming	Object-oriented programming
Behaviors	Classes (extending `UniversalActor`)
Actors	Objects (instances of behavior classes)
Messages	Asynchronous method invocations
Tokens	Message return values

Figure 9.2
Modeling actors in an object-oriented programming language.

AMST	SALSA	
send(a, pr(m, v))	`a <- m(v);`	Send named message
new(b)	`new B();`	Create new actor
ready(e)	`s = e; return;`	Behavior change

Figure 9.3
AMST syntax and equivalent SALSA syntax.

- *Coordination constructs* AMST uses asynchronous message sending as the only primitive form of communication. SALSA provides a number of higher-level constructs that facilitate coordinating otherwise independent activities between actors.
- *Distribution and mobility* AMST does not explicitly model actor locations and mobility. SALSA has a notion of *universal actor names* that enables transparent actor migration and location-independent communication.

In section 9.1, we cover the syntax of SALSA. Section 9.2 specifies the operational semantics of SALSA. Section 9.3 covers programming idioms and patterns used in SALSA programs, including higher-level coordination constructs. Section 9.4 goes over concurrent, distributed, and mobile programming examples in SALSA. Sections 9.5 and 9.6 conclude with a discussion and exercises.

9.1 SALSA Programming Language Syntax

9.1.1 Concurrent Systems Programming

A summary of the key AMST actor language primitives and the equivalent SALSA programming language syntax is given in figure 9.3. AMST can use simple values as messages; on the other hand, SALSA actors use potential method invocations as messages. Sending the message is asynchronous: The sender does not block but instead continues with its sequential computation. The message is typically buffered, and when the recipient actor eventually receives the message, the corresponding method is actually executed. Creating a new actor takes its behavior and returns the newly created actor's name. In AMST, behaviors are λ calculus abstractions, while in SALSA, the behavior is the name of a statically defined class. Finally, in AMST an actor becomes ready to receive a new message with a new behavior e by executing `ready(`e`)`. In SALSA, internal state is modeled directly as internal variables which can be reassigned new values and persist across message receptions. Returning from a method implicitly makes the actor ready to receive a new message.

Figure 9.4 specifies the partial syntax of atoms, behavior names, variables, and other auxiliary domains: primitive operators, actor names, tokens, universal actor names and locations, message names, and message property names. SALSA uses the same Java primitive types: booleans, characters, as well as different numeric types (`byte, short, int, long, float, double`) and arrays. SALSA

$\mathcal{A}_v$	=	{ `null` }	*Void*
$\mathcal{A}_b$	=	{ `true`, `false`}	*Booleans*
$\mathcal{A}_i$	=	{ ..., -2, -1, 0, 1, 2, ...}	*Integers*
$\mathcal{A}$	::=	$\mathcal{A}_v \mid \mathcal{A}_b \mid \mathcal{A}_i \mid \ldots$	***Atoms***
$\mathcal{B}_p$	=	{ `void`, `boolean`, `int`, `char`, ...}	*Primitive types*
$\mathcal{B}_j$	=	{ `Object`, `Integer`, `String`, ...}	*Java class names*
$\mathcal{B}_u$	=	{ A, B, C, ...}	*User-defined behaviors*
$\mathcal{B}$	::=	$\mathcal{B}_p \mid \mathcal{B}_j \mid \mathcal{B}_u$	***Behavior names***
$\mathcal{X}_k$	=	{ `self`, `token`, `this`, `super`, `standardOutput`, ...}	*Key words*
$\mathcal{X}_u$	=	{ x, y, z, ...}	*User-defined variables*
$\mathcal{X}$	::=	$\mathcal{X}_k \mid \mathcal{X}_u$	***Variables***
$\mathcal{F}$	=	{ +, *, ==, >, ...}	*Primitive operators*
$\mathcal{D}$	=	{ a, b, c, ...}	*Actor names*
$\mathcal{T}$	=	{ t, t_0, t_1, ...}	*Tokens*
$\mathcal{U}$	=	{ u, u_0, u_1, ...}	*Universal actor names*
$\mathcal{L}$	=	{ s, s_0, s_1, ...}	*Universal actor locations*
$\mathcal{M}$	=	{ `migrate`, m, n, o, ...}	*Message names*
$\mathcal{M}_p$	=	{ `waitfor`, `priority`, ...}	*Message properties*

Figure 9.4
SALSA programming language syntax (1/2): Atoms, behavior names, variables, and auxiliary domains.

also supports Java's operations on primitive types, and its standard class library. For standard I/O streams interaction, SALSA provides special actors called `standardOutput`, `standardInput`, and `standardError`. SALSA actors can receive a `migrate` message to move between locations. Messages can also have properties for synchronization and coordination.

Figure 9.5 specifies SALSA's core language syntax. *Values* include atoms, variables, actor names, tokens, universal actor names and locations. It is assumed that these sets are pairwise disjoint; that is,

$$\forall\, \mathcal{S}_1, \mathcal{S}_2 \in \{\mathcal{A}, \mathcal{X}, \mathcal{D}, \mathcal{T}, \mathcal{U}, \mathcal{L}\} : \; \mathcal{S}_1 \neq \mathcal{S}_2 \implies \mathcal{S}_1 \cap \mathcal{S}_2 = 0$$

Expressions are either values, function applications (including prefix, infix, and precedence operators), internal object field or method accesses, actor creation, or name dereferencing. *Statements* include local variable declarations with optional initialization ($\mathcal{S}_d$,) blocks of statements, assignments, message sending statements, conditionals, loops, and return statements. *Programs* consist of a behavior name (used to create new instances), and a body, which includes state variable declarations, constructors, and message handlers.

Message sending statements are annotated pure message-sending statements with optional continuations ($\mathcal{S}_m[\mathcal{S}_c]$). Annotations include setting a synchronization token after message processing, and message properties. Pure message sending statements ($\mathcal{S}_p$) are single asynchronous message sends or join blocks. *Continuations* ($\mathcal{S}_c$) are either first-class continuations or token-passing continuations. For example, `token t = a <- m();` means that a message `m` is sent to actor `a` asynchronously, and when the message is delivered and the handler `m` is actually executed, the returned value will be available as token `t`. A *join block* specifies that any associated continuation should wait until all the messages in the join block have been executed. For example, `join{ a1 <- m1(); a2 <- m2();} @ a <- m();` will send messages `m1` and `m2` concurrently to actors `a1` and `a2`, but message `m` to actor `a` will be received only when both `m1` and `m2` have been received and processed. This `join` statement is asynchronous: Execution continues with the next statement immediately after sending the messages inside the join block. *Token-passing continuations* are chained sequences of asynchronous message sending statements causally connected; for example, `a1 <- m1() @ a2 <- m2(token);` means that message `m2` will be sent to actor `a2` only when message `m1` has been processed by actor `a1`: indeed, the argument to `m2` is the *token* that proves that `m1` has finished execution: it is set as the returned value of `m1`. Finally, *first-class continuations* allow an actor's message handler to *delegate* returning a value to another actor. For example, `b <- m2() @ currentContinuation;` executed in actor `a`'s `m1` message handler means that the return value of `m1` will be produced by `b`'s `m2` message handler, which should then have a compatible return type with `m1`.

$\mathcal{V}$	::=	$\mathcal{A} \mid \mathcal{X} \mid \mathcal{D} \mid \mathcal{T} \mid \mathcal{U} \mid \mathcal{L}$	***Values***
$\mathcal{E}$	::=		***Expressions***
		$\mathcal{V}$	
	|	$\mathcal{F}(\mathcal{E},\ldots,\mathcal{E})$	*Function application*
	|	$\mathcal{E}\ \mathcal{F}\ \mathcal{E}$	*Infix*
	|	$(\mathcal{E})$	*Precedence*
	|	$\mathcal{E}.\mathcal{X}$	*Object field access*
	|	$\mathcal{E}.\mathcal{M}(\mathcal{E},\ldots,\mathcal{E})$	*Object method access*
	|	`new` $\mathcal{B}(\mathcal{E},\ldots,\mathcal{E})$ `[at (` $\mathcal{U},\mathcal{L}$ `)]`	*Actor creation*
	|	`reference` $\mathcal{U}$	*Reference from UAN*
$\mathcal{S}_d$	::=	$\mathcal{B}\ \mathcal{X}$ [= $\mathcal{E}$]	*Variable declaration*
$\mathcal{S}_p$	::=	$\mathcal{E}$ `<-` $\mathcal{M}(\mathcal{E},\ldots,\mathcal{E})$	*Single msg send*
	|	`join {` $\mathcal{S};\ldots;\mathcal{S}$ `}`	*Join block*
$\mathcal{S}_m$	::=		***Message Send***
		[`token` $\mathcal{T}$ =]	*Setting token*
		$\mathcal{S}_p[:\mathcal{M}_p(\mathcal{E},\ldots,\mathcal{E}):\ldots:\mathcal{M}_p(\mathcal{E},\ldots,\mathcal{E})]$	*Msg properties*
$\mathcal{S}_c$	::=		***Continuation***
		`@ currentContinuation`	1st*-class continuation*
	|	`@` $\mathcal{S}_m[\mathcal{S}_c]$	*Token-passing continuation*
$\mathcal{S}$	::=		***Statements***
		$\mathcal{S}_d$	
	|	`{` $\mathcal{S};\ldots;\mathcal{S}$ `}`	*Sequencing*
	|	$[\mathcal{E}.]\mathcal{X} = \mathcal{E}$	*Variable assignment*
	|	$\mathcal{S}_m[\mathcal{S}_c]$`;`	*Message sending*
	|	`if (` $\mathcal{E}$ `)` $\mathcal{S}$ `else` $\mathcal{S}$	*Conditional execution*
	|	`while (` $\mathcal{E}$ `)` $\mathcal{S}$	*While loop*
	|	`for (` $[\mathcal{S}];[\mathcal{E}];[\mathcal{S}]$ `)` $\mathcal{S}$	*For loop*
	|	`return` $[\mathcal{E}]$`;`	*Message end*
$\mathcal{H}$	::=	$\mathcal{B}\ \mathcal{M}(\mathcal{B}\ \mathcal{X},\ldots,\mathcal{B}\ \mathcal{X})$ `{` $\mathcal{S};\ldots;\mathcal{S}$ `}`	***Message handlers***
$\mathcal{C}$	::=	$\mathcal{B}(\mathcal{B}\ \mathcal{X}\ldots\mathcal{B}\ \mathcal{X})$ `{` $\mathcal{S};\ldots;\mathcal{S}$ `}`	***Constructors***
$\mathcal{P}$	::=	`behavior` $\mathcal{B}\{\mathcal{S}_d;\ldots;\mathcal{S}_d;\ \mathcal{C}\ldots\mathcal{C}\ \mathcal{H}\ldots\mathcal{H}\}$	***Programs***

Figure 9.5
SALSA programming language syntax (2/2): Values, expressions, statements, message handlers, constructors, and programs.

Consider the AMST *ticker* example from section 4.1:

$$ticker = \texttt{rec}(\lambda b.\lambda t.\lambda n.\lambda m.\texttt{seq}(\texttt{send}(t, \texttt{nil}), \texttt{ready}(b(t)(n+1)))).$$

We can write it in SALSA as follows:

```
behavior Ticker{
  int n;
  Ticker(int n){
    this.n = n;
  }
  void tick(){
    n++;
    self<-tick();
  }
}
```

The `Ticker` behavior has a state variable, `n`; a constructor, which following Java's convention uses the same name as the behavior; and a message handler `tick` that changes the actor's internal state and sends itself a message to continue ticking. Notice that we do not need to explicitly keep an actor's own name, since the keyword `self` represents it. In fact, when a message has no explicit recipient, it is sent to `self`. So, `self<-tick();` and simply `tick();` are equivalent. Notice also that we can use the `this` keyword to refer to the actor's state variables as opposed to the constructor/method formal arguments that may have the same name.

In AMST, it is created and started as follows:

$$\texttt{letrec}\ t = \texttt{new}(ticker(t)(0))\ \texttt{in}\ \texttt{send}(t, \texttt{nil}).$$

Equivalent code in SALSA follows:

```
Ticker ticker = new Ticker(0);
ticker <- tick();
```

9.1.2 Distributed and Mobile Systems Programming

SALSA concurrent programs can be directly used for distributed and mobile systems programming. SALSA's run-time system consists of a *name service* and *theaters*, which are Java virtual machines extended with actor creation, migration, and communication services. SALSA's actors can be assigned *Universal Actor Names* (UAN). UANs are strings that serve as unique identifiers to enable location-independent communication with universal actors, mediated by the naming service. For example, a *calendar* actor may be written as follows:

```
behavior Calendar implements ActorService{
  Appointment[] getAppointments(){
    ...
  }
  ...
}
```

The `ActorService` empty interface is used to annotate behaviors whose instances are not to be garbage collected. The reason is that it is possible to create references to instances of behaviors implementing this interface from their UANs.

A calendar instance can be created as follows:

```
Calendar myCalendar = new Calendar() at (uan, host);
```

`uan` represents the unique name of the calendar actor, which has Uniform Resource Identifier (URI) syntax, for example: `uan://wcl.cs.rpi.edu/~cvarela/calendar`, and the `host` represents the initial location of this actor, which is typically a string with a Domain Name System (DNS) domain name optionally followed by a listening port, for example ``` ``a.wcl.cs.rpi.edu:4040'' ```. The naming service (in this example, a daemon running at `wcl.cs.rpi.edu` and listening on default port `3030`) is in charge of checking for uniqueness of the UAN and rejects registration of actors with already existing UANs.

Any SALSA program can now obtain references to this universal actor and send messages to it, in the following manner:

```
Calendar calendar = reference uan;
token appointments = calendar <- getAppointments();
```

Notice that the calendar actor can be migrated at any point to another theater by sending it a `migrate` message:

```
calendar <- migrate(newHost);
```

Example 9.1 An applet server can be encoded in SALSA as follows:

```
behavior Applet {...}

Applet getApplet(String uan, String host){
  return new Applet() at (uan, host);
}
```

For each request, the applet server first creates a new applet actor with the given universal actor name at the given remote host, and then returns its reference to the applet client.

9.2 SALSA Programming Language Operational Semantics

To define the operational semantics of the SALSA programming language, we follow an approach similar to the one presented in section 4.2 for the AMST language (Agha et al., 1997). Since AMST has a functional programming core based on the λ calculus and SALSA has an object-oriented core, we need to define an appropriate semantic model for the object-oriented core of SALSA, which is based on Java's. Similarly to FeatherWeight Java (Igarashi et al., 2001), we need to find a subset of SALSA that allows us to abstract over the sequential object-oriented core and focus on the concurrent actor semantics.

In section 9.2.1, we introduce FeatherWeight SALSA (FS), the SALSA language "kernel", a subset of the full language that we will use to formalize its operational semantics. Section 9.2.2 goes over the FS language's full syntax, and section 9.2.3 specifies its semantics as a set of labeled transition rules from actor configurations to actor configurations specifying valid computations. Section 9.2.4 illustrates how SALSA's main linguistic abstractions (i.e., token-passing continuations, first-class continuations, and join blocks) are translated into FS code. This translation from the full language to the kernel language allows us to specify the full language's semantics with less syntax and complexity, following an approach similar to the one used by Roy and Haridi (2004) with the Oz programming language. Section 9.2.5 extends FS to model SALSA's abstractions for distribution and mobility. The Mobile FS (MFS) language extension incorporates key SALSA language constructs including universal actors with names (UAN) and locations (UAL), remote actor creation, transparent communication, and actor migration. Finally, section 9.2.6 discusses the fairness requirements of the SALSA language. Concurrent, distributed, and mobile systems' evolution over time can be followed by applying the rules specified in the operational semantics in a manner consistent with fairness.

9.2.1 FeatherWeight SALSA

9.2.1.1 Introduction

The abbreviated syntax of FeatherWeight SALSA (FS) is illustrated in figure 9.6. `P` denotes behavior definitions. A behavior `B` includes typed state variables, a constructor, and zero or more message handlers. A constructor `K` is restricted syntactically to receive all the actor's state variables and initialize them. A message handler `M` can receive zero or more typed arguments, and it is syntactically restricted to perform the following operations: (1) update all the actor's state variables, (2) asynchronously send messages optionally declaring tokens to refer to the future returned values and optionally waiting for these tokens, and (3) become ready to process the next message updating the token corresponding to the current message. An expression

P	::=	$\mathtt{behavior\ B\ \{\bar{B}\ \bar{f};\ K\ \bar{M}\}}$	**Behavior**
K	::=	$\mathtt{B(\bar{B}\ \bar{f})\{this.\bar{f}\ =\ \bar{f};\}}$	**Constructor**
M	::=	$\mathtt{B\ m(\bar{B}\ \bar{x})\{\bar{f}\ =\ \bar{e};}$ $\mathtt{token\ \bar{t}\ =\ \bar{e}{<}{-}\bar{m}(\bar{e}):waitfor(\bar{t});}$ $\mathtt{return\ e;\}}$	**Msg handler**
e	::=	$\mathtt{x \mid f \mid t \mid self \mid new\ B(\bar{e})}$	**Expression**

Figure 9.6
FeatherWeight SALSA: Abbreviated syntax.

`e` may refer to an actual argument passed to a message handler, a field in the actor's state variables, a token to be assigned in the future upon asynchronous message processing, a reference to the actor itself, or an actor creation, which takes the actor's behavior, its initial state, and returns the newly created actor's fresh name. Notice that we use the notation $\bar{\mathtt{e}}$ to represent the possibly empty sequence of arguments $\mathtt{e_1,\ \ldots,\ e_n}$, we use $\bar{\mathtt{B}}\ \bar{\mathtt{f}}$; to represent the possibly empty sequence of declarations $\mathtt{B_1\ f_1;\ \ldots;\ B_n\ f_n;}$, we use $\bar{\mathtt{M}}$ to represent the possibly empty sequence of method handlers $\mathtt{M_1\ \ldots\ M_n}$, we use $\bar{\mathtt{B}}\ \bar{\mathtt{f}}$ to represent the possibly empty sequence of formal arguments $\mathtt{B_1\ f_1,\ \ldots,B_n\ f_n}$ (similarly with $\bar{\mathtt{B}}\ \bar{\mathtt{x}}$,) we use $\mathtt{this.\bar{f}\ =\ \bar{f};}$ to represent the possibly empty sequence of field initializations $\mathtt{this.f_1\ =\ f_1;\ \ldots;\ this.f_n\ =\ f_n;}$ (similarly with $\mathtt{\bar{f}\ =\ \bar{e};}$), and we use $\mathtt{token\ \bar{t}\ =\ \bar{e}{<}{-}\bar{m}(\bar{e}):waitfor(\bar{t});}$ to represent the possibly empty sequence of asynchronous message sends $\mathtt{token\ t_1\ =\ e_1{<}{-}\ m_1(e_{11},\ \ldots,\ e_{1n_1}):waitfor(t_{11},\ldots,t_{1j_1});\ \ldots;\ token\ t_k\ =\ e_k{<}{-}\ m_k(e_{k1},\ \ldots,\ e_{kn_k}):waitfor(t_{k1},\ldots,t_{kj_k});}$. Message properties are optional, i.e., $\mathtt{token\ t_i\ =\ e_i{<}{-}\ m_i(e_{i1},\ \ldots,\ e_{in_i}):waitfor();}$ can simply be written $\mathtt{token\ t_i\ =\ e_i{<}{-}\ m_i(e_{i1},\ \ldots,\ e_{in_i});}$. Named tokens are also optional, i.e., $\mathtt{token\ t_i\ =\ e_i{<}{-}\ m_i(e_{i1},\ \ldots,\ e_{in_i});}$ can simply be written $\mathtt{e_i{<}{-}\ m_i(e_{i1},\ \ldots,\ e_{in_i});}$ if token $\mathtt{t_i}$ is not used, and messages to the actor itself can omit the target, i.e., $\mathtt{self\ {<}{-}\ m_i(e_{i1},\ \ldots,\ e_{in_i});}$ can simply be written $\mathtt{m_i(e_{i1},\ \ldots,\ e_{in_i});}$. We also assume that sequences of actor state variables, parameter names, and message names contain no duplicate names.

Let us consider the *ticker* example in FS as illustrated in figure 9.7. Notice the syntactic restrictions on the constructor and message handlers. The ticker can be created and started by another actor's message handler in FS as follows:

```
new Ticker(0) <- tick();
```

9.2.1.2 *Actor Configurations*

Actor configurations model concurrent system components, frozen in time, as viewed by an idealized observer. An actor configuration is composed of:

```
behavior Ticker{
  int n;
  Ticker(int n){
    this.n = n;
  }
  void tick(){
    n = n+1;
    self <- tick();
    return null;
  }
  int time(){
    n = n;
    return n;
  }
}
```

Figure 9.7
Ticker example in FeatherWeight SALSA.

- a set of individually named actors,
- messages en route, and
- a behavior table that includes all actor behavior definitions.

An *actor configuration*, κ, denoted $\alpha \parallel \mu \parallel \beta$ contains an actor map, α, which is a function mapping actor names to actor states including its behavior name, its state, and currently executing expression if any; a multiset of messages, μ; and a behavior table, β, which is a function mapping behavior names B to behavior definitions P. We may omit the behavior table when clear from context, and denote an actor configuration simply as $\alpha \parallel \mu$. An actor with behavior B and state $\bar{v}$ ready to process a message is denoted as $B(\bar{v})$, and an actor with behavior B processing a message is denoted as $B(\bar{e}) : e$, where $\bar{e}$ represents the current actor's state, and e the currently executing actor expression. A message to actor named a to execute message handler m with arguments $\bar{v}$ is denoted as $\langle a \Leftarrow m(\bar{v}) \rangle$.

The ticker example computation can be modeled with actor configurations as follows:[1]

$$\emptyset, [\texttt{B}_0\texttt{():\ new\ Ticker(0)<-tick();}]_{a_0} \parallel \emptyset \parallel \beta$$

$$= \emptyset, [\mathsf{R}_0 \blacktriangleright \texttt{new\ Ticker(0)} \blacktriangleleft]_{a_0} \parallel \emptyset \parallel \beta$$

$$\xrightarrow{[\text{new}]} \emptyset, [\mathsf{R}_0 \blacktriangleright \texttt{a} \blacktriangleleft]_{a_0}, [\texttt{Ticker(0)}]_a \parallel \emptyset \parallel \beta$$

$$= \emptyset, [\mathsf{R}_1 \blacktriangleright \texttt{a<-tick();} \blacktriangleleft]_{a_0}, [\texttt{Ticker(0)}]_a \parallel \emptyset \parallel \beta$$

$$\xrightarrow{[\text{snd}]} \quad \alpha, [\texttt{Ticker(0)}]_a \parallel \{\langle a \Leftarrow \mathit{tick}()\rangle\} \parallel \beta \tag{9.1}$$

$$\xrightarrow{[\text{rcv}]}$$

$$\alpha, [(\texttt{Ticker(n+1): self<-tick();return null;})\{(0,\texttt{a})/(\texttt{n},\texttt{self})\}]_a \parallel \emptyset \parallel \beta$$

$$= \alpha, [\texttt{Ticker(0+1): a<-tick();return null;}]_a \parallel \emptyset \parallel \beta$$

$$\xrightarrow{[\text{seq}]} \quad \alpha, [\texttt{Ticker(1): a<-tick(); return null;}]_a \parallel \emptyset \parallel \beta$$

$$= \alpha, [\mathsf{R}_2 \blacktriangleright \texttt{a<-tick();} \blacktriangleleft]_a \parallel \emptyset \parallel \beta$$

$$\xrightarrow{[\text{snd}]} \quad \xrightarrow{[\text{seq}]} \quad \xrightarrow{[\text{ret}]} \quad \alpha, [\texttt{Ticker(1)}]_a \parallel \{\langle a \Leftarrow \mathit{tick}()\rangle\} \parallel \beta$$

$$\xrightarrow{[\text{rcv}]}$$

$$\vdots$$

Initially, we have a configuration with an actor a_0 (with behavior B_0) that is to create the ticker with initial state 0 and send it a `tick()` message. We assume there are no more actors in the configuration or messages in the network. The actor expression for actor a_0 can be decomposed into a reduction context R_0 filled with a redex as will be explained in section 9.2.3.2. The redex denotes the next reducible expression, in this case, `new Ticker(0)`, which will enable the transition labeled **new**, which creates a new actor. The configuration after the **new** transition contains two actors: a_0 and a, a newly created actor with behavior `Ticker(0)`. The new actor expression for a_0 can be decomposed into a reduction context R_1 filled with redex `a<-tick()`, which enables the transition labeled **snd**. After the **snd** transition, we get a configuration whose network component includes the message $\langle a \Leftarrow \mathit{tick}()\rangle$. This configuration with an actor a ready to receive messages with behavior `Ticker(0)`, and a message $\langle a \Leftarrow \mathit{tick}()\rangle$ in the network, enables the transition labeled **rcv**. The **rcv** transition looks up the behavior table β to find a message handler for `tick()` and uses the message handler body (which we can see in figure 9.7) for the actor expression after message reception. This message reception substitutes references to the actor's internal state with the current actor's state, denoted by the substitution $\{0/\texttt{n}\}$, substitutes formal arguments with actual arguments (in this example, the `tick()` message has no arguments), and substitutes the keyword `self` with the actor's name, denoted by the substitution $\{\texttt{a}/\texttt{self}\}$. The **rcv** transition resembles β reduction in the λ calculus, in a similar way to the AMST actor language presented in chapter 4. A sequential computation step models the state change from $(n+1)\{0/n\}$ to 1. After message reception, the actor expression representing the behavior for the ticker actor a, can be decomposed into a reduction context R_2 filled with redex `a <- tick()` which enables the **snd** transition rule. The actor configuration after the **snd** transition can evolve after a sequential transition (**seq**) and a message end transition (**ret**) to a configuration containing a ticker ready with internal state 1, and a network with a message $\langle a \Leftarrow tick()\rangle$. The final actor configuration has the same form as configuration 9.1 which allows the computation to proceed indefinitely.

9.2.1.3 *Tokens and Partial Messages*

We will extend the syntax of (*full*) messages to denote *partial* messages and synchronization tokens. The partial message syntax

$$\langle(t_0, \ldots, t_n) : a \Leftarrow m(\bar{v}) \uparrow^{t}\rangle$$

denotes that tokens t_0 to t_n as well as any tokens in $\bar{v}$ must be *resolved* (i.e., converted to nontoken values) before message $m(\bar{v})$ is considered full and can be processed by actor a. Furthermore, it denotes that upon processing of message m, token t should be replaced in any other partial messages in the network by the returned value of the message handler m.

Let us consider the following FS code where message m_2 cannot be processed by actor a_2 until message m_1 has been processed by actor a_1:

```
token t1 = a1 <- m1();
token t2 = a2 <- m2(t1);
```

and its computation:

$$\alpha, [\mathsf{R}_0 \blacktriangleright \texttt{token t}_1 = \texttt{a}_1\texttt{<-m}_1\texttt{();token t}_2 = \texttt{a}_2\texttt{<-m}_2\texttt{(t}_1\texttt{);} \blacktriangleleft]_{a_0} \parallel \emptyset$$

$$= \alpha, [\mathsf{R}_1 \blacktriangleright \texttt{token t}_1 = \texttt{a}_1\texttt{<-m}_1\texttt{();} \blacktriangleleft]_{a_0} \parallel \emptyset$$

$$\xrightarrow{[\mathbf{snd}]} \quad \alpha, [\mathsf{R}_1 \blacktriangleright \texttt{null} \blacktriangleleft]_{a_0} \parallel \{\langle() : a_1 \Leftarrow m_1() \uparrow^{t_1}\rangle\}$$

$$\xrightarrow{[\mathbf{seq}]} \quad \alpha, [\mathsf{R}_2 \blacktriangleright \texttt{token t}_2 = \texttt{a}_2\texttt{<-m}_2\texttt{(t}_1\texttt{);} \blacktriangleleft]_{a_0} \parallel \{\langle() : a_1 \Leftarrow m_1() \uparrow^{t_1}\rangle\}$$

$$\xrightarrow{[\mathbf{snd}]} \quad \alpha' \parallel \{\langle() : a_1 \Leftarrow m_1() \uparrow^{t_1}\rangle, \langle() : a_2 \Leftarrow m_2(t_1) \uparrow^{t_2}\rangle\}.$$

We have omitted the behavior table β for readability. This computation path used two message sending transitions (labeled [**snd**]). Notice that the final actor configuration has two messages in its network: $\langle() : a_1 \Leftarrow m_1() \uparrow^{t_1}\rangle$, which is a *full* message, since it depends on no tokens and can be received by actor a_1 whenever it is ready, and $\langle() : a_2 \Leftarrow m_2(t_1) \uparrow^{t_2}\rangle\}$, a *partial* message, since m_2's argument is a token (t_1) and cannot be received by a_2 until the token has been resolved.

We will also extend the notation for actor states to $B(\bar{e}) : e \downarrow_t$ to denote that after processing the current message, the token t should be set to the message handler's returned value. For example, assuming that α' has an actor named a_1 ready with behavior B_1, which has a message handler `int m1(){ return 1;}`, then the previous computation may continue as follows:

$$\alpha' \parallel \{\langle() : a_1 \Leftarrow m_1() \uparrow^{t_1}\rangle, \langle() : a_2 \Leftarrow m_2(t_1) \uparrow^{t_2}\rangle\}$$

$$= \alpha'', [\texttt{B}_1\texttt{()}]_{a_1} \parallel \{\langle() : a_1 \Leftarrow m_1() \uparrow^{t_1}\rangle, \langle() : a_2 \Leftarrow m_2(t_1) \uparrow^{t_2}\rangle\}$$

$$\xrightarrow{[\mathrm{rcv}]} \alpha'', [\texttt{B}_1\texttt{(): return 1;} \downarrow_{t_1}]_{a_1} \parallel \{\langle() : a_2 \Leftarrow m_2(t_1) \uparrow^{t_2}\rangle\}$$

$$\xrightarrow{[\mathrm{ret}]} \alpha'', [\texttt{B}_1\texttt{()}]_{a_1} \parallel \{\langle() : a_2 \Leftarrow m_2(1) \uparrow^{t_2}\rangle\}.$$

Notice that in the final actor configuration, the message $\langle() : a_2 \Leftarrow m_2(1) \uparrow^{t_2}\rangle$ is now *full* and can be received by a_2, since a_1 has finished processing m_1, resolving the token $\texttt{t}_1$ to the value 1.

Let us now consider the following FS code:

```
token t1 = a1 <- m1();
token t2 = a2 <- m2():waitfor(t1);
```

In this case, the token t_1 is not used as an argument in the message m_2. Nonetheless, the message m_2 should not be received by a_2 until m_1's completion by a_1, as specified by the `waitfor(t1)` message property. The corresponding partial message is denoted as $\langle(t_1) : a_2 \Leftarrow m_2() \uparrow^{t_2}\rangle\}$, which upon token resolution becomes the full message $\langle(1) : a_2 \Leftarrow m_2() \uparrow^{t_2}\rangle\}$.

9.2.2 FS Syntax

After the introduction to FeatherWeight SALSA in section 9.2.1, we proceed to define the full programming language syntax as shown in figure 9.8. The main abstractions are values, expressions, and programs. Values include atoms, natural numbers, variable names (with `self` as a special variable name for an actor to refer to itself), actor names, and token names. We will assume that these sets of names are disjoint. Expressions can be values, primitive polyadic function applications, sequences of expressions, branching, message sending with optional synchronization tokens, actor creation, and token resolution (`return e;`). Programs consist of a behavior name, a (possibly empty) sequence of typed state variables, a constructor, and a (possibly empty) set of message handlers. Constructors are restricted to only initialize an actor's state. Message handlers are assumed to first update all the actor's state variables in the same order as defined, then optionally send messages asynchronously, and end with a token resolution expression.

9.2.3 FS Operational Semantics

In order to specify the FS programming language operational semantics, we will define a number of semantic domains including actor configurations, reducible expressions (also known as *redexes*), and reduction contexts, which enable us to define the reduction rules that formally specify valid computations in our language.

$\mathcal{A}$	=	{ `true`, `false`, `null`, ...}	*Atoms*
$\mathcal{N}$	=	{ 0, 1, 2, ...}	*Natural numbers*
$\mathcal{X}$	=	{ `self`, x, y, z, ...}	*Variables*
$\mathcal{D}$	=	{ a, b, c, ...}	*Actor names*
$\mathcal{T}$	=	{ t, t_0, t_1, ...}	*Tokens*
$\mathcal{M}$	=	{ m, n, o, ...}	*Message names*
$\mathcal{B}$	=	{ A, B, C, ...}	*Behavior names*
$\mathcal{F}$	=	{ +, *, ==, ...}	*Primitive operations*
$\mathcal{V}$	::=	$\mathcal{A} \mid \mathcal{N} \mid \mathcal{X} \mid \mathcal{D} \mid \mathcal{T}$	***Values***
$\mathcal{E}$	::=		***Expressions***
		$\mathcal{V}$	
	|	$\mathcal{F}(\mathcal{E}, \ldots, \mathcal{E})$	*Function application*
	|	$\mathcal{E}; \mathcal{E}$	*Sequencing*
	|	`if (` $\mathcal{E}$ `)` $\mathcal{E}$ `else` $\mathcal{E}$	*Conditional execution*
	|	`token` $\mathcal{T}$ = $\mathcal{E}$ `<-` $\mathcal{M}(\mathcal{E}, \ldots, \mathcal{E})$ `:waitfor(`$\mathcal{T}, \ldots, \mathcal{T}$`)`	*Message send*
	|	`new` $\mathcal{B}(\mathcal{E}, \ldots, \mathcal{E})$	*Actor creation*
	|	`return` $\mathcal{E}$	*Set token, get ready*
$\mathcal{H}$	::=	$\mathcal{B}\ \mathcal{M}(\mathcal{B}\ \mathcal{X}, \ldots, \mathcal{B}\ \mathcal{X})$ $\{\mathcal{X} = \mathcal{E}; \ldots; \mathcal{X} = \mathcal{E}; \mathcal{E}; \ldots; \mathcal{E};\}$	***Message handlers***
$\mathcal{C}$	::=	$\mathcal{B}(\mathcal{B}\ \mathcal{X} \ldots \mathcal{B}\ \mathcal{X})$ `{this.`$\mathcal{X}$ = $\mathcal{X}$`; ... this.`$\mathcal{X}$ = $\mathcal{X}$`; }`	***Constructors***
$\mathcal{P}$	::=	`behavior` $\mathcal{B}$ $\{\mathcal{B}\ \mathcal{X}; \ldots; \mathcal{B}\ \mathcal{X}; \mathcal{C}\ \mathcal{H} \ldots \mathcal{H}\}$	***Programs***

Figure 9.8
FS language syntax.

9.2.3.1 *FS Semantic Domains*

Figure 9.9 illustrates the notation for actor configurations, each composed of an actor map, a network, and a behavior table. The actor map is a function α from actor names to actor states. An actor state may be idle and ready, denoted by the actor's behavior name and the values of its state variables, or it may be processing a message, denoted by the behavior name and the expressions to be evaluated for each state variable, as well as the expression corresponding to the message handler in execution and the token to be set after message processing. A network μ is a multiset of messages. A message $\langle(v_0,\ldots,v_n) : a \Leftarrow m(v'_0,\ldots,v'_m) \uparrow^t\rangle$ is *full* if $\forall v \in \{v_0,\ldots,v_n,v'_0,\ldots,v'_m\} : v \notin \mathcal{T}$; otherwise, it is *partial* and cannot be received by a until all pending tokens are resolved. The behavior table β maps behavior names to their textual programs. We will use $\beta(B,m) =$ `B' m(B̄ x̄){f̄ = ē; ē';}` to denote that the program $\beta(B)$ has a message handler for m containing that text.

9.2.3.2 *FS Reducible Expressions and Reduction Contexts*

In order to evaluate an actor expression using a standard left-first, call-by-value evaluation strategy, we decompose it into a *reducible expression* inside a *reduction context*. The syntax for redexes and reduction contexts for FS expressions is shown in figure 9.10.

Lemma 9.1 An actor expression, e (in $\mathcal{E}$), is either a value v, or otherwise it can be uniquely decomposed into a *reduction context*, R, filled with a *redex*, r, denoted as $e = \mathsf{R} \blacktriangleright \mathsf{r} \blacktriangleleft$.

α	$=$	$\mathcal{D} \xrightarrow{f} \mathcal{S}$	***Actor maps***
$\mathcal{S}$	$::=$		***Actor states***
		$\mathcal{B}(\mathcal{V},\ldots,\mathcal{V})$	*Actor idle and ready*
	$\mid$	$\mathcal{B}(\mathcal{E},\ldots,\mathcal{E}) : \mathcal{E} \downarrow_{\mathcal{T}}$	*Actor processing*
μ	$=$	$\{\{\mathcal{G}\}\}$	***Network***
$\mathcal{G}$	$::=$	$\langle(\mathcal{V},\ldots,\mathcal{V}) : \mathcal{D} \Leftarrow \mathcal{M}(\mathcal{V},\ldots,\mathcal{V}) \uparrow^{\mathcal{T}}\rangle$	*Message*
β	$=$	$\mathcal{B} \xrightarrow{f} \mathcal{P}$	***Behavior table***
$\mathcal{K}$	$::=$	$\alpha \parallel \mu \parallel \beta$	***Actor configurations***

Figure 9.9
FS semantic domains.

$\mathcal{E}_r$	::=		***Redexes***
		$\mathcal{F}(\mathcal{V},\ldots,\mathcal{V})$	*Function application*
	|	$\mathcal{V};\mathcal{E}$	*Sequencing*
	|	`if (` $\mathcal{V}$ `)` $\mathcal{E}$ `else` $\mathcal{E}$	*Conditional execution*
	|	`token` $\mathcal{T}$ `=` $\mathcal{V}$ `<-` $\mathcal{M}(\mathcal{V},\ldots,\mathcal{V})$ `:waitfor(`$\mathcal{T},\ldots,\mathcal{T}$`)`	*Message send*
	|	`new` $\mathcal{B}(\mathcal{V},\ldots,\mathcal{V})$	*Actor creation*
	|	`return` $\mathcal{V}$	*Set current token*
$\mathcal{R}$	::=		***Reduction Contexts***
		$\square$	*Hole*
	|	$\mathcal{F}(\mathcal{V},\ldots,\mathcal{V},\mathcal{R},\mathcal{E}\ldots,\mathcal{E})$	*Function application*
	|	$\mathcal{V};\mathcal{R}$	*Sequencing*
	|	$\mathcal{R};\mathcal{E}$	
	|	`if (` $\mathcal{R}$ `)` $\mathcal{E}$ `else` $\mathcal{E}$	*Conditional execution*
	|	`token` $\mathcal{T}$ `=` $\mathcal{V}$ `<-` $\mathcal{M}(\mathcal{V},\ldots,\mathcal{V},\mathcal{R},\mathcal{E},\ldots,\mathcal{E})$ `:waitfor(`$\mathcal{T},\ldots,\mathcal{T}$`)`	*Message send*
	|	`token` $\mathcal{T}$ `=` $\mathcal{R}$ `<-` $\mathcal{M}(\mathcal{E},\ldots,\mathcal{E})$ `:waitfor(`$\mathcal{T},\ldots,\mathcal{T}$`)`	
	|	`new` $\mathcal{B}(\mathcal{V},\ldots,\mathcal{V},\mathcal{R},\mathcal{E},\ldots,\mathcal{E})$	*Actor creation*
	|	`return` $\mathcal{R}$	*Set current token*
	|	$\mathcal{B}(\mathcal{V},\ldots,\mathcal{V}) : \mathcal{R} \downarrow_{\mathcal{T}}$	*Ready*
	|	$\mathcal{B}(\mathcal{V},\ldots,\mathcal{V},\mathcal{R},\mathcal{E}\ldots,\mathcal{E}) : \mathcal{E} \downarrow_{\mathcal{T}}$	

Figure 9.10
FS reducible expressions and reduction contexts.

The redex r denotes the next subexpression to evaluate. The reduction context R denotes the surrounding expression. R contains exactly one *hole* (by construction) at the location of the redex r. For example, the actor expression `new Ticker() <- tick()` can be decomposed into reduction context $\square$ `<- tick()` filled with redex `new Ticker()`. We denote this decomposition as:

`new Ticker() <- tick()` $=$ $\square$ `<- tick()` ▶ `new Ticker()` ◀.

We extend the notion of decomposition of actor expressions to actor states as follows:

Lemma 9.2 An actor state, e (in $\mathcal{S}$), is either ready, denoted $B(\bar{v})$, or otherwise it can be uniquely decomposed into a *reduction context*, R, filled with a *redex*, r, denoted as $e = \mathsf{R} \blacktriangleright \mathsf{r} \blacktriangleleft$.

For example, the actor state `B0(): new Ticker(0)<-tick();` $\downarrow_t$ can be decomposed into reduction context R_0 = `B0():`□`<-tick();` $\downarrow_t$ filled with redex r_0 = `new Ticker(0)`. We denote this decomposition as:

$$\texttt{B}_0\texttt{(): new Ticker(0)<-tick();}\ \downarrow_t\ = \texttt{B}_0\texttt{():}\square\texttt{<-tick();}\ \downarrow_t \blacktriangleright \texttt{new Ticker(0)} \blacktriangleleft,$$

or simply:

$$\texttt{B}_0\texttt{(): new Ticker(0)<-tick();}\ \downarrow_t\ = \mathsf{R}_0 \blacktriangleright \texttt{new Ticker(0)} \blacktriangleleft .$$

9.2.3.3 FS Reduction Rules

Redexes are of two kinds: *purely sequential redexes* and *actor redexes*. Figure 9.11 depicts standard reduction rules for purely sequential redexes. These include standard evaluation strategies including primitive operations, sequencing, and branching.

The transition rules depicted in figure 9.12 are of the form $\kappa_1 \xrightarrow{l} \kappa_2$ over actor configurations, where κ_1 is the initial configuration, κ_2 is the final configuration, and l is the transition label. There are five rules, all of which apply to an actor a, which we call *in focus*: the first one, labeled [**seq**] specifies internal sequential progress within the actor. The other four rules specify creation of actors, and communication and synchronization with other actors, and apply respectively to actor redexes `new B(v̄)`, `token t = a' <- m(v̄):waitfor(t̄)`, `return v`, and to an actor ready with state `B(v̄)`.

The rule labeled [**new**] specifies actor creation, which applies when the focus actor a's redex is `new B(v̄)`: actor a creates a new actor a'. The state of a' is set to `B(v̄)`, an actor ready to receive messages. The actor a's redex is replaced by the new actor's name `a'`. a' must be *fresh*, that is, $a' \notin dom(\alpha) \cup \{a\}$, which is denoted as a precondition for the rule to apply.

The rule labeled [**snd**] specifies asynchronous message sending, which applies when the focus actor a's redex is `token t = a' <- m(v̄):waitfor(t̄)`: actor a sends a message containing value $m(\bar{v})$ to its acquaintance a'. This message can be received by a' only when synchronization tokens $\bar{t}$ and tokens in the message arguments $\bar{v}$ have been resolved. Furthermore, when the message m is processed,

$$\begin{array}{rcll} f(v_1,\ldots,v_n) & \rightarrow_s & v & \text{if } f \in \mathcal{F}, v = [\![f]\!](v_1,\ldots,v_n) \\ \texttt{v;e} & \rightarrow_s & \texttt{e} & \\ \texttt{if (true) e else \_} & \rightarrow_s & \texttt{e} & \\ \texttt{if (false) \_ else e} & \rightarrow_s & \texttt{e} & \end{array}$$

Figure 9.11
FS reduction rules for sequential computation.

$$\frac{\texttt{e} \rightarrow_s \texttt{e}'}{\alpha, [\mathsf{R} \blacktriangleright \texttt{e} \blacktriangleleft]_a \parallel \mu \parallel \beta \xrightarrow{[\text{seq}]} \alpha, [\mathsf{R} \blacktriangleright \texttt{e}' \blacktriangleleft]_a \parallel \mu \parallel \beta}$$

$$\frac{\text{fresh } \texttt{a}' \qquad a' \in \mathcal{X}}{\alpha, [\mathsf{R} \blacktriangleright \texttt{new B}(\bar{\texttt{v}}) \blacktriangleleft]_a \parallel \mu \parallel \beta \xrightarrow{[\text{new}]} \alpha, [\mathsf{R} \blacktriangleright \texttt{a}' \blacktriangleleft]_a, [\texttt{B}(\bar{\texttt{v}})]_{a'} \parallel \mu \parallel \beta}$$

$$\frac{\text{fresh } \texttt{t}' \qquad t' \in \mathcal{T}}{\begin{array}{l}\alpha, [\mathsf{R} \blacktriangleright \texttt{token t = a' <- m}(\bar{\texttt{v}})\texttt{:waitfor}(\bar{\texttt{t}}) \blacktriangleleft]_a \parallel \mu \parallel \beta \\ \xrightarrow{[\text{snd}]} \quad \alpha, [\mathsf{R}\{t'/t\} \blacktriangleright \texttt{null} \blacktriangleleft]_a \parallel \mu \uplus \{\langle(\bar{t}) : a' \Leftarrow m(\bar{v}) \uparrow^{t'}\rangle\} \parallel \beta\end{array}}$$

$$\alpha, [\texttt{B}(\bar{\texttt{v}}) : \mathsf{R} \blacktriangleright \texttt{return v} \blacktriangleleft \downarrow_t]_a \parallel \mu \parallel \beta \xrightarrow{[\text{ret}]} \alpha, [\texttt{B}(\bar{\texttt{v}})]_a \parallel \mu\{v/t\} \parallel \beta$$

$$\frac{\begin{array}{c}\beta(B, m) = \texttt{B}' \ \texttt{m}(\bar{\texttt{B}} \ \bar{\texttt{x}})\{\bar{\texttt{f}} = \bar{\texttt{e}};\ \bar{\texttt{e}}';\} \\ \forall v \in \bar{v}' \cup \bar{v}'' : v \notin \mathcal{T}\end{array}}{\begin{array}{l}\alpha, [\texttt{B}(\bar{\texttt{v}})]_a \parallel \{\langle(\bar{v}'') : a \Leftarrow m(\bar{v}') \uparrow^{t}\rangle\} \uplus \mu \parallel \beta \\ \xrightarrow{[\text{rcv}]} \quad \alpha, [(\texttt{B}(\bar{\texttt{e}}):\bar{\texttt{e}}')\{(\bar{\texttt{v}}, \bar{\texttt{v}}', \texttt{a})/(\bar{\texttt{f}}, \bar{\texttt{x}}, \texttt{self})\} \downarrow_t]_a \parallel \mu \parallel \beta\end{array}}$$

Figure 9.12
FS operational semantics.

token t' should be set to the message handler's returned value. Actor a continues execution replacing occurrences of t for t', and the network μ is extended with the new message $\langle(\bar{t}) : a' \Leftarrow m(\bar{v}) \uparrow^{t'}\rangle$.[2] We use "fresh t'" to denote the creation of a token name that is new, so that it cannot possibly conflict with previously created tokens using the same name, t.

The rule labeled **[ret]** specifies end of message processing, which applies when the focus actor a's redex is `return v`: It sets the corresponding token t to value v, and makes the actor ready to receive new messages. Notice that the substitution $\{v/t\}$ applies to the network μ, i.e., it is applied to all the messages in the multiset of messages. Also the reduction context R is discarded.

Last, the rule labeled **[rcv]** specifies message reception, which applies when the focus actor a's state is $\texttt{B}(\bar{\texttt{v}})$, and there is a message in μ directed to a, e.g., $\langle(\bar{v}'') : a \Leftarrow m(\bar{v}') \uparrow^{t}\rangle$. The actor's behavior B must have a message handler named m with formal arguments $\bar{x}$ that updates the actor's state to $\bar{e}$ and proceeds with actor expression $\bar{e}'$. Furthermore, this rule can trigger only when all the tokens in $\bar{v}''$ and any tokens in $\bar{v}'$, the message arguments, have been resolved. The actor a's new state becomes $(\texttt{B}(\bar{\texttt{e}}):\bar{\texttt{e}}')\{(\bar{\texttt{v}}, \bar{\texttt{v}}', \texttt{a})/(\bar{\texttt{f}}, \bar{\texttt{x}}, \texttt{self})\} \downarrow_t$, that is, its message handler m is executed notifying completion by setting token t. The substitution of variables allows access to the previous state $\bar{v}$ by using the field names $\bar{f}$, replaces formal arguments $\bar{x}$ with actual arguments $\bar{v}'$, and references to `self` are replaced with the actor's name a.

9.2.4 Linguistic Abstractions: From SALSA to FS

We proceed to describe how SALSA's main linguistic abstractions (from section 9.1) are converted to FS code. This strategy allows us to formalize the SALSA language abstractions by translation to the simpler core FS language. We show how to translate token-passing continuations, first-class continuations, and join blocks.

9.2.4.1 Token-Passing Continuations

Token-passing continuations enable synchronization between actors a_1 and a_2 by delaying the processing of a message m_2 in actor a_2 after a_1 has completed processing message m_1. For example, the code

```
a1 <- m1()@
a2 <- m2(token);
```

guarantees that when m_2 is processed, m_1 has completed execution. The `token`—representing the returned value in the m_1 message handler—is the "proof" that m_1 has completed, and in this case, is passed to m_2 as an argument.

We can convert the SALSA token-passing continuation code into the following equivalent FS code:

```
token t1 = a1 <- m1();
token t2 = a2 <- m2(t1);
```

whose computation was illustrated in section 9.2.1.3.

This translation from SALSA to FS eliminates the need for `@` syntax and eliminates the need for `token` as a keyword in the message arguments, which simplifies FS. The translation uses only *named tokens* (e.g., t_1 and t_2) and a uniform syntax for message sending.

Let us consider one more SALSA token-passing continuation example:

```
hello()@
world();
```

This is translated into the following FS code:

```
token t1 = self <- hello();
token t2 = self <- world():waitfor(t1);
```

In this second example, the token-passing continuation is used for synchronization, i.e., `hello()` should finish processing before `world()` is received, but no (token) value is passed as an explicit argument. The partial message generated by the `world()` message sending statement, assuming that it is being executed by an actor named a is denoted as follows: $\langle (t_1) : a \Leftarrow world() \uparrow^{t_2} \rangle$, specifying that the token t_1 must be set before the message `world()` can be received by actor a. Furthermore, when actor a finishes processing the `world()` message, any occurrences of token t_2 in the network will be set to the returned value of `world()`.

9.2.4.2 *First-Class Continuations*

First-class continuations enable a message to delegate returning a value (to set pending tokens) to another actor's message. For example, `b <- m2() @ currentContinuation;` executed in actor `a`'s `m1` message handler means that the return value of `m1` will be produced by `b`'s `m2` message handler, which should then have a compatible return type with `m1`. This is illustrated by the code

```
behavior A{ ...
  int m1(){
     b <- m2() @
       currentContinuation;
  }
}

behavior B{ ...
  int m2(){ return 1; }
}
```

which allows the "client" code

```
token t = a<-m1(); c<-m3(t); ...
```

to behave just like

```
token t = b<-m2(); c<-m3(t); ...
```

would, where any appearances of token t will be set to a value only after actor b has finished processing message m_2.

To obtain the desired semantics of first-class continuations, we convert the SALSA first-class continuation code

```
b <- m2()@
currentContinuation;
```

into the following equivalent FS code:

```
token t' = b <- m2();
return t';
```

This translation from SALSA to FS eliminates the need for `currentContinuation` as a keyword in the language, and instead it uses *named tokens* (e.g., t') and a uniform syntax for message sending and returning values.

Let us illustrate our example following the operational semantics:

$$\alpha, [\texttt{A()}]_a, [\texttt{D() : token t} = \texttt{a<-m}_1\texttt{(); token t}_2 = \texttt{c<-m}_3\texttt{(t);}]_d \parallel \emptyset$$

$$\xrightarrow{[snd]} \xrightarrow{[seq]} \xrightarrow{[snd]} \alpha', [\texttt{A()}]_a \parallel \{\langle() : a \Leftarrow m_1() \uparrow^t\rangle, \langle() : c \Leftarrow m_3(t) \uparrow^{t_2}\rangle\}$$

$$\xrightarrow{[rcv]} \alpha', [\texttt{A() : token t}' = \texttt{b<-m}_2\texttt{(); return t}'\texttt{;} \downarrow_t]_a \parallel \{\langle() : c \Leftarrow m_3(t) \uparrow^{t_2}\rangle\}$$

$$\xrightarrow{[snd]} \xrightarrow{[seq]}$$

$$\alpha', [\texttt{A() : return t'};\ \downarrow_t]_a \parallel \{\langle() : c \Leftarrow m_3(t) \uparrow^{t_2}\rangle, \langle() : b \Leftarrow m_2() \uparrow^{t'}\rangle\}$$

$$\xrightarrow{[ret]} \alpha', [\texttt{A()}]_a \parallel \{\langle() : c \Leftarrow m_3(t) \uparrow^{t_2}\rangle, \langle() : b \Leftarrow m_2() \uparrow^{t'}\rangle\}\{t'/t\}$$

$$= \alpha', [\texttt{A()}]_a \parallel \{\langle() : c \Leftarrow m_3(t') \uparrow^{t_2}\rangle, \langle() : b \Leftarrow m_2() \uparrow^{t'}\rangle\},$$

where it becomes clear that actor c's message m_3 cannot be received until actor b has finished processing message m_2 as desired.

9.2.4.3 *Join Blocks*

Join blocks enable a barrier synchronization between actors $a_1, a_2, \ldots, a_n$ and an actor a by delaying the processing of a message m in actor a after $a_1, \ldots, a_n$ have completed processing their messages $m_1, \ldots, m_n$. For example, the code

```
join {a1 <- m1(); a2 <- m2();...; an <- mn();}@
a <- m(token);
```

guarantees that when m is processed, $m_1, \ldots, m_n$ have completed execution. The `token`—representing an array of the returned values in the $m_1, \ldots, m_n$ message handlers—is the "proof" that $m_1, \ldots, m_n$ have completed, and in this case, is passed to m as an argument.

To obtain the semantics of SALSA join blocks, we use the following translation into FS:

```
new JoinDirector([a1,...,an],[m1,...,mn],a,m)  <- act();
```

We create a special actor with the `JoinDirector` behavior, for which pseudocode is shown in figure 9.13. The join director's job is to send all the messages inside the join block and collect all the tokens as they come asynchronously from the actors participating in the barrier synchronization abstraction. Once all n tokens have been set, the join director notifies the customer of the join block by sending it an array with the collected tokens. An example of this protocol is illustrated in the diagram in figure 9.14. The full code for the `JoinDirector` behavior also considers synchronization tokens in message arguments and `waitfor` message properties.

```
behavior JoinDirector{
  Actor[] as;     // actors inside join block
  Message[] ms;  // and corresponding messages
  Actor c;        // customer actor
  Message cm;     // and corresponding message
  Object[] ts;   // tokens to send to customer
  int res;        // results received so far

  JoinDirector(Actor[] as, Message[] ms, Actor c, Message cm){
    this.as = as; this.ms = ms; this.c = c; this.cm = cm;
    this.ts = new Object[as.size];
    this.res = 0;
  }

  // send messages to all actors in join block with
  // a continuation to acknowledge completion to JD.
  void act(){
    for(int i=0; i<as.size; i++){
      token ti = as[i] <- ms[i]();
      self <- ack(i,ti);
    }
  }

  // receive acknowledgement of completion from each actor
  // accumulate tokens and notify customer on completion
  void ack(int i, Object ti){
    ts[i] = ti;
    res = res + 1;
    if (res == as.size)
      c <- cm(ts);
  }
}
```

Figure 9.13
`JoinDirector` behavior used in translation of SALSA join blocks.

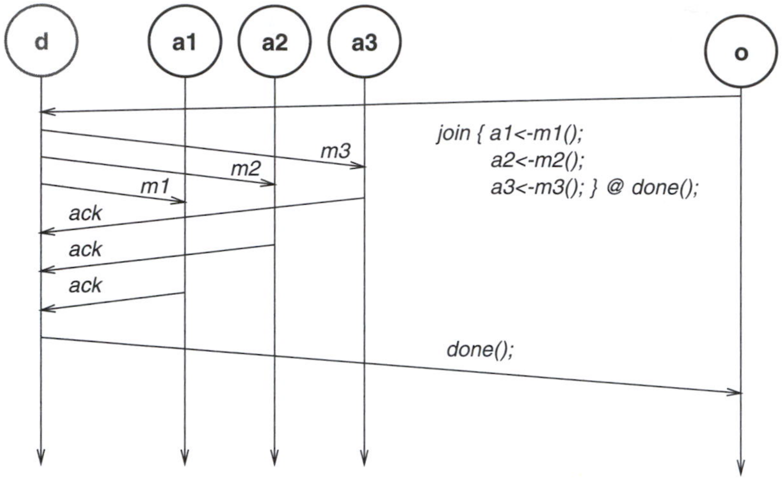

Figure 9.14
Example of join continuation protocol.

9.2.4.4 Summary

Figure 9.15 summarizes the translation of the main SALSA linguistic abstractions into FS. It is assumed that tokens `t`, t_1, t_2 and behavior `JoinDirector` are *fresh*, that is, they do not collide with any existing names.

9.2.5 Operational Semantics of Distribution and Mobility

To model distributed and mobile computing, we introduce Mobile FeatherWeight SALSA (MFS), an extension of FS to incorporate the notion of universal actor names, universal actor locations or sites, actor distribution, and actor mobility.

9.2.5.1 MFS Syntax

The syntax of MFS is extended from FS's syntax in figure 9.8 as shown in figure 9.16. We add a new `nn` atom to denote *"no name,"* an atom representing the name of anonymous actors, i.e., universal actors created with no name. We add special variable names `name` and `here` for a universal actor to obtain its own name and current location. We add a special `migrate` message name to enable universal actor migration. We add sets $\mathcal{U}$ and $\mathcal{L}$, to represent universal actor names and locations respectively, which are also values. Like in FS, it is assumed that all the sets that form values are pairwise disjoint. Finally, we modify actor expressions in two ways. First, we modify the actor expression to create a new actor, so that it also receives a universal actor name and location, and second, we add a new expression `reference u` to obtain an actor's name (or reference) from its universal actor name. The previous

Token-passing continuations

```
a1 <- m1() @ a2 <- m2(token);
  ≜ token t1 = a1 <- m1(); token t2 = a2 <- m2(t1);
a1 <- m1() @ a2 <- m2();
  ≜ token t1 = a1 <- m1(); token t2 = a2 <- m2():waitfor(t1);
```

First-class continuations

```
a <- m() @ currentContinuation;
  ≜ token t = a <- m(); return t;
```

Join blocks

```
join {a1 <- m1(); a2 <- m2();...; an <- mn();} @ a <- m(token);
  ≜ new JoinDirector([a1,...,an],[m1,...,mn],a,m) <- act();
```

Figure 9.15
SALSA linguistic abstractions and FS translations.

FS syntax for actor creation becomes syntactic sugar for MFS universal anonymous actor creation in the same location as the creator:

$$\texttt{new B}(\bar{\texttt{v}}) \quad \triangleq \quad \texttt{new B}(\bar{\texttt{v}})\ \texttt{at (nn, here)}.$$

9.2.5.2 *MFS Operational Semantics*

We extend the actor configurations' actor map α from section 9.2.3 (figure 9.9), to include a name and a location for each actor as follows:

$$\alpha = \mathcal{D} \xrightarrow{f} \mathcal{S}@(\mathcal{U}, \mathcal{L}),$$

where $\alpha(a) = e@(n, s)$, if and only if e is actor a's current state and n and s represent the actor a's universal actor name and current site or location.

As a consequence of modifying the language expressions, we also need to modify the reducible expressions and reduction contexts from figure 9.10 as shown in figure 9.17.

Finally, we specify the operational semantics of MFS as shown in figure 9.18. There are five rules, all of which apply to an actor a named n at location s, which as previously we call *in focus*. The first rule subsumes concurrent (but not distributed or mobile) computation from FS (denoted by $\kappa_1 \xrightarrow{l}_{FS} \kappa_2$), and applies to internal

$\mathcal{A}$	=	{ `true`, `false`, `null`, nn, ...}	*Atoms*
$\mathcal{X}$	=	{ `self`, name, here, x, y, z, ...}	*Variables*
$\mathcal{M}$	=	{ `migrate`, m, n, o, ...}	*Message names*
$\mathcal{U}$	=	{ u, u_0, u_1, ...}	*Universal actor names*
$\mathcal{L}$	=	{ s, s_0, s_1, ...}	*Actor locations*
$\mathcal{V}$	::=	$\mathcal{A} \mid \mathcal{N} \mid \mathcal{X} \mid \mathcal{D} \mid \mathcal{T} \mid \mathcal{U} \mid \mathcal{L}$	***Values***
$\mathcal{E}$	::=	...	***Expressions***
	|	`new` $\mathcal{B}(\mathcal{E},\ldots,\mathcal{E})$ `at` $(\mathcal{U},\mathcal{L})$	*Universal actor creation*
	|	`reference` $\mathcal{U}$	*Get reference from UAN*

Figure 9.16
MFS language syntax.

$\mathcal{E}_r$	::=	...	***Redexes***
	|	`new` $\mathcal{B}(\mathcal{V},\ldots,\mathcal{V})$ `at` $(\mathcal{U},\mathcal{L})$	*Actor creation*
	|	`reference` $\mathcal{U}$	*Get reference*
$\mathcal{R}$	::=	...	***Reduction Contexts***
	|	`new` $\mathcal{B}(\mathcal{V},\ldots,\mathcal{V},\mathcal{R},\mathcal{E},\ldots,\mathcal{E})$ `at` $(\mathcal{U},\mathcal{L})$	*Actor creation*
	|	`reference` $\mathcal{R}$	*Get reference*

Figure 9.17
MFS redexes and reduction contexts.

sequential computation (labeled [**seq**]), message sending (labeled [**snd**]), and end of message processing (labeled [**ret**]), all of which are not affected by the actor's name and location. We modify two rules: the actor creation (labeled [**new**]) and the message reception (labeled [**rcv**]) rules. And we create two new rules: one for actor migration (labeled [**mig**]), and one for obtaining actor references from universal actor names (labeled [**ref**]).

The actor creation rule (labeled [**new**]) specifies universal actor creation with behavior `B(v̄)` named n' at location s'. The actor map α is updated with a new actor a'. The new actor name, a', and the programmer-given universal actor name, n', must be *fresh*, i.e., $\forall a_i \in dom(\alpha) \cup \{a\} : ((a' \neq a_i) \wedge ((n' = \mathrm{nn}) \vee (\alpha(a_i) = e_i \downarrow_{t_i} @(n_i, s_i) \implies n' \neq n_i)))$. Anonymous actors use nn to denote that they have no name. Furthermore, the location s' must be valid, i.e., $s' \in \mathcal{L}$. In the creating actor (the actor in focus), the redex gets replaced by the new actor name, a'.

The actor migration rule (labeled [**mig**]) specifies actor migration from location s to location s'. It is activated when the actor in focus is ready with behavior `B(v̄)` and

$$\frac{\alpha, [\mathtt{e}]_a \parallel \mu \parallel \beta \xrightarrow{l}_{FS} \alpha, [\mathtt{e'}]_a \parallel \mu' \parallel \beta \qquad l \in \{[\mathrm{seq}], [\mathrm{snd}], [\mathrm{ret}]\}}{\alpha, [\mathtt{e}@(n,s)]_a \parallel \mu \parallel \beta \xrightarrow{l} \alpha, [\mathtt{e'}@(n,s)]_a \parallel \mu' \parallel \beta}$$

$$\frac{a', n' : \mathit{fresh} \qquad s' \in \mathcal{L}}{\alpha, [\mathsf{R} \blacktriangleright \mathtt{new\ B(\bar{v})\ at\ (n',s')} \blacktriangleleft @(n,s)]_a \parallel \mu \parallel \beta \xrightarrow{[\mathrm{new}]} \alpha, [\mathsf{R} \blacktriangleright \mathtt{a'} \blacktriangleleft @(n,s)]_a, [\mathtt{B(\bar{v})}@(n',s')]_{a'} \parallel \mu \parallel \beta}$$

$$\frac{\forall v \in \bar{v}' : v \notin \mathcal{T} \qquad s' \in \mathcal{L}}{\alpha, [\mathtt{B(\bar{v})}@(n,s)]_a \parallel \{\langle(\bar{v}') : a \Leftarrow \mathit{migrate}(s') \uparrow^t\rangle\} \uplus \mu \parallel \beta \xrightarrow{[\mathrm{mig}]} \alpha, [\mathtt{B(\bar{v})}@(n,s')]_a \parallel \mu\{\mathtt{null}/t\} \parallel \beta}$$

$$\alpha, [\mathsf{R} \blacktriangleright \mathtt{reference\ n'} \blacktriangleleft @(n,s)]_a, [\mathtt{e}@(n',s')]_{a'} \parallel \mu \parallel \beta \xrightarrow{[\mathrm{ref}]} \alpha, [\mathsf{R} \blacktriangleright \mathtt{a'} \blacktriangleleft @(n,s)]_a, [\mathtt{e}@(n',s')]_{a'} \parallel \mu \parallel \beta$$

$$\frac{\beta(B,m) = \mathtt{B'\ m(\bar{B}\ \bar{x})\{\bar{f} = \bar{e};\ \bar{e}';\}} \qquad \forall v \in \bar{v}' \cup \bar{v}'' : v \notin \mathcal{T} \qquad \theta = \mathtt{\{(\bar{v},\bar{v}',a,n,s)/(\bar{f},\bar{x},self,name,here)\}}}{\alpha, [\mathtt{B(\bar{v})}@(n,s)]_a \parallel \{\langle(\bar{v}'') : a \Leftarrow m(\bar{v}') \uparrow^t\rangle\} \uplus \mu \parallel \beta \xrightarrow{[\mathrm{rcv}]} \alpha, [(\mathtt{B(\bar{e})} : \mathtt{\bar{e}'})\theta \downarrow_t @(n,s)]_a \parallel \mu \parallel \beta}$$

Figure 9.18
MFS operational semantics.

the network contains a full message $\langle(\bar{v}') : a \Leftarrow \mathit{migrate}(s') \uparrow^t\rangle$. The message is full when all its synchronization tokens have been resolved. Furthermore, the location s' must be valid. In the resulting configuration, actor a is ready with the same behavior and name, but it is at the new location s'. Additionally, the token t has been resolved in the network by setting it to `null`, signaling completion of the migration process.

The rule to get references to actors from their universal actor names is labeled [ref]. It applies when the redex of the actor in focus is `reference n'` and the actor map contains an actor a' whose universal actor name is n'. The redex of the actor in focus becomes the actor reference (or name) `a'`, which can be used to send messages to the actor.

The message reception rule (labeled [rcv]) specifies universal actor message reception, which is the same as in the FS language, except that the special variables referring to key words `name` and `here` are replaced by the universal actor's name n and its current location s. We use θ to represent the extended substitution.

9.2.5.3 Linguistic Abstractions: From SALSA to MFS

Any valid concurrent computation is also valid in the distributed and mobile context. In particular, sending and receiving messages is based on actor names, not on actor locations, which enables location-independent and migration-transparent communication. Therefore, all the translations of the SALSA linguistic abstractions to the concurrent FS language introduced in section 9.2.4 (summarized in figure 9.15) also apply to the distributed and mobile MFS language. The default translation of join blocks creates the join director as an anonymous actor in the same location as the actor executing the join block, which may not be the most efficient means of achieving multi-actor coordination in the context of distributed (and mobile) actors. Compiler and middleware optimizations may be used to locate the join director "closer" to the actors being coordinated or to the customer actors which depend on the join block synchronization token.

While in the MFS language, we use variables for universal actor names (UAN) for simplicity in specifying its operational semantics, in the SALSA implementation, we actually convert `String` representations of universal actor names into internal actor references. The intention is that UANs be human-readable and writable in business cards and documents, and stored in directories or indices, similarly to URLs in the web context. This facilitates creating references to universal actors and therefore promotes openness in worldwide computing. In MFS, we also use variables for locations or sites, while the SALSA implementation uses Internet domains (DNS names or IP addresses) and port numbers. These domain names and ports uniquely denote Internet hosts that are executing *theaters* or actor virtual machines (using the JVM), which are listening for incoming requests for creation, communication, and migration of universal actors.

9.2.6 Fairness

The fairness requirement on valid SALSA program computation sequences and paths follows the exact form as the one presented in the context of the AMST language in section 4.2.4.

SALSA programming language implementations must satisfy *fairness* to properly follow the language semantics. This can generally be accomplished in one of two ways: If an actor is implemented as a thread, the underlying thread scheduling system must be fair. If multiple actors share a thread, both the actor scheduling system and the underlying thread scheduling system must then ensure fairness.

9.3 SALSA Programming Patterns

Activities in actor systems happen in response to messages. These activities are typically independent from each other and can happen concurrently and in any order.

Causality conditions constrain these otherwise independent activities to occur in a partial order. Actor systems have only two causality conditions:

- *Actor creation* If activity p in actor a preceeds the creation of actor b, then activity p must preceed every activity q in actor b.
- *Message sending* If activity q in actor b happens in response to a message m from actor a, then all activities that preceed the message sending from a also must preceed q.

Asynchronous messaging and state encapsulation are important properties for systems modularity: they enable easier distribution and dynamic reconfiguration of software subcomponents, which in turn promote scalability and fault tolerance. However, programming only with pure asynchronous messaging is very low level and prone to error.

In the SALSA programming language, there are higher level coordination constructs that enable building more complex interaction patterns, without sacrificing modularity. We present these language abstractions in the following sections.

9.3.1 Token-passing Continuations and Named Tokens

Continuations have been used in functional programming languages as a way to tell a function how to proceed after the function is computed. For example, there may be a *success* continuation specifying how to continue the computation if no errors are encountered and a *failure* continuation specifying how to handle anomalies, such as division by zero.

Token-passing continuations in SALSA also enable to establish causality conditions among otherwise independent activities. Since actor messages in SALSA are modeled as potential method invocations, it is natural to want to use the result of invoking a method, even if this invocation will happen asynchronously and in the future. We call the result of a future message invocation, a *token*, and we allow the use of the token only as an argument to future messages.

Consider, for example, the code

```
checking <- getBalance()@
savings <- transfer(checking, token);
```

In this example, we send a `getBalance` message to a `checking` account actor, and we specify the continuation as sending the message `transfer` to the `savings` account actor with two parameters: first, the `checking` account actor name, and second, the `token` that represents the return value of the `getBalance` message to the checking account actor.

This example, could also have been written as

```
token balance = checking <- getBalance();
savings <- transfer(checking, balance);
```

Named tokens enable arbitrary data-flow computations to be specified. For example, consider the following code:

```
token t1 = a1 <- m1();
token t2 = a2 <- m2();
token t3 = a3 <- m3( t1 );
token t4 = a4 <- m4( t2 );
a <- m(t1,t2,t3,t4);
```

Actor `a`'s processing of message `m` will be delayed until messages `m1,...,m4` have been processed. `m4` can proceed concurrently with `m1` and `m3`. `m3` can also proceed concurrently with `m2` and `m4`, but `m3` can happen only after `m1` has been processed and likewise, `m4` can happen only after `m2` has been processed (see figure 9.19).

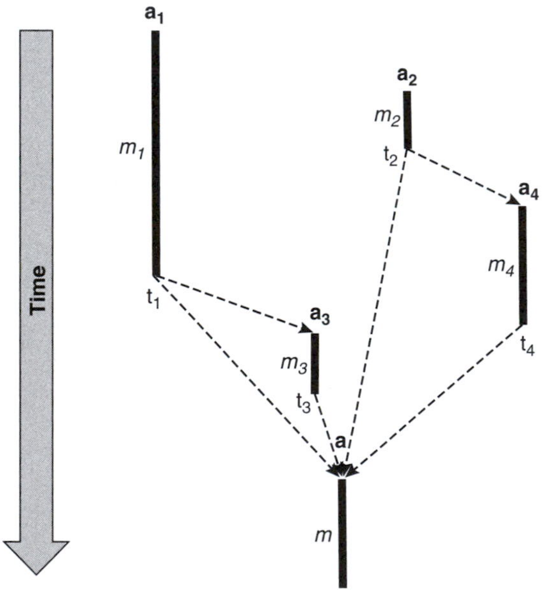

Figure 9.19
Message dependencies according to named tokens. Thick vertical lines denote messages processed by actors. Dashed lines are causal connections entailed by passed tokens.

9.3.2 Join Continuations

Join blocks in SALSA enable to program *rendezvouz*-like interaction patterns. Several independent activities are barrier-synchronized so that only after all of them have finished execution does a given join continuation become enabled.

For example, consider the following code:

```
Searcher[] actors = { searcher0, searcher1, searcher2 };
join {
  for (int i=0; i < actors.length; i++){
    actors[i] <- find( phrase );
  }
} @ customer <- output( token );
```

This code sends the `find( phrase )` message to each actor in the `actors` array and after all the searcher actors have processed their respective messages, the `output` message is sent to the `customer` actor. The set of individual results (or `tokens`) is combined as a single array of tokens and sent as an argument to the `output` message.

9.3.3 Delegation through First-Class Continuations

First-class continuations enable actors to delegate computation to a third party independently of the current processing context. For example, consider the following code fragment:

```
behavior A{
  int m(...){
    b <- n(...) @ currentContinuation;
  }
  ...
}
```

An instance `a` of this behavior `A`, when processing message `m` asks (delegates) actor `b` to respond to this message `m` on its behalf by processing its message `n`. In this example, actor `b`'s message handler for `n` should return a value of type `int`.

Let us consider an example:

```
behavior Calculator {

  int fib(int n) {
    Fibonacci f = new Fibonacci();
    f <- compute(n) @ currentContinuation;
  }
```

```
  int add(int n1, int n2) {return n1+n2;}

  void act(String args[]) {
    fib(15) @
      standardOutput <- println(token);
    fib(5) @ add(token,3) @
      standardOutput <- println(token);
  }
}
```

The `Calculator` behavior delegates the computation of Fibonacci numbers (`fib`) to a newly created `Fibonacci` actor. In response to the `act` message, the calculator actor sends itself two messages. The first one requests the calculation of `fib(15)` with the continuation specified as printing the result to standard output. The second request (`fib(5)`) specifies a different continuation: to add the result to the number `3` by sending itself an `add` message with the token (result of `fib(5)`) and the number `3` as arguments, and then send the result to the `standardOutput` actor for printing.

The `Fibonacci` behavior could be encoded as follows:

```
behavior Fibonacci {

  int compute(int n) {
    if (n == 0) return 0;
    else if (n <= 2) return 1;
    else {
      Fibonacci fib = new Fibonacci();
      Calculator calc = new Calculator();
      token x = fib <- compute(n-1);
      compute(n-2) @
        calc <- add(x,token) @
          currentContinuation;
    }
  }

}
```

Notice that the `Fibonacci` behavior creates two helper actors to perform the computation: an actor with the `Fibonacci` behavior to compute `fib(n-1)` and an actor with the `Calculator` behavior to compute the addition of `fib(n-1)` (produced by the helper actor) and `fib(n-2)` (produced by itself). Notice how the `currentContinuation` keyword enables passing the current continuation, which is different at the top level and at each recursive step.

9.4 Common Examples

9.4.1 Reference Cell in SALSA

A reference cell in SALSA can be written as follows:

```
behavior Cell{
  Object content;
  Cell(Object c){
    content = c;
  }
  Object get(){
    return content;
  }
  void set(Object c){
    content = c;
  }
}
```

The SALSA cell client code can be written as follows:

```
Cell c = new Cell("hello");
c <- get() @
  standardOutput <- print(token);
c <- set("world");
```

The return value of the `get` message (or `token`) will be passed as an argument to the `print` message sent to the `standardOutput` actor. Notice that since message processing is asynchronous, this code does not ensure that the `get` message will be received or processed before the `set` message. To do that, a token-passing continuation may be used for sequencing as follows:

```
Cell c = new Cell("hello");
c <- get() @
  standardOutput <- print(token) @
  c <- set("world");
```

In this case, the `set` message will only be processed after the `print` message is finished. However, these two messages should be able to execute concurrently, so another version of the code follows:

```
Cell c = new Cell("hello");
token t = c <- get() @
  c <- set("world");
standardOutput <- print(t);
```

In this new version of the code, completion of the `get` message will set the token `t` to its return value. The `set` message will wait until token `t` has been resolved (because of the `@` syntax.) Furthermore, the `print` message will also wait for the completion of `get` due to the causality imposed by its argument, token `t`. As desired, there is no causality between messages `set` and `print` anymore.

9.4.2 Mutual Exclusion in SALSA

Two actors can mutually exclude themselves from accesing a shared resource concurrently, i.e., they can ensure that only one of them is using the resource at a given point in time, by using a *semaphore* as follows:

```
behavior Semaphore {

  UniversalActor holder = null;

  boolean get(UniversalActor holder){
    if (this.holder == null){
      this.holder = holder;
      return true;
    } else return false;
   }

  void release() { this.holder = null; }
}
```

The semaphore contains a state that represents who currently holds access to the shared resource, or `null` if the resource is available. The semaphore replies `true` to the customer requesting access if allowed, and `false` otherwise.

A customer that keeps trying to get access to the shared resource may be encoded as follows:

```
behavior Customer {

  Semaphore sem;

  Customer(Semaphore sem){
    this.sem = sem;
  }
```

```
  void go(){
    sem <- get(self) @
      use(token);
  }

  void use(boolean ok){
    if (ok) {
      join {
        ... // critical code section
      } @ sem <- release();
    }
    else { go(); }
  }
}
```

Two customer actors `c1` and `c2` that mutually exclude each other during the critical code sections, can be written as

```
Semaphore s = new Semaphore();
Customer c1 = new Customer(s);
Customer c2 = new Customer(s);

c1<-go();
c2<-go();
```

Clearly, the example could be enhanced so that an actor is notified when the resource becomes available, instead of busy-waiting as coded above (see exercise 3).

9.4.3 Dining Philosophers in SALSA

The famous dining philosopher example can be encoded in SALSA as shown in figure 9.20.

The philosopher first attempts to get the left chopstick, then the right chopstick, then eats, and releases the chopsticks. If it fails to obtain a chopstick, it keeps trying. The chopstick can be encoded as follows:

```
behavior Chopstick extends Semaphore{}.
```

It is possible to encode the chopstick so that it keeps track of a waiting philosopher if it is not available, and so that it notifies the waiting philosopher when it becomes available. It is also possible to encode the dining philosophers in such a way that they do not deadlock (all picking up the left chopstick and waiting forever for the right one to become available.) These are left as exercises for the reader (see exercises 3 and 4).

```
behavior Philosopher{

  Chopstick left, right;

  Philosopher(Chopstick left, Chopstick right){
    this.left = left; this.right = right;
  }

  boolean pickLeft(){
    left <- get(self) @ currentContinuation;
  }

  boolean pickRight(){
    right <- get(self) @ currentContinuation;
  }

  void eat(){
    pickLeft() @
    gotLeft(token);
  }

  void gotLeft(boolean leftOk){
    if (leftOk) {
      pickRight() @
      gotRight(token);
    } else
      eat();
  }

  void gotRight(boolean rightOk){
    if (rightOk) {
      join {
        standardOutput <- println ("eating...");
        left <- release();
        right <- release();
      } @ standardOutput <- println ("thinking...") @
      eat();
    } else
      gotLeft(true);
  }

}
```

Figure 9.20
Dining philosophers in SALSA.

9.4.4 Mobile Reference Cell in SALSA

The code for a mobile reference cell in SALSA is almost identical to the code given in section 9.4.1. The ability to migrate is automatically inherited from the root `UniversalActor` behavior that all SALSA behaviors extend. One important difference for actors that are meant to provide a *service*, is that they should implement the `ActorService` interface. This empty interface simply tells the SALSA run-time system not to garbage collect actors with this behavior.

```
behavior Cell implements ActorService{
  Object content;

  Cell(Object initialContent) {
    content = initialContent;
  }

  Object get() {
    standardOutput <- println ("Returning:"+content);
    return content;
  }

  void set(Object newContent) {
    standardOutput <- println ("Setting:"+newContent);
    content = newContent;
  }
}
```

The `standardOutput` actor refers to the standard output stream in the actor's *current* location. Therefore, as the `Cell` actors migrate, the messages get printed in different hosting environments.

The following code illustrates how to create a cell, migrate it to a different hosting environment, and access it there:

```
behavior MovingCellTester {

  void act( String[] args ) {
    if (args.length != 3){
      standardError <- println("Usage:
        salsa MovingCellTester <UAN> <Host1> <Host2>");
      return;
    }
```

```
    Cell c = new Cell("Hello") at (args[0], args[1]);

    standardOutput <- print( "Initial Value:" ) @
    c <- get() @ standardOutput <- println( token ) @
    c <- set("World") @
    standardOutput <- print( "New Value:" ) @
    c <- get() @ standardOutput <- println( token ) @
    c <- migrate(args[2]) @
    c <- set("New World") @
    standardOutput <- print( "New Value at New Location:" ) @
    c <- get() @ standardOutput <- println( token );
  }
}
```

9.5 Discussion and Further Reading

The SALSA programming language (Varela and Agha, 2001) is the result of studying how to introduce a well-founded model of concurrency, the actor model, to an object-oriented programming audience. SALSA's run-time system is the result of studying how to develop worldwide computing systems using distributed and mobile actors over the Internet. SALSA was created by Carlos Varela and Gul Agha between 1998 and 2001 (Varela, 1998; Varela and Agha, 1998, 2001; Varela, 2001).

The operational semantics of SALSA in chapter 9 has followed closely the structure of chapter 4. The key difference is the use of a sequential non-shared-memory subset of Java for modeling individual actor computation instead of the call-by-value λ calculus. We have abstracted over many details in the full SALSA language, inherited from Java, including syntax and semantics for arrays, interfaces, inheritance, typing, and polymorphism. We have also skipped discussion on nonessential message properties and mobile actor garbage collection. We refer the reader to Varela et al. (2007) for a more detailed explanation of the language's capabilities and more thorough examples.

The SALSA programming language and framework have enabled research on several distributed computing areas. We refer interested readers to related publications on advanced topics, including decentralized naming services (Tolman and Varela, 2005), distributed systems visualization (Desell et al., 2004), adaptive systems through dynamic reconfiguration (Desell et al., 2004; Maghraoui et al., 2006), distributed and mobile garbage collection (Wang and Varela, 2006), applications malleability (Desell et al., 2006; Maghraoui et al., 2007; Desell et al., 2007), and fault-tolerant distributed computing (Field and Varela, 2005; Boodman, 2008). SALSA has also been used as a basis for developing applications in computational physics and astronomy (Wang et al., 2006; Desell et al., 2007, 2008a,b; Cole et al., 2008).

A number of libraries have been created—for example, Kilim (Srinivasan and Mycroft, 2008), Scala (Haller and Odersky, 2007), ProActive (Caromel et al., 2004), Actor Foundry (Astley, 1999), and Actalk (Briot, 1989)—for the development of actor systems. However, there are several advantages of using an actor programming language instead of an actor library:

- Certain semantic properties can be guaranteed at the language level. For example, an important property of an actor is that it provides complete encapsulation of data and processing. Ensuring that multiple threads are not actively mutating shared state is useful in guaranteeing safe and efficient actor migration. Another important semantic property is that an actor should never block: that is a key difference between SALSA *tokens* and other synchronization approaches, such as ProActive *futures*.
- By generating code from applications written in an actor language, it is possible to ensure that proper interfaces are always used to create and communicate with actors. In other words, programmers cannot incorrectly use the host language which has been used to build the actor library. For example, in SALSA (as opposed to in library approaches like Scala's) it is not possible to synchronously invoke methods on actors, which breaks state encapsulation.
- Finally, using an actor language improves the readability of programs developed. Writing actor programs using a library often involves using constructs of the defining language to encode actor operations. For example, one may use method invocation to perform actor creation, or message sending. It is unnatural for programmers to continually relate the actor semantics with the syntax of the defining language.

9.6 Exercises

1. Write an actor behavior in SALSA that computes the product of numbers in the leaves of a binary tree (see e.g., *treeprod(t)* in section 4.1.1.) Your program should compute the product concurrently and use a join continuation.
2. Model a concurrent computation in FeatherWeight SALSA that creates a `Ticker` actor (see figure 9.7 for its implementation) and sends it two messages: a `tick()` message and a `time()` message.

- What value is returned by the `time()` message?
- Is a value *always* returned?[3]

3. Modify the *mutual exclusion* example in SALSA (see section 9.4.2) so that it does *not* use busy-waiting. Instead of continuously asking, the semaphore customer gets notified when the resource becomes available.

4. Modify the *dining philosophers* example in SALSA (see section 9.4.3) so that philosophers cannot deadlock.
5. How would you implement token-passing continuations in terms of actor creation and message passing?
6. How would you implement join blocks in terms of actor creation and message passing?
7. How would you implement first-class continuations in terms of actor creation and message passing?
8. The join director behavior illustrated in figure 9.13 does not contact the customer actor until it has received all the results from its coordinated actors. Modify the `JoinDirector` definition to tolerate non-Byzantine failures as follows:
(a) the customer actor is notified once a *majority* of responses has been received.
(b) a *timeout* is used to notify the customer actor of partial results if not all results have arrived by the designated timeout.

9. Write a *distributed queue* abstract data type in SALSA.
10. Create a *dining nomad philosophers* example in SALSA. Philosophers eat in a *dining room* and think in a *thinking room*, assuming different rooms are in different sites.
11. Create a *mobile address book* behavior that keeps track of contacts (name, email, phone). Start it in a site, query it, update it, migrate it to another site, and query it and update it again.
12. Develop a *work stealing* framework in SALSA to distribute computations over the Internet.

Notes

1. We use $\alpha, [e]_a$ to denote the extended map α', which is the same as α except that it maps a to e, i.e., $\alpha'[a] = e \wedge \forall a' \neq a, \alpha'[a'] = \alpha[a']$. We use $\emptyset$ to denote empty maps and multisets.

2. We use $\uplus$ to denote multiset union.

3. Find out about *unbounded nondeterminism*, a property that distinguishes actor computation from other models of concurrent computation such as the π calculus and from more general models of computation such as Turing machines.

10 Programming with Join Patterns

Programming with *join patterns* as coordination abstractions can be accomplished in the JoCaml programming language (Fessant, 1998; Conchon and Fessant, 1999; Mandel and Maranget, 2008). Join patterns can also be used as abstractions in other high-level programming languages; for example, Cω is an extension of C# with join definitions. JoCaml is an extension of the Objective Caml language (Leroy et al., 2008), itself an object-oriented dialect of the ML functional programming language. JoCaml was developed to program concurrent and distributed systems using join calculus abstractions.

The most significant semantic differences between JoCaml and the join calculus presented in chapter 5 are the following:

- *Synchronous and asynchronous channels* While the join calculus exclusively models synchronous join pattern matching and asynchronous output of molecules, JoCaml supports the notion of *synchronous channels*, which are modeled as asynchronous communication channels with an implicit *continuation*, in the *continuation-passing style* of functional programming. A special `reply` primitive in join definitions and semicolon (`;`) in otherwise asynchronous message sending processes are used to create an implicit continuation and to send a value over it.
- *Pattern matching* The join calculus admits only a limited form of patterns, where *formal arguments* on join definitions get matched by *actual arguments* in molecule solutions using simple substitutions of names to names. JoCaml, being an extension of Objective Caml, inherits its extensive pattern matching capabilities. Join patterns therefore can use arbitrarily complex Objective Caml patterns in its join definitions. However, join patterns remain nondeterministic, while Objective Caml patterns are deterministic.
- *Distribution and mobility* JoCaml follows the distribution and mobility model of the distributed join calculus (Fournet et al., 1996). This includes the notion of a tree of locations with creation, migration, termination, and failure detection capabilities.

In section 10.1, we cover the syntax of JoCaml. Section 10.2 specifies the operational semantics of JoCaml. Section 10.3 covers programming idioms and patterns used in JoCaml programs. Section 10.4 goes over concurrent, distributed, and mobile programming examples in JoCaml. Sections 10.5 and 10.6 conclude with a discussion and exercises.

10.1 JoCaml Programming Language Syntax

10.1.1 Concurrent Systems Programming

A summary of the key join calculus primitives and the equivalent JoCaml programming language syntax is given in figure 10.1. A join calculus atom is a JoCaml expression resulting from spawning a process, using the `spawn` keyword. A molecule, or parallel composition of processes P and Q in the join calculus, is written as `p & q` in JoCaml. Join calculus definitions use join patterns that look like atom and molecule patterns in JoCaml, such as `x(u) & y(v)`. These definitions can be composed in JoCaml using the `or` operator (equivalent to using $\wedge$ in the join calculus.) JoCaml also supports an `and` operator for definitions of pairwise disjoint channel names.

For example, consider the join calculus expression from chapter 5:

def $ready\langle printer\rangle \mid job\langle file\rangle \triangleright printer\langle file\rangle$ in $ready\langle laser\rangle \mid job\langle f1\rangle$.

An equivalent JoCaml program is written as follows:

```
def ready(printer) & job(file) = printer(file) in
  spawn ready(laser) & job(f1)
```

JoCaml extends the primitive types of Objective Caml with an asynchronous channel type: `Join.chan`. JoCaml also inherits Objective Caml's operations on values of primitive types.

Figure 10.2 specifies JoCaml's core language syntax extensions to Objective Caml. *Expressions* are extended with process spawning. Process spawning as

Join Calculus	JoCaml	
$x\langle y\rangle$	`spawn x(y)`	Atom
$P \mid Q$	`p & q`	Molecule
def $x\langle u\rangle \mid y\langle v\rangle \triangleright P$ in Q	`def x(u) & y(v) = p in q`	Definition
$D_1 \wedge D_2$	`d1 or d2`	Multiset

Figure 10.1
Join calculus syntax and equivalent JoCaml syntax.

```
Expr         ::=                                  Expression
                   OExpression                    Objective Caml expression
               |   spawn Process                  Asynchronous execution
               |   JoinDef in Expr                Local channel definition

Process      ::=                                  Process
                   0                              Empty process
               |   Process & Process              Parallel composition
               |   Expr1 Expr2                    Asynchronous send
               |   Expr; Process                  Sequencing
               |   reply [Expr] to Id             Reply to synchronous send
               |   if Expr then Process           Conditional
                   [else Process]
               |   match Expr with                Pattern matching
                   (| OPattern [when Expr]
                     -> Process)+
               |   let [rec] OBinding             Local definition
                   (and OBinding)* in Process
               |   for Id = Expr                  Concurrent loop
                   (to | downto) Expr
                   do Process done
               |   JoinDef in Process             Local channel definition

JoinDef      ::=   def ReactionSet                Join Definition
                   (and ReactionSet)*
ReactionSet  ::=   Reaction (or Reaction)*
Reaction     ::=   JoinPattern = Process
JoinPattern  ::=   Channel (& Channel)*
Channel      ::=   Id (OPattern)
```

Figure 10.2
JoCaml programming language syntax.

an expression evaluates to `()` and executes the process given as an argument asynchronously. *Processes* are executed producing no result. The empty process and parallel composition are denoted `0` and `p & q` respectively. The expression `e1 e2` evaluates `e1` to an asynchronous channel and `e2` to a value and sends the value to the channel. The process `e; p` evaluates `e` first, then it executes `p`. The expression `e` must be of `unit` type. The expression `reply e to c` sends the value of `e` as a reply over synchronous channel `c`. Conditional expressions enable guarding a process by a boolean expression. Pattern matching and local definitions have the same name-value

`begin` *Process* `end`	$\triangleq$	*Process*
`(` *Process* `)`	$\triangleq$	*Process*
$Expr_1$ `(`$Expr_2$`)`	$\triangleq$	$Expr_1\ Expr_2$

Figure 10.3
JoCaml programming language syntactic sugar.

binding behavior as the Objective Caml counterparts but on processes rather than on expressions. Loop expressions execute iterations concurrently. Local channels can be defined inside both expressions and processes.

Join definitions specify the creation of channels, their binding to names, and the process to execute when reactions are enabled. A join definition may specify one or more *disjoint* sets of reactions (separated by the `and` operator). That is, the sets of channel names defined by each set of reactions must be pairwise disjoint. Each *reaction set* consists of a group of reactions (separated by the `or` keyword) that may share defined names, thereby creating a need for synchronization. However, a channel name may not be declared more than once in a single reaction's join pattern. A *reaction* consists of a join pattern and a process. When the join pattern is matched by incoming messages on defined channels, the guarded process *may* be executed. If multiple join patterns are matched, only one of the guarded processes is chosen nondeterministically and executed. If the guarded process includes a `reply e to c` construct, then the defined channel `c` is *synchronous*. *Join patterns* are equivalent to the molecule patterns in the join calculus, except that arbitrary patterns from Objective Caml may be used in the matching process.

The *OPattern* and *OBinding* non-terminals are inherited from Objective Caml, and refer to patterns and let bindings respectively. We refer the reader to Leroy et al. (2008) for these definitions. JoCaml also inherits syntactic sugar from Objective Caml as shown in figure 10.3. Processes may be surrounded by parentheses or `begin` and `end` delimiters for clarity. Furthermore, asynchronous communication can use the more familiar function invocation syntax from functional programming.

10.1.2 Distributed and Mobile Systems Programming

JoCaml concurrent programs can be directly used for distributed systems programming. Since the language entirely relies on asynchronous communication (synchronous communication is modeled as asynchronous communication and an implicit continuation), JoCaml programs can run on a single machine or on several machines transparently. Channel names can be used as part of both local and remote messages and locality is transparent.

JoCaml's distribution model consists of a *name server* (`Join.Ns`) and *sites* (`Join.Site`). Sites are bytecode executables generated by the compiler and linked to the distributed run-time. JoCaml values, including channel names, can be registered and looked up in the name server using plain strings. For example, a *square* function can be created and registered as follows:

```
spawn begin
  def f (x) = reply x*x to f in
  Join.Ns.register Join.Ns.here "square" (f: int -> int);
  Join.Site.listen (Unix.ADDR_INET
                      (Join.Site.get_local_addr(),12345));
  def x () & y () = reply to x in x;
  0
end ;;
```

The `Join.Site.listen` function creates a TCP/IP socket to wait for incoming connections. Here, we assume that the program is executed in the server `a.wcl.cs.rpi.edu`. The line defining channels `x` and `y` is a way to make the program wait indefinitely without ever halting (since no other process could possible write on `y` because of `y`'s lexical scope).

Another process (in a different run-time) that looks up and uses the *square* function can be created as follows:

```
spawn begin
  let server =
    let server_addr = Unix.gethostbyname
                          "a.wcl.cs.rpi.edu" in
    Join.Site.there
              (Unix.ADDR_INET
               (server_addr.Unix.h_addr_list.(0),12345))
  in
  let ns = Join.Ns.of_site server in
  let sqr = (Join.Ns.lookup ns "square" : int -> int) in
  print_int (sqr 2);
  0
end;;
```

The program first connects to `a.wcl.cs.rpi.edu:12345` with the function `Join.Site.there` to get the abstract value `server`, which represents thc run-time on `a.wcl.cs.rpi.edu`. The name server is then extracted with the library function `Join.Ns.of_site` and queried with `Join.Ns.lookup`. After this operation `sqr` is an alias for the remote channel `f`.

Regarding mobility, JoCaml introduces the notion of *locations* that encapsulate a set of definitions and running processes.[1] Locations have a name that can be communicated in messages, registered in the name server, and used as arguments to primitives that dynamically control how they are related.

For example, a location containing a *square* definition can be written as follows:

```
let loc this_location
  def square (x) = reply x*x
do {
  print_int (square 2);
  0
} ;;
```

This location can be registered in the name server as follows:

```
spawn begin
  Join.Ns.register Join.Ns.here "sq_location"
                     (this_location: Join.location);
  Join.Site.listen (Unix.ADDR_INET
                     (Join.Site.get_local_addr(),12345));
  def x () & y () = reply to x in x;
  0
end;;
```

Distributed computations are organized as trees of nested locations. Processes and definitions are attached to a location and once the location is created, no new bindings and processes may be made in the location from outside the location. Mobility is modeled as the movement of a location from one enclosing location to another. Similarly to mobile ambients (see chapter 6), location movement is *subjective*, that is, triggered by a process inside the location to be moved.

For example, a mobile agent that goes to the site where the square definition is located, can be written as follows:

```
let loc mobile
  do {
    let sq_loc =
        (Join.Ns.lookup ns "sq_location" : Join.location) in
    go sq_loc;
    let sqr = (Join.Ns.lookup ns "square" : int -> int) in
    print_int (sqr 2);
  }
```

Applet Server Example An applet server can be encoded in JoCaml as follows:

```
def cell there =
  def log s = print_string ("cell "^s^"\n");
              flush stdout;
              reply to log
in
  let loc applet
    def get () & some(x) = log ("is empty"); none() &
                            reply x to get
    and put(x) & none() = log ("contains "^x); some(x) &
                           reply to put
  do { go there; none (); 0 } in

  reply get, put ;;

spawn begin
  Join.Ns.register Join.Ns.here "cell"
                           (cell: Join.location Join.chan);
  Join.Site.listen (Unix.ADDR_INET
                    (Join.Site.get_local_addr(),12345));
  def x () & y () = reply to x in x;
  0
end;;
```

A cell applet has two states: either `none()` or `some(x)`, and two methods `get` and `put`. For each request, the cell applet server first creates a new cell applet, migrates it to the given `there` client location, and then returns a reference to the applet methods. Notice that the applet can communicate from the client back to the server through the `log` channel within its lexical scope.

An applet client can be written as follows:

```
let cell =
    (Join.Ns.lookup ns "cell" : Join.location Join.chan) in

let loc user
  do {
    let get,put = cell user in
    put("world");
    put("hello, "^get());
    print_string (get());
    0
  }
```

The applet client first gets a reference to the `cell` applet server using the name server, it then creates a `user` location where the cell applet will be hosted, it requests a new cell applet from the server, and then it interacts with the cell through its exported `put` and `get` methods.

10.2 JoCaml Programming Language Operational Semantics

10.2.1 Operational Semantics of Concurrent Execution

The operational semantics of JoCaml is given by a set of *heating* and *cooling* reversible rules, denoted by $\rightleftharpoons$, and by a single *reduction* rule, denoted by $\longrightarrow$, as shown in figure 10.4. These rules operate on *solutions* of the form $\mathcal{R} \vdash \mathcal{M}$, where we only display the reaction rules and molecules in the solution that participate in the transition. These are taken from the multisets $\mathcal{R}$ and $\mathcal{M}$ respectively.

The first three rules are reversible, and correspond to a notion of structural equivalence, including reflection. The last rule is the only reduction rule in JoCaml. We assume that the semantics of pure Objective Caml expressions is preserved, that is, if an expression e can evolve as e' in Objective Caml, then the same "pure" Objective Caml reduction can be applied to e as a JoCaml expression inside a molecule in the solution.

The first two structural rules, (*str-join*) and (*str-and*), essentially say that the parallel composition operator for processes, `&`, and the multiset union operator for reaction rules, `or`, are both commutative and associative. We ignore the `and` definition operator since it is useful from an efficient code generation perspective, but from a semantic perspective, it can be replaced by `or`.

The third structural rule, (*str-def*), specifies the *heating* of a defining molecule, `def d in p`, which changes the multiset of reaction rules, $\mathcal{R}$, by adding a new definition `d`. The substitution σ_d is applied to both `d` and `p` to ensure that the defined variables, $\mathbf{dv}(\mathtt{d})$ are *fresh*, i.e., $dom(\sigma_d) = \mathbf{dv}(\mathtt{d}) \wedge ran(\sigma_d) \cap fv(\mathcal{R} \vdash \mathcal{M}) = \emptyset$. This substitution thus ensures that the scope of defined names is static. By applying the rule from right to left, we can also extrude the scope of defined variables, as in the π calculus.

(*str-join*)		$\vdash$	`p & q`	$\rightleftharpoons$		$\vdash$	`p, q`
(*str-and*)	`d1 or d2`	$\vdash$		$\rightleftharpoons$	`d1, d2`	$\vdash$	
(*str-def*)		$\vdash$	`def d in p`	$\rightleftharpoons$	$\mathtt{d}\sigma_d$	$\vdash$	$\mathtt{p}\sigma_d$
(*red*)	$\mathtt{j} \triangleright \mathtt{p}$	$\vdash$	$\mathtt{j}\sigma_r$	$\longrightarrow$	$\mathtt{j} \triangleright \mathtt{p}$	$\vdash$	$\mathtt{p}\sigma_r$

Figure 10.4
JoCaml operational semantics.

The reduction rule, (*red*), defines a single computation step where the join pattern `j` is matched by a molecule in the solution, using substitution σ_r, whose domain is the received variables **rv**(`j`). The molecule on the right-hand side of the reaction rule, `p`, is placed into the solution, once the substitution σ_r has been applied. We can think of defined variables as *ports*, received variables as *formal arguments*, and applying the substitution σ_r to `p` as replacing *formal arguments* by *actual arguments* according to the pattern match substitution (actually received names). Once again, we assume that Objective Caml pattern matching semantics are lifted to JoCaml patterns.

The semantics of synchronous channels (`reply to` and `;` syntactic forms) can be expressed as a translation from synchronous communication to asynchronous communication with explicit continuation channels. For example,

```
def p(v) = reply to p in
spawn p(v); q ;;
```

can be translated into *continuation-passing style* as follows:

```
def c() = q
and p(v c) = c() in
spawn p(v c) ;;
```

where we essentially pass a *continuation* channel `c` as an extra argument to messages on channel `p` to notify `q` of completion. Notice that the translation does not use any of the synchronous communication primitives.

10.2.2 Operational Semantics of Distribution, Mobility, and Failure Detection

JoCaml's operational semantics of distribution and mobility is based on the *distributed join calculus* (Fournet et al., 1996), which extends the join calculus with primitives for locations, mobility, and failure detection. Figure 10.5 illustrates the new primitives in the distributed join calculus and their equivalent JoCaml primitives.

The semantics for distributed and mobile computing in JoCaml follows the semantics for the distributed join calculus. The distributed join calculus extends the join calculus by enabling execution over a tree of nested (and possibly failed) locations. These locations are modeled using a distributed reflexive chemical abstract machine, which is a multiset of *solutions* of the form $\mathcal{R}_i \vdash \mathcal{M}_i$ separated by $\|$. Each local solution evolves in the same way as in the join calculus. However, solutions can also interact by having molecules migrate automatically to where they can react according to definitions (see rule (*comm*) in figure 10.6). Synchronization across multiple locations is avoided by allowing only *well-formed* machines where every name is defined in at most one solution.

Distributed Join Calculus	JoCaml	
$go\langle a, k\rangle$	`go a; p`	Migration
$halt\,\langle\rangle$	`halt ()`	Termination
$fail\langle a, k\rangle$	`fail a; p`	Failure detection
$a[D : P]$	`let loc a d do p`	Creation

Figure 10.5
Distributed join calculus syntax and equivalent JoCaml syntax.

(*comm*) $\vdash$ `x(y)` $\|$ `j=p` $\vdash$ $\longrightarrow$ $\vdash$ $\|$ `j=p` $\vdash$ `x(y)`
(x $\in$ **dv**(j))

(*str-loc*) `let loc a d do p` $\vdash_\varphi$ $\rightleftharpoons$ $\vdash_\varphi$ $\|$ `d` $\vdash_{\varphi a}$ `p`
(a frozen)

(*move*) `let loc a d do p & go b; q` $\vdash_\varphi$ $\|$ $\vdash_{\psi b}$ $\longrightarrow$
$\vdash_\varphi$ $\|$ `let loc a d do p & q` $\vdash_{\psi b}$

(*halt*) `let loc a d do p & halt()` $\vdash_\varphi$ $\longrightarrow$ `failed loc a` $\vdash_\varphi$

(*detect*) $\vdash_\varphi$ `fail a ; p` $\|$ $\vdash_{\psi a}$ $\longrightarrow$ $\vdash_\varphi$ `p` $\|$ $\vdash_{\psi a}$
(ψa location failed)

Figure 10.6
JoCaml operational semantics for distribution and mobility.

Location trees are modeled by assigning names to locations (e.g., a, b, ...) and using strings of names to denote nested locations (e.g., $\varphi = ab$ denotes location b is inside location a.) Running locations are labeled local solutions $\mathcal{R} \vdash_\varphi \mathcal{M}$. When a location fails, all its sublocations are failed as well. Thus, all the rules in figure 10.6 assume that location φ is alive.

Creating a new location adds a new solution to the multiset with the appropriate label (see rule (*str-loc*) in figure 10.6). The (a frozen) side condition means that there can be no sublocations of a in the multiset of solutions when this structural equivalence rule takes place. This ensures that locations remain organized in a well-formed tree, when the rule is applied from right to left.

Location migration is modeled as a subjective move (see section 6.2) whereby a process inside location a moves its enclosing location to another location b. Rule (*move*) specifies how location a moves from φa to ψba. Enclosed processes, such as p in this rule and inner locations also move along with a.

Location failures and recovery are supported by two new primitives: *halt* and *fail*. Halting a location makes it permanently inert (see rule (*halt*) in figure 10.6). We denote it by using the `failed` keyword. Failed sublocations can make no progress as no reduction or heating/cooling rules apply. The `fail` primitive detects when a location a or any of its parent locations has failed (see rule (*detect*)).

10.3 JoCaml Programming Patterns

10.3.1 Objective Caml Pattern Matching in Join Patterns

A key feature of JoCaml is its ability to use Objective Caml patterns inside join definition patterns. For example, to merge two sorted lists, you may use the following definition:

```
def merge([],[]) = reply [] to merge
or  merge(xs,[]) = reply xs to merge
or  merge([],xs) = reply xs to merge
or  merge(x::xs,y::ys) =
      if x>y then reply x::merge(xs,y::ys) to merge
      else reply y::merge(x::xs,ys) to merge
in
spawn merge([1;3;4],[2,3]) ;;
```

The nondeterminism semantics inherent in join calculus patterns is respected in JoCaml. Consider for example:

```
def c([]) = echo_string "Nil"
or  c(_)  = echo_string "Anything"
in
  spawn c([]) ;;
```

The execution is free to print `Nil` or `Anything`. However, there is no requirement of *fairness* (see chapter 4) in selecting among multiple matching patterns over time.

Objective Caml patterns on the other hand are resolved deterministically: the first textual pattern to match will always be chosen. Consider, for example,

```
def c(x) =
  match x with
| [] -> echo_string "Nil"
| _  -> echo_string "Anything"
in
  spawn c([]) ;;
```

Any valid execution must always print `Nil`.

10.3.2 π Calculus Channels

Asynchronous π calculus channels can be modeled in JoCaml as follows:

```
let new_pi_channel () =
  def send(x) & receive() = reply x to receive in
  send, receive ;;
```

For example, the π calculus expression

$$(\nu c)(\nu d)(\bar{c}1 \mid \bar{c}2 \mid c(x).\bar{d}(x+x) \mid d(y).\bar{p}y)$$

can then be written in JoCaml as follows:

```
spawn begin
  let sc, rc = new_pi_channel ()
  and sd, rd = new_pi_channel () in
    sc(1) & sc(2) & (let x = rc() in sd(x+x)) &
    (let y = rd() in print_int y; 0)
end ;;
```

This code can print 2 or 4 depending on which process communicates first: $\bar{c}1$ or $\bar{c}2$.

Synchronous π calculus channels can easily be modeled by making `send` synchronous:

```
let new_sync_pi_channel () =
  def send(x) & receive() = reply x to receive &
                            reply to send
  in
    send, receive ;;
```

The π calculus expression

$$(\nu c)(\bar{c}a.P \mid c(x).Q)$$

can be modeled as follows:

```
spawn begin
  let sc, rc = new_sync_pi_channel () in
    (sc(1); print_string "Send 1 succeeded"; 0) &
    (let x = rc() in print_int x; print_string " received"; 0)
end ;;
```

10.3.3 Join Continuations and Concurrent Iterators

Barrier synchronization enables concurrent activities to be synchronized on finishing execution so that another new activity only happens after they are all finished. For example, two concurrent activities can be barrier-synchronized in JoCaml as follows:

```
def join1() & join2() = reply to join1 & reply to join2
in
spawn begin
  (print_string "(" ; join1() ; print_string "a" ; join1() ;
   print_string ")" ; 0) &
  (join2() ; print_string "b" ; join2() ; 0)
end ;;
```

The code when executed prints `(ab)` or `(ba)`. However, neither `a` nor `b` will print until after `(` has been printed, due to the first synchronization, and likewise `)` will not be printed until after both `a` and `b` have been printed, due to the second synchronization on channels `join1` and `join2`.

Waiting for n concurrent events to complete can be coded as follows:

```
def count(n) & tick() = count(n-1)
or  count(0) & wait() = reply to wait
;;
```

In this code, `tick` is used to notify completion of an event, and `wait` is used to be notified of completion of all events. The code assumes that at most n ticks are ever sent, otherwise, the first join pattern (`count(n) & tick()`) could fire on the $n+1^{th}$ tick, preventing the second join pattern (`count(0) & wait()`) from ever being fired.

An example of using these channels follows:

```
let n = 9 in
  def print_tick(i) = print_int i; tick()
  in
  print_string "(";
  spawn begin
          count(n) &
          for int i = 1 to n do print_tick(i) done
        end;
  wait();
  print_string ")" ;;
```

This example will print numbers 1...9 in arbitrary order, but properly enclosed by parentheses.

A generalization of waiting for n events is collecting the results from n concurrent events. The following higher-order code takes `f` as a function to combine the n results and `y0` as the collection operation identity.

```
let create_collector f y0 n =
  def count(y,n) & collect(x) = count(f x y,n-1)
  or  count(y,0) & wait() = reply y to wait in
  spawn count(y0,n) ;
  collect, wait ;;
```

For example, summing the first n numbers can be implemented as follows:

```
let n = 10
and add, total = create_collector (+) 0 n
in
spawn for i = 1 to n do add(i) done;
print_int (total()) ;;
```

The code prints `55`.

Producing a list of squares in arbitrary order can be done as follows:

```
let n = 10
and square x = x*x
and digits = [1;2;3;4;5;6;7;8;9;10]
and iter f xs = List.iter (fun x -> spawn f(x)) xs
and squares xs =
    let add, total = create_collector
                         (fun x xs -> x::xs) [] (List.length xs)
    def add_square(x) = add(square(x)) in
    iter add_square xs;
    total ()
in
squares digits ;;
```

The code uses the asynchronous list iterator `List.iter` which takes an arbitrary function and a list, and calls the function on all the list elements, in this case, spawning n `add_square` processes, which themselves produce n `add` processes that get collected by the `total` channel created in the collector.

10.4 Common Examples

10.4.1 Reference Cell in JoCaml

A reference cell in JoCaml can be written as follows:

```
let cell c0 =
  def content(c) & get() = content(c) & reply c to get
   or content(_) & set(c) = content(c) & reply to set in
  spawn content(c0) ;
  (get, set) ;;
```

The JoCaml cell client code can be written as follows:

```
let cg, cs = cell 0 ;;


print_int (cg()) ;;
cs(5) ;;
print_int (cg()) ;;
```

The style of putting together all the methods to access an encapsulated data structure, is reminiscent of *object-based programming*. Here, the `content` channel is encapsulated, and the `get` and `set` methods are returned as a tuple.

10.4.2 Mutual Exclusion in JoCaml

You can define a semaphore in JoCaml to ensure that only one process is accessing a resource at a given point in time, as follows:

```
let semaphore () =
  def sem() & get() = reply to get
  and release() = sem() & reply to release
  in spawn sem();
  (get, release) ;;
```

Notice that we can use the `and` operator since channels defined in the first pattern (`sem` and `get`) are disjoint with the channel defined in the second pattern (`release`).

Two processes that mutually exclude each other during some critical code sections can be encoded as follows:

```
let loop (f, s, n) =
  for i = 1 to n do f(s) done
and echo (s) = print_string s; 0
in
```

```
let sg, sr = semaphore () in
spawn  (sg(); loop(echo,"a",10); sr(); 0)
&      (sg(); loop(echo,"b",10); sr(); 0)
```

Notice that `loop` is a higher-order function that takes a channel `f`, a string `s` and a number `n`, and sends `n` asynchronous messages over channel `f` with parameter `s`. The semaphore ensures that `a`s and `b`s in the output are not intermixed.

10.4.3 Dining Philosophers in JoCaml

The famous dining philosopher example can be encoded in JoCaml as follows:[2]

```
def phil(i,l,r) =
  def eat(i) = print_int i; print_string "eating..."; 0
  and l() & r() = eat(i) & l() & r() in 0
and chopstick(c) = c()
in
spawn (phil(0,c0,c1) & phil(1,c1,c0) &
       chopstick(c0) & chopstick(c1)) ;;
```

It is possible to encode this example in a way that philosophers can deadlock, by explicitly picking up one chopstick at a time. The given encoding will not deadlock, since the join pattern matching is atomic: either both left and right chopsticks are picked, or none is.

10.4.4 Mobile Reference Cell in JoCaml

A mobile reference cell can be written in JoCaml as follows:

```
def cell initial_loc c0 =

  let loc mobile_cell
    def content(c) & get() = content(c) & reply c to get
     or content(_) & set(c) = content(c) & reply to set
    and migrate(loc) = go loc & reply to migrate
  in begin
    go initial_loc;
    content(c0); 0
  end

  reply get, set, migrate ;;

spawn begin
  Join.Ns.register Join.Ns.here "cell"
```

```
                          (cell: Join.location 'a Join.chan);
  Join.Site.listen (Unix.ADDR_INET
                          (Join.Site.get_local_addr(),12345));
  def x () & y () = reply to x in x;
  0
end;;
```

The cell can be used as follows:

```
let cell =
    (Join.Ns.lookup ns "cell" : Join.location 'a Join.chan) in

let loc user
  do {
    let get,put,mig = cell user "world" in
    put("hello, "^get());
    print_string (get());
    mig(there);
    put("hello, new world");
    print_string (get());
    0
  }
```

The cell will be created in the client's location, used, migrated to a new `there` location, and used in the new location.

10.5 Discussion and Further Reading

The JoCaml programming language (Fessant, 1998; Conchon and Fessant, 1999; Mandel and Maranget, 2008) is the result of studying how to create a practical implementation of the join calculus, while enjoying the benefits of functional programming, in particular, pattern matching, as well as existing libraries in Objective Caml (Leroy et al., 2008). JoCaml was created by Fabrice Le Fessant and Sylvain Conchon in 1998-1999 (Conchon and Fessant, 1999), and it has been further developed by Luc Maranget, Cédric Fournet, Alan Schmitt, Ma Qin, and Louis Mandel (Mandel and Maranget, 2008).

The operational semantics of JoCaml in chapter 10 has followed closely the structure of chapter 5 as well as the semantics of the distributed join calculus (Fournet et al., 1996). We have abstracted over many details in the full JoCaml language, some inherited from Objective Caml, including pattern matching, exceptions, modules, and types. We refer the reader to Mandel and Maranget (2008) for a more detailed explanation of the language capabilities and for more thorough examples.

JoCaml has enabled research on effective compilation of join patterns (Ma and Maranget, 2004; Fessant and Maranget, 1998), and distributed garbage collection (Conchon and Fessant, 1999), and it has been used for an asynchronous highly concurrent implementation of mobile ambients (Fournet et al., 2000) as well as for distributed 3D-image rendering (Mandel and Maranget, 2007).

10.6 Exercises

1. Write a program in JoCaml that computes the product of numbers in the leaves of a binary tree (see, e.g., *treeprod(t)* in section 4.1.1) using join patterns.
2. Write a *distributed binary tree* abstract data type in JoCaml.
3. Modify the dining philosophers example in JoCaml (see section 10.4.3) to:
(a) print “thinking” messages.
(b) receive `n` and a create a table with *n* philosophers.
4. Modify the dining philosophers example in JoCaml (see section 10.4.3) so that philosophers *can* deadlock.
5. Create a *dining nomad philosophers* example in JoCaml. Philosophers eat in a *dining room* and think in a *thinking room*, assuming different rooms are in different sites.
6. Create a *mobile address book* behavior that keeps track of contacts (name, email, phone). Start it in a site, query it, update it, migrate it to another site, and query it and update it again.
7. Develop a *farmer/worker* framework in JoCaml to distribute computations over the Internet.
8. Use the location failure detection primitive in JoCaml to re-create *workers* when their location fails.
9. Compare JoCaml locations with *mobile ambients*. What are the main differences?
10. How would you implement *mobile ambients* using JoCaml? Discuss how you would represent mobile ambients, and how to emulate the ambient calculus primitive operations (`in` *n*, `out` *n*, `open` *n*) using JoCaml's location and mobility primitives.

Notes

1. JoCaml release 3.11 (December 2008) does not support mobility, so the description herein applies to the abstractions in an earlier JoCaml beta release (January 2001) that did incorporate mobility. It is likely that future releases of JoCaml will support mobility in a way similar to the earlier beta release.

2. However, the author's last known JoCaml implementation, version 3.11.2, does not support nested `def` definitions.

11 Social Networking Example

In this chapter, concluding part II, we develop a simplified social networking application which attempts to capture the essence of *real-world* social networking distributed systems such as Twitter or Facebook. In particular, the application illustrates the principles of a *publish-subscribe* protocol. We develop the application in all the programming languages that we have discussed in the second part of this book to enable the reader to study, compare, and contrast the different concurrent programming models and languages using a practical real-world scenario.

Section 11.1 specifies the application requirements at a high level. Section 11.2 presents the design of the distributed application. Sections 11.3, 11.4, and 11.5 present the implementation of the social networking application in the Pict, SALSA, and JoCaml programming languages respectively. Section 11.6 illustrates a testing scenario to check that the implementations in the different programming languages satisfy the specifications. Sections 11.7 and 11.8 conclude with a discussion and exercises.

11.1 Specification

The social network consists of the following classes of actors:

- *Agents*, which represent individual people in the system.
- *Events*, which represent individual news published by agents in the system.

Agents contain as part of their state a set of other agents or *friends*. Friendship is a symmetric relationship, that is, $f(a,b) \iff f(b,a)$. However, it is not transitive, i.e., $f(a,b) \wedge f(b,c) \not\Longrightarrow f(a,c)$. An agent's dynamic set of friends represents the *subscribers* of any events published that are related to the agent. The set of events related to an agent form its *space*, which is also part of the state of the agent.

Agents can be created with a unique name, agents can become friends after mutual agreement, agents can unilaterally remove any of their existing friends, and an agent can publish new events only in the agent's own space or in a friend's space.

Events represent the unit of publication in the social network. When an event is *published* by an agent *a* in its own space, it must be disseminated to all of *a*'s friends (by publishing the event in their space), but no other agents must learn about the event. When an event is published by an agent *a* in its friend *b*'s space, it must be disseminated to all of *a*'s friends and *b*'s friends, but no other agents in the system.

11.2 Design

Figure 11.1 illustrates our social network system design. Following the system specification, there are two kinds of behaviors in our system: `Agents` and `Events`. The internal state is denoted in *italics*. The message handlers and their signatures are denoted in normal font.

An `Agent` has a unique name, a set of confirmed friends, a set of friends that have not confirmed friendship (`wannaBe`), and a space of published events. There are

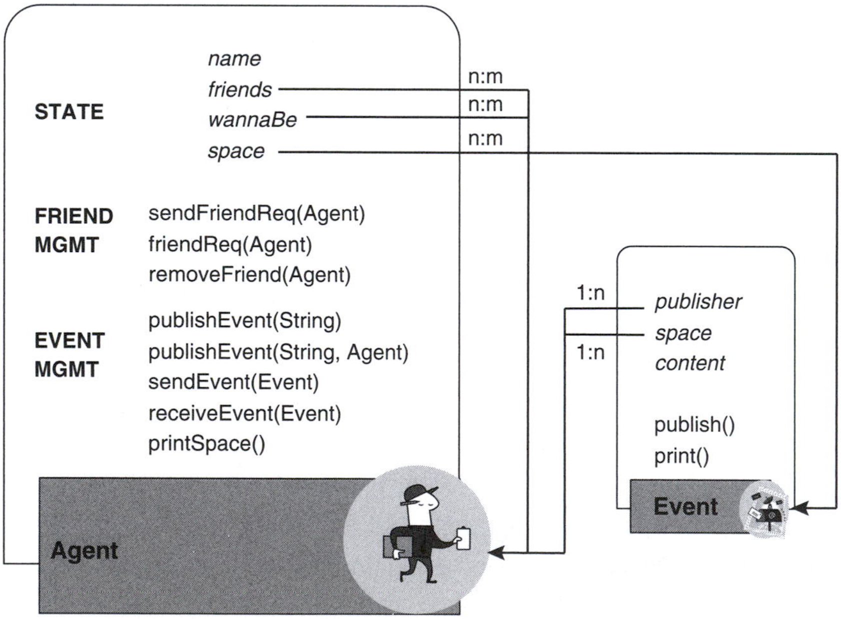

Figure 11.1
Social network design: `Agent` and `Event` attributes and message handlers.

also two types of message handlers: *friend management* message handlers and *event management* message handlers.

The friend management message handlers include three types of messages: (1) a `sendFriendReq(Agent)` message handler that takes care of adding an agent to the set of unconfirmed friends and requesting friendship, (2) a `friendReq(Agent)` message handler that receives a friendship request from another agent, and (3) a `removeFriend(Agent)` message handler that ends the friendship.

The event management message handlers include five types of messages: (1) a `publishEvent(String)` message handler to publish a new event containing a string in the agent's own space, (2) a `publishEvent(String, Agent)` message handler to publish a new event in a friend agent's space, (3) a `sendEvent(Event)` message handler to broadcast an event to all the agents' friends, (4) a `receiveEvent(Event)` message handler to receive an event from a friend and add it to the receiver's space, and (5) a `printSpace()` message handler to display all the agent's space events in the console.

An `Event` has a unique publisher agent, and a unique agent's space that it belongs to, as well as a `String` content. The event's `publish()` message handler takes care of broadcasting the event to its space, the space owner's friends and the publisher's friends. Finally, the event's `print()` message handler displays the event in the console.

11.3 Implementation in the Pict Programming Language

In this section, we illustrate the use of the Pict programming language in developing the social networking example.

11.3.1 Types and Auxiliary Functions

The user-defined types and some auxiliary functions to be used in this social networking example application can be placed in a separate file, which we will call `types.pi`. Figure 11.2 describes these types. The `Event` and `Agent` types are records that contain fields corresponding to the exported operations on elements of the data type. For example, the `Event` type includes operations to publish an event, to print the event's information to the console, as well as utilities to get the event state components. These data types closely follow the design presented in section 11.2. Notice that the types are *recursive* since we want to be able to refer to these types in the signatures of some of the operations that implement their functionality. For example, to publish an event, we want to pass a reference to the event itself to the event publisher and to the agent in whose space the event is being published.

```
type Event =
(rec E =
 [
  publish=/[E Sig]
  print=/[Sig]

  getPublisher=/[/String]
  getSpace = /[/String]
  getContent = /[/String]
 ])

type Agent =
(rec A =
  [
    toString=/[/String]

    sendFriendReq=/[A A Sig]
    friendReq=/[A A Sig]
    removeFriend=/[A A Sig]

    publishMyEvent=/[A String Sig]
    publishEvent=/[A String A Sig]
    sendEvent=/[Event Sig]
    receiveEvent=/[Event Sig]

    printSpace=/[Sig]
   ])
```

Figure 11.2
Pict types for `Agent` and `Event` actors.

Finally, figure 11.3 illustrates four utility functions. The first two—`contains` and `remove`—are *generic* functions to check for membership of an element in a list and to remove all instances of an element in a list respectively. `#X` denotes a type variable. Equality of elements of type `X` is given by the function `f`, passed as an argument, with type `/[X X /Bool]`, that is, a function that takes two elements of type `X` and returns a boolean value. Both these functions use `list.filter`, a standard higher-order function that takes a list and a predicate, and returns a new list with all the elements in the original list that satisfy the predicate. In both cases, an anonymous abstraction, denoted as `\(y:X):Bool = ...`, is passed as the predicate function.

```
import "Std/List"

{- Utility function to check for list membership -}
def contains (#X l:(List X) x:X f:/[X X /Bool]) : Bool =
  (not (null (list.filter l
             \(y:X):Bool = (f x y))))

{- Utility function to remove element from list -}
def remove (#X l:(List X) x:X f:/[X X /Bool]) : (List X) =
  (list.filter l \(y:X):Bool = (not (f x y)))

def eqAgent (a1:Agent a2:Agent) : Bool =
  (val (rec aa1) = a1
   val (rec aa2) = a2
   (==$ (aa1.toString) (aa2.toString)))

def eqEvent (e1:Event e2:Event) : Bool =
  (val (rec ee1) = e1
   val (rec ee2) = e2
   (&& > (==$ (ee1.getPublisher) (ee2.getPublisher))
         (==$ (ee1.getSpace) (ee2.getSpace))
         (==$ (ee1.getContent) (ee2.getContent))))
```

Figure 11.3
Utility functions in Pict for list operations, and Agent and Event equality testing.

The last two—eqAgent and eqEvent—are utility functions to check for agent and event equality. Two agents are equal if they have the same name. Notice that we need to explicitly "unfold" each argument agent a_i since the Agent type is recursive. We use the val (rec aa_i) = a_i syntax to get the record (i.e., aa_i) that gives us access to the agent a_i's operations (e.g., toString.) Two events are equal if they have the same publisher and space agents, and the same content. The notation (f > e_1 e_2 ... e_n e) is syntactic sugar for folding, i.e., (f e_1 (f e_2 ... (f e_n e) ...)).

11.3.2 Agent Behavior

We write the Agent behavior in a separate file called agent.pi. An Agent is defined as a record of operations acting on shared encapsulated state, with the content as illustrated in figure 11.4.

```
{-
 - Agent implementation in Pict
 -}

  import "types"
  import "event"

  def agent (n:String) : Agent =
  (new name:^String
   run name!n
   new friends:^(List Agent)
   run friends!nil
   new wannaBe:^(List Agent)
   run wannaBe!nil
   new space:^(List Event)
   run space!nil

   (rec
   [
    toString = \[res:!String] = name?n = ( res!n | name!n )

    sendFriendReq = ...
    friendReq = ...
    removeFriend = ...

    publishMyEvent = ...
    publishEvent = ...
    sendEvent = ...

    printSpace = ...
   ]))
```

Figure 11.4
Agent implementation in Pict.

State is modeled as internal channels carrying the state variables: a `name` channel carries the agent's name as a `String`, channels `friends` and `wannaBe` carry a list of agents each, and a `space` channel carries a list of events in the agent's space.

Each operation exported by the agent definition uses a similar pattern: to get the current state of the agent by reading the information over the relevant channel, to perform operation-specific actions such as sending data over response channels or to the console, and to reestablish the invariant of keeping the internal channels populated with the (potentially modified) agent's state to be able to satisfy subsequent requests. For example, the `toString` operation is implemented as an anonymous abstraction that reads the agent's name from its corresponding channel (`name?n`), and concurrently writes it over the response channel (`res!n`) and reestablishes the invariant by writing it back on the same channel (`name!n`).

Figure 11.5 defines the agent operations related to friendship management.

The `sendFriendReq` operation is implemented as an anonymous abstraction that attempts to establish friendship with an agent `a`. It also takes a reference to the agent itself (`self`) as the first argument and a channel to signal completion of the operation (`c`) as the last argument. First, it reads the current list of friends from the respective channel (`friends?f`). Then, it concurrently reestablishes the invariant (`friends!f`), and checks whether the agent `a` is already a friend. For this purpose, it uses the generic `contains` utility with specific type `#Agent` and equality function `eqAgent`. If the agent `a` is already a friend, a message is sent to the console. Otherwise, it needs to add the agent `a` to the list of potential friends who have not confirmed friendship (`wannaBe`) and send a friendship request to the agent `a`. To modify its state, it first reads the current list of potential friends (`wannaBe?w`), and then it reestablishes the invariant by writing to the channel the new list with `a` as the first element (`wannaBe!(cons a w)`). To send the friendship request to agent `a`, it uses the unfolded record `aa`'s `friendReq` operation. It passes the (folded) agent `a` as the first argument, which will take the place of `self` in the `friendReq` operation, and it passes itself (`self`) as the second argument. Notice that the `; ()` syntax is to receive completion signals and ignore them. See section 8.3.2 for a more detailed explanation of sequencing. As a final step, a completion signal is sent over channel `c`.

The `friendReq` operation represents an external friend request from an agent `a`. Similarly to the previous operation, it gets a reference to itself (`self`) and a channel to signal operation completion (`c`) as its first and last arguments. First, it reads the current list of friends and checks whether the agent `a` is already a friend. If so, it prints a message in the console to this effect. Otherwise, it checks whether `a` is in the list of potential friends (denoting that this agent wants to be a friend of `a`) and if so, it concurrently performs three actions: (1) it reestablishes the list of potential friends removing the agent `a` from the list, (2) it adds `a` to the list of current friends, and (3) it sends a friendship confirmation request to `a`. Removing the agent from the list of

```
sendFriendReq = \[self:Agent a:Agent c:Sig] =
  (val (rec aa) = a
   friends?f = (friends!f |
     if (contains #Agent f a eqAgent) then
       ((prNL (+$ "Already friends with: " (aa.toString))); ())
     else
       (((prNL "Sending friend request..."); ()) |
        wannaBe?w = (wannaBe!(cons a w) |
                     ((aa.friendReq a self); ()) )
       ) |
    c![] ))

friendReq = \[self:Agent a:Agent c:Sig] =
  (((prNL "Received friend request..."); ()) |
  (val (rec aa) = a
   friends?f =
     if (contains #Agent f a eqAgent) then
       (friends!f |
        ((prNL (+$ "Already friends with: " (aa.toString))); ()))
     else
       wannaBe?w =
         if (contains #Agent w a eqAgent) then
           (wannaBe!(remove #Agent w a eqAgent) |
            friends!(cons a f) |
            ((aa.friendReq a self); ()) )
         else (friends!f | wannaBe!w)
      ) |
   c![] )

removeFriend = \[self:Agent a:Agent c:Sig] =
  (((prNL "Removing friend..."); ()) |
  (val (rec aa) = a
   friends?f =
     if (not (contains #Agent f a eqAgent)) then
       (friends!f |
        ((prNL (+$ "Not friends with: " (aa.toString))); ()))
     else
        (friends!(remove #Agent f a eqAgent) |
         ((aa.removeFriend a self); ()) )
    ) |
   c![] )
```

Figure 11.5
Agent operations on friend relationship in Pict.

potential friends is accomplished by using the generic `remove` utility. Notice that this utility removes all occurrences of the friend in the list. The friendship confirmation request is useful to ensure that agent `a`, which presumably initiated the friend request, also updates its list of friends. If agent `a` is neither in the list of friends nor in the list of potential friends, then the unilateral friendship request is ignored, and the invariant is reestablished (`friends!f | wannaBe!w`). For a friendship relationship to be formed, since it is to be symmetric, both agents have to initiate the intention to befriend each other by using `sendFriendReq`.

The `removeFriend` operation unilaterally removes an agent `a` from the list of friends. It also sends a request to agent `a` to remove itself from `a`'s list of friends.

Figure 11.6 defines the agent operations related to event management.

The `publishMyEvent` operation is used to publish a new event in an agent's own space. It takes a reference to the agent itself (`self`), the content of the new event as a string of characters (`s`), and a channel to signal completion of event publication (`c`). First, it creates a new event using the `event` definition described in section 11.3.3. The event's publisher and space agents are set to this agent itself. The event's content is passed on from argument `s`. Once the event is created, we use its `publish` operation to request it to publish itself. Notice that we pass the completion signal `c` to the event's publication operation to delegate the notification of completion to that operation.

The `publishEvent` operation is used to publish a new event in another agent `a`'s space. First, we check whether `a` is a friend and only then we create a new event and ask it to publish itself. Otherwise, we print a message on the console stating that `a` is not a friend (and therefore, it is not possible to publish in its space) and send a completion signal over channel `c`.

The `sendEvent` operation broadcasts an event `e` to all the agent's friends. It uses the standard generic higher-order `list.apply` function to send a `receiveEvent` message to the agent's list of friends. The anonymous abstraction that is created unfolds the recursive type of each friend agent and uses `receiveEvent` on the obtained record to notify the agent about the event `e`. The completion signal `c` is passed along to `list.apply` for notification of operation completion.

The `receiveEvent` operation is in charge of adding an event to the agent's space. Since we model the space as a set of events, this operation first checks whether the event has already been added to prevent duplicates.

Finally, the `printSpace` operation is used to print the name and all the events in the agent's space. The operation reads the name and space channels, preserves the agent's invariant by writing them back unmodified, and proceeds by printing the agent's name and its space's events. It uses `list.apply` with an anonymous abstraction to extract the event record from its recursive enclosure, and send a `print` message to each event. In this case, we used the functional programming abstraction to invoke `list.apply` and `;` for sequencing. See section 8.3.2 for a more detailed

```
publishMyEvent = \[self:Agent s:String c:Sig] =
  (val e = (event self self s)
   val (rec ee) = e
   ee.publish![e c])

publishEvent = \[self:Agent s:String a:Agent c:Sig] =
  (val (rec aa) = a
   friends?f = (friends!f |
     if (not (contains #Agent f a eqAgent)) then
       (((prNL (+$ "Not friends with: " (aa.toString))); ()) |
          c![])
     else
       (val e = (event self a s)
        val (rec ee) = e
        ee.publish![e c])
  ))

sendEvent = \[e:Event c:Sig] =
  friends?f = ( friends!f |
    list.apply![#Agent f
                \(a:Agent):[] = (val (rec aa) = a
                                 (aa.receiveEvent e)) c] )

receiveEvent = \[e:Event c:Sig] =
   (space?s =
       if (not (contains #Event s e eqEvent)) then
         space!(cons e s)
       else
         space!s |
    c![] )

printSpace = \[c:Sig] =
  space?s = name?n =
  (space!s | name!n |
    ((prNL (+$ > "*** " n "'s Events***"));
     (list.apply s \(e:Event):[] = (val (rec ee) = e
                                    (ee.print)));
     prNL![(+$ > "*** " n "'s events finished.***") c])
  )
```

Figure 11.6
Agent operations on event management in Pict.

explanation of these abstractions. The last prNL operation passed the continuation channel c explicitly for notification of operation completion.

A key invariant to maintain in all these operations is that the agent's encapsulated state channels (i.e., name, friends, wannaBe, and space) be repopulated again, and only once, after reading their values. It is important to ensure that this is the case, especially in branching commands, where it may be easy to reestablish the invariant only under certain computation paths, but not all of them, leading to potential liveness problems.

11.3.3 Event Behavior

We write the Event behavior in a separate file named event.pi with the content as described in figure 11.7. The Event definition also follows the pattern of a set of channels representing its internal state and a record of operations exported to act on it. The internal state includes: a publisher agent, the agent whose space contains the event, and the event's content. The two main operations are to publish and to print the event. Three auxiliary operations to read the event state are: getPublisher, getSpace, and getContent.

The publish operation performs three concurrent activities: (1) it sends a message to the space agent to add the event (using receiveEvent), (2) it broadcasts the event to all the space agent's friends (using sendEvent), and (3) it broadcasts the event to all the publisher agent's friends, if the publisher agent is not the same as the space agent. The publish operation can only signal completion of the publication process when all these three concurrent subactivities (1, 2, and 3) have completed. To implement this join continuation, we use three completion channels—c_1, c_2, and c_3—to be notified of each subactivity completion before sending a notification signal over completion channel c.

The print operation allows an event to print itself to the console. It reads all the state (publisher, space, and content) channels, reestablishes the invariant by writing the values back on the state channels, and prints the name of the publisher agent, the name of the agent whose space contains the event, and the event's content. Finally, it requests prNL to send a completion signal over channel c.

The three state reading operations getPublisher, getSpace, and getContent, receive a response channel res, read the internal state channel corresponding to the state variable being read, write the value back, and reply with the string representation of each state variable. getPublisher and getSpace use the agent's toString operation (see figure 11.4) whereas getContent uses the variable itself which is already a string.

As in the agent implementation, it is critical to preserve the invariant of encapsulated channels that represent the event's state (publisher, space, and content)

```
{-
 - Event implementation in Pict
 -}
  import "types"

  def event (p:Agent s:Agent c:String) : Event =
  (new publisher:^Agent  new space:^Agent  new content:^String
   run publisher!p       run space!s       run content!c
   (rec [
    publish = \[self:Event c:Sig] =
      (new c1:^[] new c2:^[] new c3:^[]
       (space?s = (space!s |
         (val (rec ss) = s
          (ss.receiveEvent![self (rchan c1)] |
           ss.sendEvent![self (rchan c2)] |
           publisher?p = (publisher!p |
             if (not (eqAgent s p)) then
               (val (rec pp) = p
                pp.sendEvent![self (rchan c3)])
             else
               c3![]
          )))) |
      c1?[] = c2?[] = c3?[] =
      (c![] |
       content?x = (content!x |
     ((prNL (+$ x " published!")); ()))))))

   print = \[c:Sig] =
     publisher?p = space?s = content?x =
       (publisher!p | space!s | content!x |
        (val (rec pp) = p
         val (rec ss) = s
         prNL![(+$ > (pp.toString) " wrote in "
                     (ss.toString) "'s space: " x) c]
        ))
```

Figure 11.7
Event implementation in Pict.

```
getPublisher = \[res:!String] =
  publisher?p = ( publisher!p |
                  (val (rec pp) = p
                   res!(pp.toString)) )

getSpace = \[res:!String] =
  space?s = ( space!s |
              (val (rec ss) = s
               res!(ss.toString)) )

getContent = \[res:!String] = content?x = (content!x | res!x)

]))
```

Figure 11.7
Continued.

always holding the state's current value after the end of each operation. That is, every time that we read a state channel, we must write back to it exactly once. Since in this example, the state of an event is immutable, we could accomplish this by simply writing the state's value back to the state channel right after we read it (e.g., `publisher?p = ( publisher!p | ...))`.

11.4 Implementation in the SALSA Programming Language

In this section, we illustrate the use of the SALSA programming language in developing the same social networking example.

11.4.1 Agent Behavior

We write the `Agent` behavior in a separate file called `Agent.salsa` with the content as shown in figure 11.8.[1]

An `agent` is defined as an actor with internal state variables, a constructor, and message handlers. Notice that we represent the dynamic set of friends, unconfirmed friends, and events as Java `Vectors`, which are generic and already provide standard methods to test for membership and to add and remove elements: `contains`, `add`, and `remove`, respectively. Notice also that we do not need to explicitly pass `self`, since it is a keyword in the language. We also do not need to explicitly represent continuation or response channels, but rather simply use `return` and associated return types in the message signatures (see, e.g., `toString` message handler.)

```
behavior Agent{
  String name;     // Unique name
  Vector friends; // Friend agents
  Vector wannaBe; // Agents I want to befriend
  Vector space;    // Events

  Agent(String name){  // Constructor
    this.name = name;
    friends = new Vector();
    wannaBe = new Vector();
    space = new Vector();
  }

  String toString() { return name; }

  void sendFriendReq(Agent a){ ... }

  void friendReq(Agent a){ ... }

  void removeFriend(Agent a){ ... }

  // publish event in own space
  void publishEvent(String s){ ... }

  // publish event in friend's space
  void publishEvent(String s, Agent a){ ... }

 // send event to friends
  void sendEvent(Event e){ ... }

  void receiveEvent(Event e){ ... }

  void printSpace(){ ... }}
```

Figure 11.8
Agent implementation in SALSA.

The `Agent` behavior has a single constructor, which receives the new agent's `name` and initializes the agent's state variables to the received name and empty vectors. `this.name` refers to the actor instance variable whereas `name` refers to the constructor's incoming argument.

Figure 11.9 defines the agent operations related to friendship management.

The `sendFriendReq` message handler receives an agent `a` with whom the agent wants to establish a friendship relationship. If `a` is already a friend, it sends a message to the `standardError` actor for printing in the console. The + operation

```
void sendFriendReq(Agent a){
   if (friends.contains(a))
     standardError <- println("Already friends with: "+a);
   else {
     wannaBe.add(a);
     a <- friendReq(self);
   }
 }

 void friendReq(Agent a){
   if (friends.contains(a))
     standardError <- println("Already friends with: "+a);
   else
     if (wannaBe.contains(a)){
       wannaBe.remove(a);
       friends.add(a);
       a <- friendReq(self);
     }
 }

 void removeFriend(Agent a){
   if (!friends.contains(a))
     standardError <- println("Not friends with: "+a);
   else {
     friends.remove(a);
     a <- removeFriend(self);
   }
 }
```

Figure 11.9
Agent operations on friend relationship in SALSA.

automatically uses a's toString message handler to obtain its string representation. Java Vector methods contains and add can be invoked directly from the message handler, since an actor's internal state variables can be Java objects. If a is not yet a friend, it gets added to the wannaBe vector, and a friendReq message is sent to a with self as its argument.

The friendReq message handler is only significant when coming from an agent a that we already want to befriend (in wannaBe). In such a case, we remove a from the vector of unconfirmed friends and add it to the vector of friends. Furthermore, we send a friendship confirmation message to a (a<-friendReq(self)) so that the agent a can also update its vector of friends.

Essentially, since friendship is a symmetric relationship, a sendFriendReq must be initiated by both agents a and b, before friendship can be established. Without loss of generality, suppose that a is the first to process the sendFriendReq(b) message. a will put b in its wannaBe vector and send b a friendReq(a) message. If b has concurrently processed the sendFriendReq(a) message, then a will be in its wannaBe vector, and b will update its friends to contain a, and send a confirmation message friendReq(b) to a, which will cause a to update its friends to contain b. There are two extra friendReq messages that will be sent to each other after updating their vectors of friends. These two confirmation requests will cause two warning messages to be printed. If b has not yet processed its own sendFriendReq(a) (or does not want to be a friend of a's), the friendReq(a) request is silently ignored. When b decides to become a friend of a's, by processing its own sendFriendReq(a) message, it will add a to its wannaBe vector, and send a friendReq(b) message to a. This will cause a to add b to its friends, send a confirmation message to b, which will cause a to be added to b's friends and a final confirmation message that will print a warning. In all cases, the handshaking protocol terminates with both a and b in each other's friends vector as desired.

The removeFriend message handler unilaterally removes an agent a from the vector of friends. It also sends a message to agent a to remove itself from a's list of friends.

Figure 11.10 defines the agent operations related to event management.

The publishEvent message handler has two different signatures. In the first one, it receives a string s to be published in the agent's own space, and in the second one, it also receives an agent a in whose space it is to publish the event. The first message handler creates a new event actor using its constructor described in section 11.4.2. The event's publisher and space agents are set to self and its contents to the incoming argument s. Then, it sends the event a publish() message using the currentContinuation keyword to delegate to it the notification of event publication completion, that is, the publishEvent message is only considered finished when the

```
// publish event in own space
void publishEvent(String s){
  Event e = new Event(self, self, s);
  e <- publish() @
  currentContinuation;
}

// publish event in friend's space
void publishEvent(String s, Agent a){
  if (!friends.contains(a))
    standardError <- println("Not friends with: "+a);
  else {
    Event e = new Event(self, a, s);
    e <- publish() @
    currentContinuation;
  }
}

// send event to friends
void sendEvent(Event e){
  java.util.Iterator i = friends.iterator();
  join {
    while (i.hasNext()){
      Agent a = (Agent) i.next();
      a <- receiveEvent(e);
  } @ standardOutput <- println("Sent event!") @
  currentContinuation;
}

void receiveEvent(Event e){
  if (!space.contains(e))
    space.add(e);
}
```

Figure 11.10
Agent operations on event management in SALSA.

```
void printSpace(){
  java.util.Iterator i = space.iterator();
  token t = standardOutput <- println
              ("*** "+name+"'s Events***");
  while (i.hasNext()){
    Event e = (Event) i.next();
    t = e <- print():waitfor(t);
  }
  standardOutput <- println
    ("*** "+name+"'s events finished.***"):waitfor(t) @
  currentContinuation;
}
```

Figure 11.10
Continued.

corresponding event e's `publish` message is actually finished, not just when the message has been sent to `e`. For a more detailed explanation of `currentContinuation`, please refer to section 9.3.3. The second message handler has the same behavior, except it first checks whether `a` is in the agent's vector of friends, as a precondition to enable publication in `a`'s space.

The `sendEvent` message handler uses an `Iterator` to send an event `e` to all the agent's friends. It uses the `receiveEvent` message to notify each friend agent of the event. These messages are sent sequentially but can be processed concurrently. A join continuation is used to ensure that all the `receiveEvent` messages have been received and processed before notifying completion of the `sendEvent` message processing. For more details on join continuations, please refer to section 9.3.2.

The `receiveEvent` message handler simply adds an event `e` to the agent's space, if it is not already there.

Finally, the `printSpace` message handler prints the agent's name and uses an `Iterator` to print its space's events. A token `t` is used to ensure that `print` messages in events get processed sequentially (contrast the `while` loop in this message handler to the one used in the `sendEvent` message handler). The `printSpace` message notifies completion after the line containing "`events finished`" is printed on the console. For more details on token-passing continuations, please refer to section 9.3.1.

11.4.2 Event Behavior

We write the `Event` behavior in a separate file named `Event.salsa` with the content as shown in figure 11.11.

```
behavior Event{
  Agent publisher; // Publisher agent
  Agent space;     // Agent's space where event belongs
  String content;  // Event's content

  Event(Agent publisher, Agent space, String content){
    this.publisher = publisher;
    this.space = space;
    this.content = content;
  }

  void publish(){
    join {
      space <- receiveEvent(self);
      space <- sendEvent(self);
      if (space != publisher)
        publisher <- sendEvent(self);
    } @ standardOutput <- println (content+" published!") @
    currentContinuation;
  }

  String formString(String p, String s, String c){
    return p+" wrote in "+s+"'s space: "+c+"\n";
  }

  String toString(){
    token p = publisher <- toString();
    token s = space <- toString();
    formString(p,s,content) @
    currentContinuation;
  }

  void print(){
    toString() @
    standardOutput <- print(token) @
    currentContinuation;
  }
}
```

Figure 11.11
Event implementation in SALSA.

The `Event` constructor receives and initializes the event's state variables: `publisher`, `space`, and `content`.

The `publish` message handler first adds the event to the space it belongs to by sending a `receiveEvent` message to the space owner agent. Second, it requests the space owner to broadcast the event to the space owner's friends. Finally, if the event's publisher is not the same as the space owner, then the publisher broadcasts the event to its friends as well. A join continuation ensures that the `receiveEvent` and `sendEvent` messages have been received and processed before printing the "`published!`" message to the console and signaling `publish` message completion.

The `print` message handler uses an auxiliary `toString` message which itself uses an auxiliary `formString` message to build the string to print. Notice that event printing will occur at the current location of the event actor, since `standardOutput` is dynamically bound to the current actor's location's standard output stream. In a distributed or mobile setting, the `toString` message is more appropriate to use in the `Agent`'s `printSpace` message handler (instead of `print`), so that all events are printed in the agent's current location.

11.4.3 Distributed and Mobile Version

The social network design and implementation allow for agents and events to be located (and migrated to) *anywhere* on the Internet. It suffices to mark agent behaviors to implement the `ActorService` interface, give agents a valid Universal Actor Name at creation time (see e.g., section 9.4.4) and to be running the appropriate naming service and theaters (SALSA VM environments, see section 9.1.2) before program execution.

11.5 Implementation in the JoCaml Programming Language

In this section, we illustrate the use of the JoCaml programming language in developing the same social networking example. The implementation follows a very similar strategy to the Pict implementation described in section 11.3.

11.5.1 Types and Auxiliary Functions

The user-defined types to be used in this application are shown in figure 11.12. The `event` and `agent` types are records that contain fields corresponding to the exported operations on elements of the data type. These data types closely follow the design presented in section 11.2. Recursive types have simpler syntax in JoCaml than in Pict; however, references to `self` need to be passed on explicitly, as opposed to in SALSA. For example, the `event` type includes operations to publish an event, to print the event's information to the console, as well as utilities to get the event's

```
type event =
{
   publish: event -> unit;
   print: unit -> unit;

   getPublisher: unit -> string;
   getSpace: unit -> string;
   getContent: unit -> string;
}

type agent =
{
   toString: unit -> string;

   sendFriendReq: (agent * agent) -> unit;
   friendReq: (agent * agent) -> unit;
   removeFriend: (agent * agent) -> unit;

   publishMyEvent: (agent * string) -> unit;
   publishEvent: (agent * string * agent) -> unit;
   sendEvent: event -> unit;
   receiveEvent: event -> unit;

   printSpace: unit -> unit;
}
```

Figure 11.12
JoCaml types for `Agent` and `Event` actors.

state components. The signature of each operation tells us its type; for example, `publish`'s type is `event -> unit`, denoting that it takes an event (itself) and returns a completion signal. Conversely, `getPublisher`'s type is `unit -> string`, denoting that it takes no arguments and returns the event's publisher name. Polyadic messages are denoted by multiple types separated by `*`. For example, `publishMyEvent` takes an agent and a string and returns a completion signal (`(agent * string) -> unit`).

Figure 11.13 illustrates five utility functions. The first three—`contains`, `remove`, and `iter`—are *generic* recursive functions to check for membership of an element in a list, to remove all instances of an element in a list, and to apply a function to all elements of a list, respectively. We use pattern matching syntax to decompose a list into its head and tail when it is not empty. Type inference in JoCaml eliminates

```
(* Utility function to check for list membership *)
let rec contains l x eq =
  match l with
    [] -> false
  | h::t -> if eq h x then true
            else contains t x eq;;

(* Utility function to remove element from list *)
let rec remove l x eq =
  match l with
    [] -> []
  | h::t -> if eq h x then t
            else h::remove t x eq;;

(* Utility function to apply f to all elements of a list *)
let rec iter f l =
  match l with
    [] -> ()
  | h::t -> f h;
            iter f t;;

let eqAgent a1 a2 =
  let a1s = a1.toString() in
  let a2s = a2.toString() in
    compare a1s a2s = 0;;

let eqEvent e1 e2 =
  let e1c = e1.getContent() in
  let e2c = e2.getContent() in
  let e1p = e1.getPublisher() in
  let e2p = e2.getPublisher() in
  let e1s = e1.getSpace() in
  let e2s = e2.getSpace() in
    compare e1c e2c = 0 &&
    compare e1p e2p = 0 &&
    compare e1s e2s = 0;;
```

Figure 11.13
Utility functions in JoCaml for list operations, and `Agent` and `Event` equality testing.

the need to annotate types. The last two—`eqAgent` and `eqEvent`—are utility functions to check for agent and event equality. They use the standard string comparison utility function `compare`.

11.5.2 Agent Behavior

We write the `Agent` behavior with the content as illustrated in figure 11.14.

An `Agent` is defined as a record of operations acting on shared encapsulated state. State is modeled as internal join definition channels carrying the state: a `name` channel carries the agent's name as a `string`; channels `friends` and `wannaBe` carry a list of agents each; and a `space` channel carries a list of events in the agent's space. The data type operations are exported as synchronous channels on the internal join definition.

Each operation exported by the agent definition uses a similar pattern: to get the current relevant state of the agent by reading the information over the appropriate channel, to perform operation-specific actions such as sending data over response channels or to the console, and to reestablish the invariant of keeping the internal channels populated with the (potentially modified) agent's state to satisfy subsequent requests. For example, the `toString()` operation is implemented as a join definition that reads the agent's name from its corresponding channel (`name(n)`), and concurrently writes it over the response channel (`reply n to toString`) and reestablishes the invariant by writing the name back on the same channel (`name(n)`).

Figure 11.15 defines the agent operations related to friendship management.

The `sendFriendReq` operation attempts to establish a friendship relation with agent `a`. This operation also takes a reference to the agent itself as an argument. The process reads the list of friends (`f`) and the list of unconfirmed friends (`w`) from their respective state channels. Since `f` is not modified in this operation, it is written back to the agent's state immediately (`friends(f)`). If the agent `a` is already in `f`, a message is printed on the console, and the state is reestablished by writing `w` back to its corresponding `wannaBe` channel. Otherwise, agent `a` is added to the list of unconfirmed friends, and a `friendReq` message is sent to agent `a` with its own reference and `self` as arguments. The `; 0` syntax discards the completion signal from `a`. For more details on sequencing syntax, please refer to section 10.2.1. Finally, an operation completion signal is sent over channel `sendFriendReq`. Thus, the type of `sendFriendReq` is as expected: `(agent * agent) -> unit`.

The `friendReq` operation represents an external friend request from agent `a`. It also reads state variables `f` and `w`. The operation is only significant if `a` is in `w`. In such case, it updates the list of friends to include `a` and removes `a` from the list of unconfirmed friends. It also sends a `friendReq` message to `a` with `a` and `self` as arguments to confirm friendship, in order to complete the symmetric friendship establishment protocol outlined in section 11.4.1. It is important to remember to

```
(*
 * Agent implementation in JoCaml
 *)

let agent n =
  def name(n) & toString() = name(n) & reply n to toString

   or friends(f) & wannaBe(w) & sendFriendReq(self,a) =
      ...
   or friends(f) & wannaBe(w) & friendReq(self,a) =
      ...
   or friends(f) & removeFriend(self,a) =
      ...

   or publishMyEvent(self,s) =
      ...
   or friends(f) & publishEvent(self,s,a) =
      ...
   or friends(f) & sendEvent(e) =
      ...
   or space(s) & receiveEvent(e) =
      ...

   or name(n) & space(s) & printSpace() =
      ...
  in
  spawn name(n) & friends([]) & wannaBe([]) & space([]);
  {toString=toString;
   sendFriendReq=sendFriendReq;
   friendReq=friendReq;
   removeFriend=removeFriend;
   publishMyEvent=publishMyEvent;
   publishEvent=publishEvent;
   sendEvent=sendEvent;
   receiveEvent=receiveEvent;
   printSpace=printSpace;
  } ;;
```

Figure 11.14
Agent implementation in JoCaml.

```
or friends(f) & wannaBe(w) & sendFriendReq(self,a) =
   friends(f) &
   (if contains f a eqAgent then
    begin
      print_endline ("Already friends with: "^(a.toString())) ;
      wannaBe(w)
    end
    else
    begin
      wannaBe(a::w) &
      (a.friendReq(a, self); 0)
    end) &
   reply to sendFriendReq

or friends(f) & wannaBe(w) & friendReq(self,a) =
   (if contains f a eqAgent then
    begin
      print_endline ("Already friends with: "^(a.toString())) ;
      friends(f) & wannaBe(w)
    end
    else
      if contains w a eqAgent then
      begin
        wannaBe(remove w a eqAgent) &
        friends(a::f) &
        (a.friendReq(a,self); 0)
      end
      else
        begin
          friends(f) & wannaBe(w)
        end) &
   reply to friendReq
```

Figure 11.15
Agent operations on friend relationship in JoCaml.

```
or friends(f) & removeFriend(self,a) =
   (if not (contains f a eqAgent) then
    begin
      print_endline ("Not friends with"^(a.toString())) ;
      friends(f)
    end
    else
    begin
      friends(remove f a eqAgent) &
      (a.removeFriend(a,self); 0)
    end) &
   reply to removeFriend
```

Figure 11.15
Continued.

reestablish the state invariants in all branches of the code by writing back `f` and `w` into their respective channels (`friends(f) & wannaBe(w)`).

Just like in Pict and SALSA, the `removeFriend` operation unilaterally removes an agent `a` from the list of friends. It also sends a message to agent `a` to remove itself from `a`'s list of friends.

Figure 11.16 defines the agent operations related to event management.

The `publishMyEvent` operation is in charge of event publication in the agent's own space. It creates a new event `e` with `self` as both the publisher agent and the space agent, and with the incoming string argument `s` as its content. Then, it replies to the synchronous channel `publishMyEvent` with the result from invoking the `publish` operation on the new event `e`. This has the same effect as explicitly passing the continuation channel `c` in Pict, or using `currentContinuation` in SALSA. Notice that this operation does not need to read any of the agent's state variables.

The `publishEvent` operation to publish an event in another agent `a`'s space has similar behavior except that it confirms that `a` is a friend beforehand. It reads the agent's list of friends `f` and preserves the state invariant by writing it back on the `friends` channel. If `a` is not a friend agent, it replies to the synchronous channel denoting operation completion after printing a message on the console.

The `sendEvent` operation needs to broadcast the received event `e` to all the agent's friends. So, we read and write back the agent's list of friends `f`. We create an auxiliary procedure `receiveE`, which lexically captures `e` in its closure, and takes a friend agent `a` as its only argument. We can then use the `iter` higher-order utility function to iterate over all the agent's friends `f`, sending them a `receiveEvent(e)` message. Finally, we reply on the synchronous channel `sendEvent` to signal operation completion.

```
or publishMyEvent(self,s) =
   let e = event self self s in
     reply e.publish(e) to publishMyEvent

or friends(f) & publishEvent(self,s,a) =
   friends(f) &
   if not (contains f a eqAgent) then
   begin
     print_endline ("Not friends with"^(a.toString()));
     reply to publishEvent
   end
   else
     let e = event self a s in
     reply e.publish(e) to publishEvent

or friends(f) & sendEvent(e) =
   friends(f) &
   (let receiveE a = a.receiveEvent(e) in
    iter receiveE f;
    reply to sendEvent)

or space(s) & receiveEvent(e) =
   reply to receiveEvent &
   if not (contains s e eqEvent) then
     space(e::s)
   else space(s)

or name(n) & space(s) & printSpace() =
   name(n) & space(s) &
   begin
     print_endline ("*** "^n^"'s Events***");
     let printE e = e.print() in
       iter printE s;
     print_endline ("*** "^n^"'s events finished.***");
     reply to printSpace
   end
```

Figure 11.16
Agent operations on event management in JoCaml.

The `receiveEvent` operation reads the agent's space `s` and adds the event `e` if it is not already in the space. It signals completion on the synchronous channel `receiveEvent` concurrently. This is safe to do, since no operations that read the agent's space (e.g., another `receiveEvent`) will be able to continue until the space channel is written to.

Finally, the `printSpace` operation reads the agent's name `n` and space `s`, and prints them on the console before replying to the synchronous channel `printSpace`. Similarly to the `sendEvent` operation, it creates an auxiliary procedure `printE` to take an event argument `e` and print it, and uses the higher-order `iter` function to print all the events in the agent's space.

As in Pict, it is critical to liveness to write state variables back on channels after reading them in each operation. It is particularly important to consider branching instructions, where at every branch, we must write state values back. For example, in the `receiveEvent` operation, if the event `e` is already in the agent's space `s`, it is easy to forget to write `s` back on the `space` channel. Such a mistake would prevent any future operations that read the space from proceeding, impeding progress.

11.5.3 Event Behavior

We write the `Event` behavior as described in figure 11.17. The `Event` definition also follows the pattern of a join definition with a set of channels representing its internal state and a record of operations exported to act on it. The internal state includes: a `publisher` agent, the agent whose `space` contains the event, and the event's `content`. The two main operations are to `publish` and to `print` the event. Three auxiliary operations to read the event state are: `getPublisher`, `getSpace`, and `getContent`.

The `publish` operation sends a message to the space agent to add the event (using `receiveEvent`) and it also broadcasts the event to all the space agent's friends and the publisher agent's friends (using `sendEvent`). Finally, it replies on the synchronous channel `publish` to signal operation completion.

The `print` operation reads the state channels `publisher`, `space`, and `content` and writes them back to reestablish the state invariant; it uses the `toString` operation on agents (see figure 11.14) to print the event's information on the console; and finally, it replies on the synchronous channel `print` to signal operation completion.

The three state reading operations `getPublisher`, `getSpace`, and `getContent` read the corresponding state channel, write its value back, and reply to the synchronous channel the string representation of the state. In the case of publisher `p` and space `s` agents, using the `toString` operation on agents as before, and in the case of the content `c` using the string itself.

As in the case of Pict, maintaining the invariant of the state channels being repopulated after each operation was relatively easier than in the case of the agent,

```
(*
 * Event implementation in JoCaml
 *)
let event p s c =

  def publisher(p) & space(s) & content(c) & publish(self) =
      publisher(p) & space(s) & content(c) &
      (s.receiveEvent(self);
       s.sendEvent(self);
       if not (eqAgent s p) then
         p.sendEvent(self);
       reply to publish)

   or publisher(p) & space(s) & content(c) & print() =
      publisher(p) & space(s) & content(c) &
      (print_endline
        (p.toString()^" wrote in "^s.toString()^"'s space: "^c);
       reply to print)

   or publisher(p) & getPublisher() =
      publisher(p) &
      reply p.toString() to getPublisher

   or space(s) & getSpace() =
      space(s) &
      reply s.toString() to getSpace

   or content(c) & getContent() =
      content(c) &
      reply c to getContent

  in
  spawn publisher(p) & space(s) & content(c);
  {publish=publish;
   print=print;
   getPublisher=getPublisher;
   getSpace=getSpace;
   getContent=getContent;
  } ;;
```

Figure 11.17
Event implementation in JoCaml.

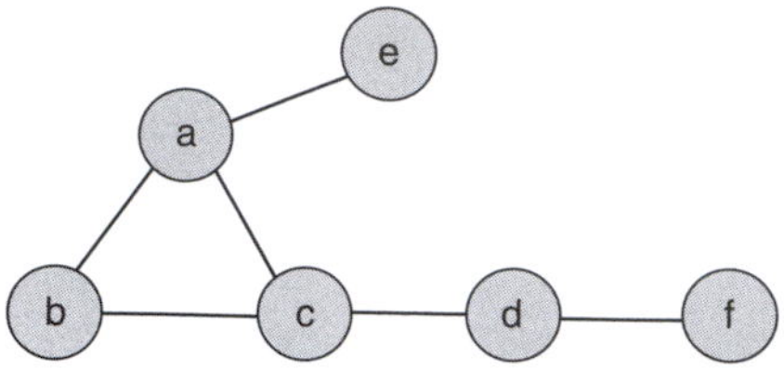

Figure 11.18
A simple social network for testing purposes.

since the event's state is immutable. We simply made sure that we wrote the state channels as soon as they were read in each operation.

11.6 Testing

We will (partially) test the concurrent programs by creating a simple social network with six agents: `a`, `b`,...,`f`; where the first three are common friends; `d` is a friend of `c` and `f`; and `e` and `f` have only one friend each, `a` and `d`, respectively (see figure 11.18). We will then let agents `a`, `c`, and `f` publish an event in their own space, and agent `c` publish two more events in `a`'s and `d`'s spaces respectively.

11.6.1 Testing the Pict Program

We place the testing code in a separate file named `socnet.pi` with the content as shown in figure 11.19.

11.6.2 Testing the SALSA Program

We place the testing code in a separate file named `SocialNetwork.salsa` with the content as shown in figure 11.20.

11.6.3 Testing the JoCaml Program

The testing code is shown in figure 11.21.

11.6.4 Program Output

After program execution in any of the three programming languages, we get the following (partial) output:

```
*** d's Events***
c wrote in d's space: c_e3
c wrote in a's space: c_e2
c wrote in c's space: c_e1
```

```
f wrote in f's space: f_e1
*** d's events finished.***
*** e's Events***
c wrote in a's space: c_e2
a wrote in a's space: a_e1
*** e's events finished.***
*** f's Events***
c wrote in d's space: c_e3
f wrote in f's space: f_e1
*** f's events finished.***
```

Notice that agents must learn only about their friends' events. In particular, agent d learns only about events originating from its friends f and c, and it does not learn about agent a's event. Agent e learns only about its friend a's events: event a_{e1} and event c_{e2}—posted by c in a's space. Agent e does not learn about f's event or c's events unrelated to a. Finally, agent f learns about its own event and c's posting on d's space, since d is f's friend. However, agent f does not learn about a's event or c's events unrelated to d. This demonstrates that information flow happened as expected.

11.7 Discussion and Further Reading

In this section, we used a modern distributed application—social networking—as a driving scenario for illustrating key aspects of programming distributed computing systems. The sample application illustrates how to model different types of concurrency units and coordination patterns using processes, actors, and join pattern definitions in the Pict (Pierce and Turner, 2000), SALSA (Varela and Agha, 2001), and JoCaml (Conchon and Fessant, 1999) programming languages respectively.

We focused on two key aspects common to many distributed applications: first, *mutual agreement* of agents, in our case, establishing the friend relationship, with the possibility of unilaterally breaking it, and second, *information flow* restrictions where only agents directly associated to an event (either as its *source* or its *target*) and their peers get the event information. That is, the dynamic topology of agents, determined in the sample application by the friend relationship, directly influences how information flows in the distributed system.

Agents and events were modeled following the "simple concurrent object" pattern in the Pict tutorial (Pierce, 1998). In the Pict implementation, we also used advanced language features including lists, polymorphism, anonymous functions, and recursive types (Pierce, 1998). The SALSA implementation used actor naturally model agents and events (Varela et al., 2007). To implement coo

```
{-
 - Social network implementation in Pict
 -}

  import "event"
  import "agent"

    val a = (agent "a")    val (rec aa) = a
    val b = (agent "b")    val (rec bb) = b
    val c = (agent "c")    val (rec cc) = c
    val d = (agent "d")    val (rec dd) = d
    val e = (agent "e")    val (rec ee) = e
    val f = (agent "f")    val (rec ff) = f

    run ((aa.sendFriendReq a b); (bb.sendFriendReq b a);
           (aa.sendFriendReq a c); (cc.sendFriendReq c a);
           (cc.sendFriendReq c b); (bb.sendFriendReq b c);
           (aa.sendFriendReq a e); (ee.sendFriendReq e a);
           (cc.sendFriendReq c d); (dd.sendFriendReq d c);
           (ff.sendFriendReq f d); (dd.sendFriendReq d f);

           (aa.publishMyEvent a "a_e1");
           (ff.publishMyEvent f "f_e1");
           (cc.publishMyEvent c "c_e1");
           (cc.publishEvent c "c_e2" a);
           (cc.publishEvent c "c_e3" d);

           (aa.printSpace);
           (bb.printSpace);
           (cc.printSpace);
           (dd.printSpace);
           (ee.printSpace);
           (ff.printSpace); ()
      )
```

Figure 11.19
Testing code for social networking example in Pict.

```
behavior SocialNetwork{

  void act(String args){
    // create agents
    Agent a = new Agent("a");
    Agent b = new Agent("b");
    Agent c = new Agent("c");
    Agent d = new Agent("d");
    Agent e = new Agent("e");
    Agent f = new Agent("f");

    // create friendships
    join {
      a <- sendFriendReq(b);  b <- sendFriendReq(a);
      a <- sendFriendReq(c);  c <- sendFriendReq(a);
      c <- sendFriendReq(b);  b <- sendFriendReq(c);
      a <- sendFriendReq(e);  e <- sendFriendReq(a);
      c <- sendFriendReq(d);  d <- sendFriendReq(c);
      f <- sendFriendReq(d);  d <- sendFriendReq(f);
    } @

    // create events
    join {
      a <- publishEvent("a_e1");
      f <- publishEvent("f_e1");
      c <- publishEvent("c_e1");
      c <- publishEvent("c_e2",a);
      c <- publishEvent("c_e3",d);
    } @

    // print agents' spaces
    a <- printSpace() @
    b <- printSpace() @
    c <- printSpace() @
    d <- printSpace() @
    e <- printSpace() @
    f <- printSpace();
  }
}
```

Figure 11.20
Testing code for social networking example in SALSA.

```
(*
 * Social network implementation in JoCaml
 *)

let a = agent "a" ;;
let b = agent "b" ;;
let c = agent "c" ;;
let d = agent "d" ;;
let e = agent "e" ;;
let f = agent "f" ;;

a.sendFriendReq(a,b); b.sendFriendReq(b,a);
a.sendFriendReq(a,c); c.sendFriendReq(c,a);
c.sendFriendReq(c,b); b.sendFriendReq(b,c);
a.sendFriendReq(a,e); e.sendFriendReq(e,a);
c.sendFriendReq(c,d); d.sendFriendReq(d,c);
f.sendFriendReq(f,d); d.sendFriendReq(d,f);

print_endline "friendships created";

a.publishMyEvent(a,"a_e1");
f.publishMyEvent(f,"f_e1");
c.publishMyEvent(c,"c_e1");
c.publishEvent(c,"c_e2",a);
c.publishEvent(c,"c_e3",d);

print_endline "events published!";

a.printSpace();
b.printSpace();
c.printSpace();
d.printSpace();
e.printSpace();
f.printSpace();
```

Figure 11.21
Testing code for social networking example in JoCaml.

patterns, we used advanced language features including named tokens, join blocks, and first-class continuations (Varela et al., 2007), as well as inherited Java's support for vectors and iterators. The JoCaml implementation used join pattern definitions for agents and events following sample concurrent data and control structures (Mandel and Maranget, 2008). We used synchronous channels extensively (Mandel and Maranget, 2008), as well as inherited Ocaml's support for lists, records, and pattern matching (Leroy et al., 2008).

Because of space and scope constraints, we have only modeled and developed three fundamental aspects of social networking applications: concurrent execution, dynamic agent topologies, and the subsequent restricted event information flow. Many important aspects have been left out from the discussion: distributed and mobile execution including partial fault tolerance, agent name uniqueness, persistent storage for agents and events, security issues including authentication and privacy, human interfaces including web access and multimedia content, and so on.

This chapter illustrated differences and commonalities in modeling and developing concurrent systems using three different programming languages following three different models of concurrent computation. Open research issues include techniques to verify high-level semantic properties of concurrent, distributed, and mobile systems, bringing to light some of the theoretical techniques illustrated in part I. Two sample properties for the social network example follow:

1. Agents can only become friends after mutual agreement, i.e., an agent *a* should only be in the set of friends of another agent *b* (and vice versa) if both agents have independently sent a `sendFriendReq` message to each other.
2. Agents' events are private up to direct friendship at the time of event publication, i.e., if an event *e* belongs to an agent *a*'s space, then *e* must have been published by *a*, by one of *a*'s friends, or in the space of one of *a*'s friends.

11.8 Exercises

1. Modify the Pict implementation as necessary to execute the social networking example in a distributed/mobile setting.
2. Modify the SALSA implementation as necessary to execute the social networking example in a distributed/mobile setting. In particular, modify the `Agent` behavior so that events are always printed in the agent's location (and not on their own location).
3. Modify the JoCaml implementation as necessary to execute the social networking example in a distributed/mobile setting.
4. Distributed/mobile execution adds the possibility of partial failures to concurrent systems. Design and implement a fault tolerance mechanism that supports the

potential loss of friend request messages extending the friendship handshake protocol described in section 11.4.1.

5. Name uniqueness for agents is a critical property of the social networking system.

(a) Reason about correctness properties that fail if agent names are not unique.

(b) Design and implement a *decentralized* service to guarantee agent name uniqueness.

6. In a distributed execution, event replication can improve latency of access from agents. Since events are immutable actors, they can be replicated in a relatively simple manner. Modify the social networking example, replicating events so that agents can access them locally.

7. Incorporate persistence in the social networking example: save agents and events in a database or secondary storage, so that distributed system state can be recovered upon failures and machine down times.

8. Privacy of data is a critical concern in social networking systems. Model essential privacy requirements and design and implement a layered privacy system enabling data access by only agents, by agents and their direct friends, and by friends of friends.

9. Removal of a friend in the social networking example described in this chapter, does not modify the spaces of any of the agents in the system. Modify the implementations in Pict, SALSA, and JoCaml, so that friendship removal is privacy-preserving, that is, any events that should no longer be visible in the new friendship graph are removed from agents' spaces.

10. Add multimedia events to the social networking system so that pictures, audio, and video can be published. Enable tagging of agents in multimedia events.

11. Incorporate a graphical user interface to the social networking example, for example, enabling web or mobile device access to the data.

12. Think of a correctness property for the social networking system, formalize it, and prove the implementation is correct with respect to this property. *Hint:* This exercise may entail significant research in theorem proving and/or model checking systems beyond the material provided in this book.

Note

1. SALSA inherits the Java naming convention, where `modules` and `behaviors` must be written in a corresponding hierarchical directory/file structure.

References

Agha, G. (1986). *Actors: A Model of Concurrent Computation in Distributed Systems*. MIT Press.

Agha, G., I. A. Mason, S. F. Smith, and C. L. Talcott (1997). A foundation for actor computation. *Journal of Functional Programming 7*, 1–72.

Agha, G. and P. Thati (2004). An algebraic theory of actors and its application to a simple object-based language. In O. Owe, S. Krogdahl, and T. Lyche (Eds.), *From Object-Orientation to Formal Methods*, Volume 2635 of *Lecture Notes in Computer Science*, pp. 26–57. Springer.

Armstrong, J., R. Virding, C. Wikström, and M. Williams (1996). *Concurrent Programming in Erlang, Second Edition*. Prentice-Hall.

Armstrong, J., R. Virding, and M. Williams (1993). *Concurrent Programming in Erlang*. Prentice Hall.

Astley, M. (1999). *The Actor Foundry: A Java-Based Actor Programming Environment*. Open Systems Laboratory, University of Illinois at Urbana-Champaign.

Backus, J. W., F. L. Bauer, J. Green, C. Katz, J. McCarthy, A. J. Perlis, H. Rutishauser, K. Samelson, B. Vauquois, J. H. Wegstein, A. van Wijngaarden, and M. Woodger (1960, May). Report on the algorithmic language Algol 60. *Communications of the ACM 3*, 299–314.

Backus, J. W., R. J. Beeber, S. Best, R. Goldberg, L. M. Haibt, H. L. Herrick, R. A. Nelson, D. Sayre, P. B. Sheridan, H. Stern, I. Ziller, R. A. Hughes, and R. Nutt (1957, February). The Fortran automatic coding system. In *Western Joint Computer Conference: Techniques for Reliability*, IRE-AIEE-ACM '57 (Western), New York, pp. 188–198. ACM.

Barendregt, H. P. (1981). *The Lambda Calculus: Its Syntax and Semantics*. North-Holland.

Benton, N., L. Cardelli, and C. Fournet (2002). Modern concurrency abstractions for C#. In B. Magnusson (Ed.), *European Conference on Object-Oriented Programming*, Volume 2374 of *Lecture Notes in Computer Science*, pp. 415–440. Springer.

Berry, G. and G. Boudol (1990). The chemical abstract machine. In *ACM Symposium on Principles of Programming Languages*, pp. 81–94.

Boodman, B. (2008, May). *Implementing and verifying the safety of the transactor model*. Master's thesis, Rensselaer Polytechnic Institute.

Briot, J.-P. (1989). Actalk: A testbed for classifying and designing actor languages in the Smalltalk-80 environment. In *European Conference on Object-Oriented Programming, Nottingham, UK, July 10–14, 1989. Cambridge University Press 1989, ISBN 0-521-38232-7*, pp. 109–129.

Callsen, C. and G. Agha (1994). Open heterogeneous computing in ActorSpace. *Journal of Parallel and Distributed Computing*, pp. 289–300.

Cardelli, L. and A. D. Gordon (2000, June). Mobile ambients. *Theoretical Computer Science 240*(1), 177–213.

Caromel, D., L. Henrio, and B. Serpette (2004). Asynchronous and deterministic objects. In *ACM Symposium on Principles of Programming Languages*, pp. 123–134. ACM Press.

Carriero, N. and D. Gelernter (1990). *How to Write Parallel Programs*. MIT Press.

Church, A. (1941). *The Calculi of Lambda Conversion*. Princeton University Press.

Church, A. and J. Rosser (1936). Some properties of conversion. *Transactions of the American Mathematical Society 3*, 472–482.

Cole, N., H. Newberg, M. Magdon-Ismail, T. Desell, K. Dawsey, W. Hayashi, J. Purnell, B. Szymanski, C. A. Varela, B. Willett, and J. Wisniewski (2008). Maximum likelihood fitting of tidal streams with application to the Sagittarius Dwarf tidal tails. *Astrophysical Journal 683*, 750–766.

Colmerauer, A. and P. Roussel (1993). The birth of Prolog. In *History of Programming Languages Conference (HOPL-II), Preprints, Cambridge, Massachusetts, USA, April 20-23, 1993. SIGPLAN Notices 28(3), March 1993*, pp. 37–52.

Conchon, S. and F. L. Fessant (1999, October). JoCaml: mobile agents for Objective Caml. In *Proceedings of 1st International Symposium on Agent Systems and Applications/3rd International Symposium on Mobile Agents (ASA/MA)'99*, pp. 22–29. IEEE Computer Society.

Curry, H. B. (1941). Consistency and completeness of the theory of combinators. *Journal of Symbolic Logic* 6(2), 54–61.

Dahl, O.-J. and K. Nygaard (1966). Simula—an Algol-based simulation language. *Communications of the ACM* 9(9), 671–678.

Dedecker, J., T. V. Cutsem, S. Mostinckx, T. D'Hondt, and W. D. Meuter (2006). Ambient-oriented programming in AmbientTalk. In D. Thomas (Ed.), *European Conference on Object-Oriented Programming*, Volume 4067 of *Lecture Notes in Computer Science*, pp. 230–254. Springer.

Desell, T., N. Cole, M. Magdon-Ismail, H. Newberg, B. Szymanski, and C. A. Varela (2007, December). Distributed and generic maximum likelihood evaluation. In *3rd IEEE International Conference on e-Science and Grid Computing (eScience2007)*, Bangalore, India, pp. 337–344.

Desell, T., H. Iyer, A. Stephens, and C. A. Varela (2004, March). OverView: A framework for generic online visualization of distributed systems. In *Proceedings of the European Joint Conferences on Theory and Practice of Software (ETAPS 2004), Eclipse Technology eXchange (eTX) Workshop*, Volume 107 of *Electronic Notes in Theoretical Computer Science*, pp. 87–101. Barcelona, Spain.

Desell, T., K. E. Maghraoui, and C. A. Varela (2004, January). Load balancing of autonomous actors over dynamic networks. In *Proceedings of the 37th Hawaii International Conference on System Sciences, HICSS Software Technology Track*, pp. 1–10. IEEE Computer Society.

Desell, T., K. E. Maghraoui, and C. A. Varela (2006, June). Malleable components for scalable high performance computing. In *Proceedings of the HPDC'15 Workshop on HPC Grid Programming Environments and Components (HPC-GECO/CompFrame)*, Paris, pp. 37–44. IEEE Computer Society.

Desell, T., K. E. Maghraoui, and C. A. Varela (2007, June). Malleable applications for scalable high performance computing. *Cluster Computing* 10(3), 323–337.

Desell, T., B. Szymanski, and C. A. Varela (2008a, April). Asynchronous genetic search for scientific modeling on large-scale heterogeneous environments. In *Proceedings of the 17th International Heterogeneity in Computing Workshop (HCW/IPDPS'08)*, International Symposium on Parallel and Distributed Processing, Miami, FL, pp. 1–12. IEEE.

Desell, T., B. Szymanski, and C. A. Varela (2008b, July). An asynchronous hybrid genetic-simplex search for modeling the Milky Way galaxy using volunteer computing. In *Genetic and Evolutionary Computation Conference (GECCO 2008)*, Atlanta, GA, pp. 921–928. ACM.

Fessant, F. L. (1998). *The JoCaml system*. http://pauillac.inria.fr/jocaml. Software and documentation available on the Web.

Fessant, F. L. and L. Maranget (1998). Compiling join-patterns. *Electronic Notes in Theoretical Computer Science 16*(3), 205–224.

Field, J. and C. A. Varela (2005, January). Transactors: A programming model for maintaining globally consistent distributed state in unreliable environments. In *ACM Symposium on Principles of Programming Languages*, Long Beach, CA, pp. 195–208.

Fournet, C., F. L. Fessant, L. Maranget, and A. Schmitt (2002). JoCaml: A language for concurrent distributed and mobile programming. In J. Jeuring and S. L. P. Jones (Eds.), *Advanced Functional Programming*, Volume 2638 of *Lecture Notes in Computer Science*, pp. 129–158. Springer.

Fournet, C. and G. Gonthier (1996). The reflexive CHAM and the join-calculus. In *ACM Symposium on Principles of Programming Languages*, pp. 372–385.

Fournet, C., G. Gonthier, J.-J. Lévy, L. Maranget, and D. Rémy (1996). A calculus of mobile agents. In *Proceedings of the 7th International Conference on Concurrency Theory (CONCUR '96)*, Number 1119 in LNCS, pp. 406–421. Springer-Verlag.

Fournet, C., J.-J. Lévy, and A. Schmitt (2000). An asynchronous, distributed implementation of mobile ambients. In *International IFIP Conference on Theoretical Computer Science*, Volume 1872 of *Lecture Notes in Computer Science*, pp. 348–364. Springer.

Frølund, S. (1996). *Coordinating Distributed Objects: An Actor-Based Approach to Synchronization*. MIT Press.

Frølund, S. and G. Agha (1993). A language framework for multi-object coordination. In *European Conference on Object-Oriented Programming*, Volume 707 of *Lecture Notes in Computer Science*, pp. 346–360. Springer Verlag.

Gordon, A. and L. Cardelli (2003). Equational properties of mobile ambients. *Mathematical Structures in Computer Science 13*, 371–408.

Gordon, M. J. C., R. Milner, L. Morris, M. C. Newey, and C. P. Wadsworth (1978). A metalanguage for interactive proof in LCF. In *ACM Symposium on Principles of Programming Languages*, pp. 119–130.

Gosling, J., W. N. Joy, and G. L. Steele, Jr. (1996). *The Java Language Specification*. Addison-Wesley.

Gropp, W. D., E. L. Lusk, and A. Skjellum (1994). *Using MPI—Portable Parallel Programming with the Message-Passing Interface*. MIT Press.

Haller, P. and M. Odersky (2007). Actors that unify threads and events. In A. L. Murphy and J. Vitek (Eds.), *International Conference on Coordination Models and Languages (COORDINATION)*, Volume 4467 of *Lecture Notes in Computer Science*, pp. 171–190. Springer.

Hejlsberg, A., S. Wiltamuth, and P. Golde (2003). *C# Language Specification*. Addison-Wesley Longman.

Hewitt, C. (1975). How to use what you know. In *International Joint Conference on Artificial Intelligence, Tbilisi, Georgia, USSR, 3-8 September 1975*, pp. 189–198.

Hewitt, C. (1977). Viewing control structures as patterns of passing messages. *Artificial Intelligence 8*(3), 323–364.

Hewitt, C., P. Bishop, and R. Steiger (1973). A universal modular ACTOR formalism for artificial intelligence. In *International Joint Conference on Artificial Intelligence*, pp. 235–245.

Hoare, C. (1985). *Communicating Sequential Processes*. Prentice Hall.

Hopper, G. M. (1981). Keynote address. In R. L. Wexelblat (Ed.), *History of Programming Languages I*, pp. 7–20. ACM.

Hudak, P., J. Hughes, S. L. P. Jones, and P. Wadler (2007). A history of Haskell: Being lazy with class. In *ACM SIGPLAN History of Programming Languages Conference (HOPL-III), San Diego, California, USA, 9-10 June 2007*, pp. 1–55. ACM.

Hudak, P., S. L. P. Jones, P. Wadler, B. Boutel, J. Fairbairn, J. H. Fasel, M. M. Guzmán, K. Hammond, J. Hughes, T. Johnsson, R. B. Kieburtz, R. S. Nikhil, W. Partain, and J. Peterson (1992). Report on the programming language Haskell, a non-strict, purely functional language. *SIGPLAN Notices 27*(5), 1–178.

Igarashi, A., B. Pierce, and P. Wadler (2001, May). Featherweight Java: a minimal core calculus for Java and GJ. *ACM Transactions on Programming Languages and Systems 23*(3), 396–450.

Jamali, N. (2004). *Cyberorgs: A Model for Resource Bounded Complex Agents*. Ph.D. thesis, University of Illinois at Urbana-Champaign.

Kay, A. C. (1980). User interface design in the Smalltalk computing system (abstract). In *International Federation for Information Processing (IFIP) Congress*, pp. 1025.

Kernighan, B. W. and D. Ritchie (1978). *The C Programming Language*. Prentice-Hall.

Kurtz, T. E. (1981). BASIC. In R. L. Wexelblat (Ed.), *History of Programming Languages I*, pp. 515–537. ACM.

Leroy, X., D. Doligez, J. Garrigue, D. Remy, and J. Vouillon (2008, November). *The Objective Caml System Release 3.11*. INRIA. Documentation and user manual at http://caml.inria.fr.

Lieberman, H. (1981, June). *A preview of Act 1*. MIT AI memo 625.

Ma, Q. and L. Maranget (2004, April). Compiling pattern matching in join patterns. In *International Conference on Concurrency Theory*, Volume 3170 of *Lecture Notes in Computer Science*, pp. 417–431. Springer.

Maghraoui, K. E., T. Desell, B. K. Szymanski, and C. A. Varela (2006). The Internet Operating System: Middleware for adaptive distributed computing. *International Journal of High Performance Computing Applications (IJHPCA), Special Issue on Scheduling Techniques for Large-Scale Distributed Platforms 20*(4), 467–480.

Maghraoui, K. E., T. Desell, B. K. Szymanski, and C. A. Varela (2007, May). Dynamic malleability in iterative MPI applications. In *IEEE International Symposium on Cluster Computing and the Grid (CCGrid 2007), Rio de Janeiro*, pp. 591–598. IEEE Computer Society.

Mandel, L. and L. Maranget (2007, August). *Programming in JoCaml*. INRIA Research Report 6261.

Mandel, L. and L. Maranget (2008, December). *The JoCaml Language Release 3.11*. Documentation and users' manual. INRIA.

Manning, C. (1989). A peek at Acore, an actor core language. *SIGPLAN Notices 24*(4), 84–86.

McCarthy, J. (1960). Recursive functions of symbolic expressions and their computation by machine, part I. *Communications of the ACM 3*(4), 184–195.

McCarthy, J. (1978, August). History of LISP. *SIGPLAN Notices 13*(8), pp. 217–223.

Meyer, B., J.-M. Nerson, and M. Matsuo (1987). Eiffel: Object-oriented design for software engineering. In *1st European Software Engineering Conference, Strasbourg, France*, Volume 289 of *Lecture Notes in Computer Science*, pp. 221–229. Springer.

Miller, M. S., E. D. Tribble, and J. Shapiro (2005, April). Concurrency among strangers: Programming in E as plan coordination. In R. D. Nicola and D. Sangiorgi (Eds.), *Symposium on Trustworthy Global Computing*, Volume 3705 of *Lecture Notes in Computer Science*, pp. 195–229. Springer.

Milner, R. (1980). *A Calculus of Communicating Systems*, Volume 92 of *Lecture Notes in Computer Science*. Springer-Verlag.

Milner, R. (1989). *Communication and Concurrency*. Prentice Hall.

Milner, R. (1990). Functions as processes. *Journal of Mathematical Structures in Computer Science 2*(2), 119–141. Research Report 1154, INRIA Sophia Antipolis.

Milner, R. (1993). Elements of interaction—Turing award lecture. *Communications of the ACM 36*(1), 78–89.

Milner, R. (1999). *Communicating and Mobile Systems: The Pi-Calculus*. Cambridge University Press.

Milner, R., J. Parrow, and D. Walker (1992, Sept.). A calculus of mobile processes, Part I/II. *Journal of Information and Computation 100*, 1–77.

Morali, A. (2006, April). *AcTrust: A security model for trust-based computing*. Master's thesis. Technische Universität Darmstadt.

Odersky, M. (2006). The Scala experiment—Can we provide better language support for component systems? In *ACM Symposium on Principles of Programming Languages*, pp. 166–167.

Parrow, J. (2001). An introduction to the π calculus. In Bergstra, Ponse, Smolka (Eds.), *Handbook of Process Algebra*. Elsevier.

Petri, C. (1962). *Communikation mit Automaten*. Schriften des Institutes ftir Instrumentelle Mathematik.

Pierce, B. C. (1998). *Programming in the Pi-calculus: A tutorial introduction to Pict*. Available at: http://www.cis.upenn.edu/~bcpierce/papers/pict/Html/Pict.html.

Pierce, B. C. and D. N. Turner (2000). Pict: A programming language based on the Pi-Calculus. In G. Plotkin, C. Stirling, and M. Tofte (Eds.), *Proof, Language and Interaction: Essays in Honour of Robin Milner*, pp. 455–494. MIT Press.

Reisig, W. (1983). *Petri Nets*. EATCS Monographs on Theoretical Computer Science. Springer Verlag.

Ren, S. and G. A. Agha (1995). RTsynchronizer: Language support for real-time specifications in distributed systems. In *Workshop on Languages, Compilers, and Tools for Real-Time Systems (LCTES)'95, ACM SIGPLAN Notices 30*(11), 50–59.

Roy, P. V. and S. Haridi (2004). *Concepts, Techniques, and Models of Computer Programming*. MIT Press.

Sewell, P., P. T. Wojciechowski, and B. Pierce (1998, May). Location-independent communication for mobile agents: A two-level architecture. In *Internet Programming Languages: International Conference on Computer Languages (ICCL) Workshop*, Volume 1686 of *Lecture Notes in Computer Science*, Chicago, IL, pp. 1–31. Springer.

Sewell, P., P. T. Wojciechowski, and A. Unyapoth (2010, April). Nomadic Pict: Programming languages, communication infrastructure overlays, and semantics for mobile computation. *ACM Transactions on Programming Languages and Systems 32*, 12:1–12:63.

Smolka, G., M. Henz, and J. Würtz (1993). Object-oriented concurrent constraint programming in Oz. In O. Herzog, T. Christaller, and D. Schütt (Eds.), *Grundlagen und Anwendungen der Künstlichen Intelligenz (KI)*, Informatik Aktuell, pp. 44–59. Springer.

Srinivasan, S. and A. Mycroft (2008). Kilim: Isolation-typed actors for Java. In J. Vitek (Ed.), *European Conference on Object-Oriented Programming*, Volume 5142 of *Lecture Notes in Computer Science*, pp. 104–128. Springer.

Stroustrup, B. (1982). Classes: an abstract data type facility for the C language. *SIGPLAN Notices 17*(1), 42–51. ACM.

Sussman, G. J. and G. L. Steele, Jr. (1998). The first report on Scheme revisited. *Higher-Order and Symbolic Computation 11*(4), 399–404.

Talcott, C. L. (1998). Composable semantic models for actor theories. *Higher-Order and Symbolic Computation 11*(3), 281–343.

Toll, R. and C. A. Varela (2003, July). Mobility and security in worldwide computing. In *European Conference on Object-Oriented Programming Workshop on Mobile Object Systems*, pp. 1–9, Darmstadt, Germany.

Tolman, C. and C. A. Varela (2005, October). A fault-tolerant home-based naming service for mobile agents. In *XXXI Conferencia Latinoamericana de Informática*, pp. 1–13, Cali, Colombia.

Tomlinson, C., W. Kim, M. Scheevel, V. Singh, B. Will, and G. Agha (1989). Rosette: An object-oriented concurrent systems architecture. *ACM SIGPLAN Notices 24*(4), 91–93.

Varela, C. (1998, October). An actor-based approach to worldwide computing. In *Object-Oriented Programming, Systems, Languages and Applications (OOPSLA 98), Doctoral Symposium.*

Varela, C. (2001). *Worldwide Computing with Universal Actors: Linguistic Abstractions for Naming, Migration, and Coordination.* Ph.D. thesis, University of Illinois at Urbana-Champaign.

Varela, C. and G. Agha (1998, April). What after Java? From objects to actors. In *International Conference on the World Wide Web (WWW7)*, Brisbane, Australia. *Computer Networks and ISDN Systems: The International Journal of Computer Telecommunications and Networking 30*, 573–577.

Varela, C. and G. Agha (1999, April). A hierarchical model for coordination of concurrent activities. In P. Ciancarini and A. Wolf (Eds.), *Third International Conference on Coordination Models and Languages (COORDINATION)*, Volume 1594 of *Lecture Notes in Computer Science*, Berlin, pp. 166–182. Springer-Verlag.

Varela, C. A. and G. Agha (2001, December). Programming dynamically reconfigurable open systems with SALSA. In *Object-Oriented Programming, Systems, Languages, and Applications (OOPSLA) Intriguing Technology Track. ACM SIGPLAN Notices 36*(12), 20–34.

Varela, C. A., G. Agha, W. Wang, T. Desell, K. E. Maghraoui, J. LaPorte, and A. Stephens (2007, February). *The SALSA Programming Language: 1.1.2 Release Tutorial.* Technical Report 07-12, Dept. of Computer Science, Rensselaer Polytechnic Institute.

Venkatasubramanian, N., C. Talcott, and G. Agha (2001). A formal model for reasoning about adaptive QoS-enabled middleware. In J. Oliveira and P. Zave (Eds.), *Formal Methods Europe*

(FME): *Formal Methods for Increasing Software Productivity*, Volume 2021 of *Lecture Notes in Computer Science*, pp. 197–221. Springer.

Venkatasubramanian, N. and C. L. Talcott (1995). Reasoning about meta level activities in open distributed systems. In *ACM Symposium on Principles of Distributed Computing*, pp. 144–152.

Wang, W., K. E. Maghraoui, J. Cummings, J. Napolitano, B. Szymanski, and C. Varela (2006, December). A middleware framework for maximum likelihood evaluation over dynamic grids. In *IEEE International Conference on e-Science and Grid Computing*, Amsterdam, Netherlands, pp. 1–8. IEEE.

Wang, W. and C. A. Varela (2006, May). Distributed garbage collection for mobile actor systems: The pseudo root approach. In *International Conference on Grid and Pervasive Computing (GPC 2006)*, Volume 3947 of *Lecture Notes in Computer Science*, Taichung, Taiwan, pp. 360–372. Springer.

Whitaker, W. A. (1996). Ada—The project: The DOD high order language working group. In T. J. Bergin, Jr. and R. G. Gibson, Jr. (Eds.), *History of Programming Languages—II*, pp. 173–232. ACM.

Wirth, N. (1971). The programming language Pascal. *Acta Informatica 1*, 35–63.

Wojciechowski, P. T. (2000, December). *The Nomadic Pict system release 1.0-alpha: Documentation and user's manual.* Available at http://www.cs.put.poznan.pl/pawelw/npict.

Yonezawa, A., J.-P. Briot, and E. Shibayama (1986). Object-oriented concurrent programming in ABCL/1. In *ACM Conference on Object-Oriented Programming Systems, Languages, and Applications (OOPSLA'86), Portland, Oregon. SIGPLAN Notices 21(11)*, 258–268.

Index